First language attrition examines linguistic aspects of the attrition or loss of first language abilities in bilinguals through a collection of studies in various language groups. The phenomena of attrition are examined at both the individual bilingual and societal levels.

This volume is divided into three sections: Part I surveys different aspects of existing empirical evidence to arrive at theoretical generalizations about language attrition. Part II is comprised of group studies examining attrition in societal bilingualism or in groups of bilingual individuals. Part III contains individual case studies of bilingual children and adults.

The research reported in this text investigates first language attrition in a variety of linguistic areas, including syntax, morphology, semantics, phonology, and lexicon, with the following first languages: Spanish, German, Hebrew, Dyirbal, English, Breton, Dutch, Hungarian, Russian, French, and Pennsylvania German.

Although there is growing interest in bilingualism, this is the first work to examine the effects of the acquisition of a second language on linguistic abilities in the first language.

First language attrition

First language attrition

Edited by

HERBERT W. SELIGER

and

ROBERT M. VAGO

Queens College and the Graduate Center,
City University of New York

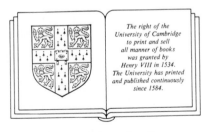

The right of the
University of Cambridge
to print and sell
all manner of books
was granted by
Henry VIII in 1534.
The University has printed
and published continuously
since 1584.

Cambridge University Press

Cambridge

New York   Port Chester

Melbourne   Sydney

Published by the Press Syndicate of the University of Cambridge
The Pitt Building, Trumpington Street, Cambridge CB2 1RP
40 West 20th Street, New York, NY 10011, USA
10 Stamford Road, Oakleigh, Melbourne 3166, Australia

© Cambridge University Press 1991

First published 1991

Printed in Great Britain at The Bath Press, Avon

British Library cataloguing in publication data
First language attrition.
1. Bilingualism
I. Seliger, Herbert W.   II. Vago, Robert M.
404.2

Library of Congress cataloguing in publication data
First language attrition/edited by Herbert W. Seliger and Robert M.
Vago.
    p.   cm.
ISBN 0 521 34426 3. – ISBN 0 521 34883 8 (pbk)
1. Language attrition.   2. Bilingualism.   I. Seliger, Herbert W.,
1937– . II. Vago, Robert Michael.
P40.5.L28F57   1991
404'.2–dc20   90–33930 CIP

ISBN 0 521 34426 3 hardback
ISBN 0 521 34883 8 paperback

To Ruchama and Anita

Contents

List of figures   *page* xi
List of tables   xiii
List of contributors   xv
Acknowledgment   xvii

Part I: Survey studies

1   The study of first language attrition: an overview   3
     HERBERT W. SELIGER AND ROBERT M. VAGO

2   First language attrition and the parameter setting model   17
     MICHAEL SHARWOOD SMITH AND PAUL VAN BUREN

3   Recapitulation, regression, and language loss   31
     KEES DE BOT AND BERT WELTENS

4   First language loss in bilingual and polyglot aphasics   53
     LORAINE K. OBLER AND NANCY R. MAHECHA

5   A crosslinguistic study of language contact and
     language attrition   67
     JULIANNE MAHER

Part II: Group studies

6   L1 loss in an L2 environment: Dutch immigrants in France   87
     KEES DE BOT, PAUL GOMMANS, AND CAROLA ROSSING

7   The sociolinguistic and patholinguistic attrition of
     Breton phonology, morphology, and morphonology   99
     WOLFGANG U. DRESSLER

8   Language attrition in Boumaa Fijian and Dyirbal   113
     ANNETTE SCHMIDT

9   Pennsylvania German: convergence and change as
     strategies of discourse   125
     MARION LOIS HUFFINES

10   Lexical retrieval difficulties in adult language attrition   139
     ELITE OLSHTAIN AND MARGARET BARZILAY

11   Spanish language attrition in a contact situation
     with English   151
     CARMEN SILVA-CORVALÁN

Part III: Case studies

12   Morphological disintegration and reconstruction in
     first language attrition   175
     DORIT KAUFMAN AND MARK ARONOFF

13   Assessing first language vulnerability to attrition   189
     EVELYN P. ALTENBERG

14   Compensatory strategies of child first language attrition   207
     DONNA TURIAN AND EVELYN P. ALTENBERG

15   Language attrition, reduced redundancy, and creativity   227
     HERBERT W. SELIGER

16   Paradigmatic regularity in first language attrition   241
     ROBERT M. VAGO

     Index   253

Figures

		page
1.1	Compound and coordinate bilingualism and attrition	5
1.2	Group and case studies of this volume	14
8.1	Age and test score correlations in Boumaa Fijian	116
8.2	Attrition stages in Traditional Dyirbal	123
10.1	Lexical retrieval options in language attrition	146
11.1	Representation of tense distinctions in system I	163
11.2	Representation of tense distinctions in system V	164
15.1	The problem with indirect negative evidence	230
15.2	Possible types of evidence for developing grammars	231
15.3	Redundancy reduction for the dative in language attrition	237

Tables

		Page
4.1	Hemispheric lesion × recovery type	60
4.2	Handedness × recovery type	60
4.3	Four educational levels × recovery type	61
4.4	Etiology × recovery type	61
6.1	Number of informants per category	88
6.2	FSI interrater reliability	91
6.3	Significant correlations with sentence types (p < .10)	92
6.4	Percentages correct for control and emigrant group per sentence type	92
6.5	Significant F ratios for sentence types	93
9.1	Pennsylvania German pronouns	128
9.2	Case of personal pronouns in dative functions (translation task)	129
9.3	Dative personal pronouns (free conversation and picture descriptions)	129
9.4	Use of the auxiliary *du* (translation task)	131
9.5	Use of the auxiliary *du* – scored (free conversation)	132
9.6	Position of past participle in independent clauses (translation data)	134
9.7	Position of past participle in independent clauses (free conversation)	134
10.1	Responses given on the first encounter of the picture of a "pond"	143
10.2	Responses given on the first encounter of the picture of a "deer"	143
10.3	Responses given on the first encounter of the picture of a "gopher"	143
10.4	Responses given on the first encounter of the picture of a "cliff"	144
10.5	Responses given on the first encounter of the picture of a "jar"	144
11.1	Verb forms examined across the continuum	156

11.2	Stages of loss of "tense–mood–aspect" morphemes	160
11.3	Stages of simplification and loss	162
11.4	Tense systems across the bilingual continuum	162
11.5	Hierarchy of markedness	165
12.1	Stages in the attrition of the L1 verbal system	176
12.2	L2 verbal insertions	180
12.3	Child's 2-C defective verbs modeled on the canonical 3-C pattern	181
12.4	Child's L1 deviant forms	183
12.5	Saliency of the prefix *i* in colloquial Hebrew	184
12.6	The first occurrence of each verb used in the iCaCe(C) form	185
13.1	Examples of each structure used in the syntactic judgement task	194
13.2	Average responses of each subject in the syntactic judgement task	195
13.3	Stimuli, verb usage task	199
13.4	Percentage of incorrect responses, gender and plural task	202
14.1	Compensatory strategies used by Joseph	217
15.1	Word order and preposition judgements	235
15.2	The double object judgements	235

Contributors

Evelyn P. Altenberg
Queens College, City University of New York

Mark Aronoff
State University of New York, Stony Brook

Margaret Barzilay
Tel Aviv University

Kees de Bot
University of Nijmegen

Wolfgang U. Dressler
University of Vienna

Paul Gommans
University of Nijmegen

Marion Lois Huffines
Bucknell University, Lewisburg, Pennsylvania

Dorit Kaufman
State University of New York, Stony Brook

Nancy R. Mahecha
The Graduate Center, City University of New York

Julianne Maher
Loyola University, New Orleans

Loraine K. Obler
The Graduate Center, City University of New York

Elite Olshtain
Tel Aviv University

Carola Rossing
University of Nijmegen

Annette Schmidt
Australian Institute of Aboriginal Studies

Herbert W. Seliger
Queens College and the Graduate Center, City University of New York

Michael Sharwood Smith
University of Utrecht

Carmen Silva-Corvalán
University of Southern California, Los Angeles

Donna Turian
Queens College, City University of New York

Robert M. Vago
Queens College and the Graduate Center, City University of New York

Paul van Buren
University of Utrecht

Bert Weltens
University of Nijmegen

Acknowledgment

This work was supported in part by a grant from the City University of New York PSC-BHE Research Award Program.

Part I
Survey studies

1 The study of first language attrition: an overview

HERBERT W. SELIGER AND ROBERT M. VAGO

1 Introduction

The primary concern of the present text is the disintegration or attrition of the structure of a first language (L1) in contact situations with a second language (L2). Bilingualism, under which we include the more general case of multilingualism, is a natural setting for the unraveling of native language abilities; pathological states such as aphasia and senile dementia are further contexts for attrition effects. Attrition phenomena develop in bilingual individuals as well as bilingual societies, in both indigenous and immigrant communities. At its extreme, attrition leads to what has come to be known as "language death" (cf. Dorian 1981; Schmidt 1985).

The articles brought together in this volume approach first language attrition from diverse angles. The survey studies in Part I draw general conclusions from empirical evidence presented in the literature, while the articles in Parts II and III discuss specific properties of L1 attrition based on the analysis of data they present. The group studies of Part II investigate attrition in societal bilingualism or in groups of bilingual individuals, while the case studies of Part III concentrate on single bilingual subjects, both children and adults. These works employ a wide range of data gathering methodologies: direct response requests such as untimed grammaticality judgement and fill-in tasks, translations, story telling prompted by pictures, paradigm elicitation, as well as free conversations (indirect). Attrition in bilingual aphasic individuals is discussed by de Bot & Weltens; Obler & Mahecha; and Dressler; in moribund languages by Schmidt and by Dressler.

In the following sections of this chapter we wish to highlight some fundamental issues raised by the study of first language attrition, with a view toward setting a background to the general topics addressed in this volume. We caution that space limitations force us to be selective; the reader is advised to consult the individual contributions and their references for details.

2   Psycholinguistic and sociolinguistic aspects of first language attrition

The languages spoken by the bilingual may be said, metaphorically, to coexist in a state of competition for a finite amount of memory and processing space in the mind of the speaker. Except for the case of the so-called balanced bilingual, the languages of the bilingual develop patterns of dominance or strength, usually in relation to the domains in which the languages are used (Fishman 1972). That is, not all the languages known to the bilingual can be said to have equal strength in all contexts of language use. In particular, the domain relationships of the languages can change such that the host or first language is weakened by the increasing frequency of use and function of the second language.

The diminished role of L1 in use and function, exacerbated by separation from the L1 speaking community in the case of immigrants, is one of the significant sociolinguistic variables in the advent and sustenance of first language attrition. Several authors address this issue in the present volume: Sharwood Smith & van Buren; de Bot & Weltens; de Bot, Gommans & Rossing; Silva-Corvalán; Schmidt; Huffines; Maher; Olshtain & Barzilay; Dressler; and Seliger.

Another important sociolinguistic factor is the subordination or recessivism of L1 to L2 in the affective domains of language, such as prestige, social status, attitude, and degrees of acculturation; cf. the articles in this volume by Olshtain & Barzilay; Schmidt; and Dressler.[1] Dressler also argues that in severe cases of language decay, social, sociolinguistic, and linguistic norms are relaxed and style differentiations tend to be reduced and neutralized into casual, informal types (cf. also Maher's article in this volume concerning the latter point).

The beginnings of first language attrition can be traced to advanced stages of bilingualism or second language acquisition. Figure 1.1 shows the changing relationships between the grammars of the bilingual's languages and the role Universal Grammar (UG) plays at three stages in bilingual development. These stages should be construed as major reference points along a more complex continuum; the sociolinguistic justification for assuming a continuum of bilingual stages is discussed in this volume by Silva-Corvalán, Schmidt, and Dressler.

At the first stage, **compound I**, the speaker is just beginning the process of acquiring an additional linguistic system (L2). A number of studies in second language acquisition have drawn attention to the fact that at this incipient stage of bilingualism, the learner utilizes the knowledge of the acquired or established language (L1) as a source for hypotheses about the target language (L2); cf. for example Gass (1979). Another source of linguistic knowledge which the learner may draw upon is UG, assuming that these universals are valid for the target language (Flynn 1987; Chomsky 1981; Cook 1984; Hyltenstam 1987). In order to simplify the present discussion we will ignore any other contributing sources for hypothesis formation.

At this first stage in bilingual development, both grammars are served by a common base of knowledge from L1, as evidenced by language learner performance in L2, demonstrating that transfer is a primary processing and acquisition strategy. However, also at this first stage there are a number of forms in the interlanguage of the second language acquirer whose sources are not in L1. Many of the same kinds of errors are found in a particular interlanguage even though they may be produced by speakers of different first languages. This has led a number of researchers to hypothesize that these errors are the result of innate principles for the acquisition of language which are independent of a specific first language.

At the second stage of linguistic evolution for the bilingual, there is a gradual separation of the two grammars of L1 and L2. This is the result of the second language learner's testing transfer hypotheses against L2 data and developing an independent set of L2 rules which are distinct from those of L1. Corder (1978) has referred to two different processes which take place in second language acquisition: "restructuring" and "recreation." Restructuring refers to the adaptation of L1 hypotheses to L2 data, that is, transfer. Recreation refers to the construction of unique rules for the target language without reference to the first language of the learner. This stage may be referred to as the **coordinate** stage of bilingual development because the grammars of the two languages begin to develop independently, even though, as can be seen in Figure 1.1, there is still a role for L1 transfer and universal principles.

The final stage of bilingual development may be referred to as **compound II**; it resembles the first stage, where the two language grammars were intermingled. At this more advanced stage, the bilingual has

Compound I bilingualism	*Coordinate bilingualism*	*Compound II bilingualism*
L1 → L2	L1 → L2	L2 → L1
UG → L2	L2 → L2	L2 → L2
	UG → L2	L1 → L2
		UG → L2?
		UG → L1

1.1   Compound and coordinate bilingualism and attrition

become quite fluent in L2, which begins to encroach on the linguistic domains of L1. In other words, the direction of transfer found in the first stage of bilingual development is reversed. In Corder's terms, there is a restructuring of the first language according to grammatical principles found in the second. It is not clear whether universal principles still influence L2 as they did in the previous stages. Rather, it appears that they impact on L1, as suggested in this volume by Silva-Corvalán; Dressler; and Vago. It is at this compound II stage that language attrition is most evident.

The intrusion of L2 elements into L1 is not necessarily indicative of attrition: it could simply be a case of code mixing or code switching. Under normal conditions of bilingual language mixing, relative autonomy is maintained for both language grammars and the bilingual speaker is able to switch to one or the other of the two languages being mixed, depending on such stimuli as topic or interlocutor. That is, while code mixing is a common phenomenon of bilingualism, it occurs within predictable and describable conditions of language variation and can be controlled by the speaker. Within the languages being mixed, autonomy is maintained so that each language is served by its own independent grammar. The degree of autonomy can be examined in various ways. One is to administer metalinguistic tests that require the bilingual to judge the grammaticality of L1 sentences which reflect the intermixing of grammatical rules from L2. The suitability of metalinguistic tasks for testing purposes is discussed in this volume by Altenberg; de Bot, Gommans & Rossing; and Seliger.

Mixing thus may remain an additional communication technique or strategy for the bilingual when in the company of other bilinguals with similar linguistic repertoires, or it may become a precursor stage for gradual language attrition or loss as the bilingual increasingly loses control of the conditions that constrain mixing.

3   Linguistic aspects of first language attrition

A profound understanding of L1 (and L2) attrition must take account of the dynamic changes that take place in linguistic form. Many, though not all, of the linguistic changes attendant to attrition are simplificatory in nature. In what follows, we would like to outline in broad terms the most salient characteristic features. We should like to emphasize that our lists are only a sampling and that any classification system is to be construed not as an end unto itself, but rather as a requisite component to attain a higher goal, namely the description and explanation of the attrition process.

The studies referred to and contained in this volume make clear that there are two principal forces bearing on the linguistic forms of attriting L1 grammars. The first one is variously called transfer, interference, convergence, interlingual effects, or crosslinguistic influences: an element (form, construction, etc.) in L1 is patterned on analogy to L2. We might refer to such changes as **externally induced**.

We will illustrate externally induced changes in the L1 grammar with Hungarian (H) and German (G) examples. The cited tokens are culled from our research notes based on data collected in natural speech settings from a native speaker of German and a number of native speakers of Hungarian.[2] All of our informants used English, their L2, as their primary language and exhibited attrition in their native languages. We omit discussing sociolinguistic background, for it has no effect on our suggested classificatory schemes.

We must, however, pause first in order to consider a question of great significance: is our corpus indicative of a deeper, systematic erosion, or merely of on-line accessing problems? We will beg this question as far as our specific data are concerned, since for purposes of classification it does not seem to matter which is the case; in particular, the categories we propose appear to be characteristic of both types of deviant forms. In general, though, effects of performance (accessing, processing, control) need to be sorted out from those of competence (tacit knowledge): it is erosion that reaches the level of competence that allows for interesting claims about and meaningful insight into the attrition process. Proper testing procedures are essential in this regard. For discussion, cf. the contributions in this volume by Sharwood Smith & van Buren, and Altenberg.

With respect to the syntax module of grammar, the most common strategy appears to be **rule generalization**: an L2 rule is extended to L1. In the representative samples given below, the L2 (English) rules for agreement, tag question, word order, and preposition preposing are applied, incorrectly, in L1; in these and subsequent examples the correct L1 patterns are indicated in parentheses. Each case is followed by a brief annotation.

(1)   (H) *Sok állatok (állat) vannak (van) a világon.*
       "There are many animals in the world."

       The subject and the predicate are pluralized, as in English. However, in Hungarian the quantifier *sok* "many" governs singular number: the correct forms are *állat* "animal" and *van* "is."

(2)   (H) *Ezt nem tudod, tudod?*
       "You don't know this, do you?"

The verb *tudod* "you know" is repeated as a tag. Tag questions of this sort are not permitted in Hungarian.

(3)   (G) ... *daß du sollst eine Matraze kaufen.*
       (... *dass du eine Matraze kaufen sollst.*)
       "... that you should buy a mattress."

According to German syntax, the auxiliary *sollst* "should" must be in final position in subordinate clauses.

(4)   (G) *Alle andere Leute hast du keine Zeit für.*
       (*Für alle andere Leute hast du keine Zeit.*)
       "You have no time for all other people."

Preposition stranding (*für* "for") is not allowed in German syntax.

In this volume several syntactic constructions are shown to be subject to attrition: word order (Schmidt; Maher; Huffines; de Bot, Gommans & Rossing), prepositional phrase (Seliger), agreement (Schmidt), subordinate clause (Maher; Schmidt).

The semantic characteristics of L2 impact on L1 in at least two significant ways. One is through **meaning extension**: the meaning of a word in L1 is generalized to include the meaning of another word in L1, on analogy to the range of meaning of the equivalent word in L2. In each of the word pairs listed in (5), meaning oppositions were neutralized in L1: the first word was used in the sense of the second. In each case, the meaning differentiations of L1 are missing in L2 (English).

(5)   a. (H) *tud* "know how to do something"
              ismer "know somebody"   →   *tud*
       b. (H) *öreg* "old (animate)"
              régi "old (inanimate)"   →   *öreg*
       c. (H) *szőr* "body hair"
              haj "scalp hair"   →   *szőr*
       d. (G) *seit* "since (temporal)"
              weil "since (causal)"   →   *seit*
       e. (G) *Sache* "thing (abstract)"
              Ding "thing (concrete)"   →   *Sache*

Loan translation (calquing) is another common transfer strategy affecting meaning: an L2 phrase or expression, especially if idiomatic, is translated literally into L1, where it is ungrammatical. In the representative examples provided in (6), the calqued L1 expressions are translations of the English glosses.

(6)   a. (H) *olajos (zsíros "fatty") haj*
                  "oily hair"

      b. (H) *rossz vagy (nincs igazad* "you don't have truth")
                  "you are wrong"

      c. (H) *vesz egy tantárgyat (tanul* "learns")
                  "takes a subject (in school)"

      d. (G) *Vergiß es (laß es bleiben* "let it stay")!
                  "Forget it!"

      e. (G) *den Flug zu machen (erreichen* "reach")
                  "to make the flight"

      f. (G) *Man muß **am ersten Platz** (vom Anfang* "from the beginning") *verrückt sein, um Linguistik zu studieren.*
                  "One has to be crazy **in the first place** to study linguistics."

As regards morphology/morphophonemics, two examples will suffice:

(7)   (G) ... *wenn du das zu mir machst*
            (... *wenn du das mir machst*)
            "... when you do it for me"

The German pronoun *mir* "to me" is already inflected for dative case. The speaker reinforced the indirect object with the preposition *zu* "to," on analogy from English.

(8)   (G) *auf Absicht (absichtlich* "intentionally")
            "on purpose"

The adverbial suffix *-lich* was replaced with the preposition *auf* "on," patterned after the English gloss.

Schmidt mentions a relevant example in this volume: in Dyirbal ergative case marking gave way to the nominative/accusative pattern of L2 (English).

   Phonological/phonetic investigations of L1 attrition are scarce, beyond impressionistic observations. Our subjects evidenced externally induced attrition in intonational patterns and in low level rules, such as the allophonic realization of phonemes (e.g. retroflexing /r/, aspirating voiceless stops) and the diphthongization of vowels. In this volume, Dressler and Schmidt discuss transfer effects in relation to allophonic distribution and word stress.

External influences are also evident in the domain of the lexicon. As any student of bilingualism, language contact, and second language acquisition knows, the lexical items, phrases, and grammatical categories of L1 and L2 can be intermingled within the span of an utterance (see the discussion in Section 2 above). This phenomenon, described under such headings as code mixing, code switching, lexical borrowing, and lexical hybridization (depending on the level of interaction), has been well studied and need not be dwelled upon here. Some cases are described in this volume by Dressler and by Turian & Altenberg.

In addition to structural changes that are explainable in terms of external influences, L1 attrition is characterized also by changes that are **internally induced**: the modification of linguistic forms is either motivated by universal principles or is related to some fact in the particular grammar of L1. The fact that in L1 attrition "unmarked" forms are better preserved than and substitute for "marked" ones, but not vice versa (Dressler and Seliger, this volume), is an example of the former, and the fact that paradigmatically related allomorphic representations may influence each other's development (Vago, this volume) is an example of the latter. Internally induced attrition phenomena encompass what elsewhere is called generalization, simplification, regularization, naturalness, intralinguistic effects, conceptual/cognitive/innate strategies, and the like. For a general discussion in this volume, cf. the contributions of Sharwood Smith & van Buren; Silva-Corvalán; Dressler; Seliger; and Vago.

We will exemplify internally induced attrition in L1 structures in the realm of morphology/morphophonemics only, since that is where the process manifests itself most profoundly. We will propose four broad subcategories.

We begin with cases of **analogical leveling**, whereby a marked feature or irregular pattern is eliminated and replaced by the unmarked, general, or regular pattern. Three sets of examples, with explanatory notes, follow.

(9)   (H) *híden (hídon)* "on (the) bridge"
       innél (innál) "you would drink"

Perhaps the most well-known rule of Hungarian phonology/morphophonemics is vowel harmony (cf. Vago 1976, 1980). In a grossly oversimplified statement, but one which is adequate for present purposes, vowel harmony specifies that front vowel roots take front vowel suffixes and back vowel roots take back vowel suffixes. However, there exist some fifty roots with the front vowels *i, í,* or *é* which take back vowel suffixes. These roots thus constitute surface exceptions to the general patterns of vowel harmony. This irregularity was removed in the above examples: in both cases the suffix vowel agrees with the root vowel in backness. (Superessive *-on* → *-en*; conditional *-ná-* → *-né-*.)

(10)   (H) *töröd (törődik)* ''cares''
        The regular 3sg present suffix is *-ø*; however, in a lexically marked subclass of verbs this suffix shows up as *-ik*. The verb for ''care'' belongs to the ''*-ik*'' conjugation class: cf. correct *törődik* above. Our subject simplified the underlying representation of this verb: the attrited form *töröd* is explained as the removal of the lexical marking for the irregular conjugation class.

(11)   (G) *er wißt (weiß)* ''he knows''
        er schleichte (schlich) ''he slunk''
        er nimmte (nahm) ''he took''
        In each case a lexically marked ''strong'' verb is regularized on analogy to the unmarked class of ''weak'' verbs. (''Ablaut'' is replaced by 3sg present *-t* or past *-t*.)

In this volume, examples of analogical leveling include the removal of lexical markings for noun classification (Schmidt) and irregular verb conjugation (Schmidt; Turian & Altenberg).

Under **paradigmatic leveling** regular alternations of morphemes are reduced, leading to more uniform paradigms. Allomorphy reduction is discussed in this volume by Schmidt for case affixes, by Dressler for pluralization and consonant mutation; for a more detailed discussion, cf. Maher's and Vago's contributions.

Category leveling neutralizes categorical distinctions by extending the domain of one category to another. In incipient stages this process is not systematic, so that substitution is subject to variation; severe cases of decay result in the elimination of the neutralized category from the grammar. Examples discussed in this volume include reductions in verbal derivational morphology (Kaufman & Aronoff), diminished productivity in word formation (Dressler), and decay in both verbal and nominal inflectional systems, especially as regards tense/aspect and case (cf. Maher's article in Part I and most of the articles in Parts II and III).

Our final classification might be called **category switch**: a category is maintained conceptually, but is expressed in a different linguistic form. Thus, Maher (this volume) makes mention of the general tendency to replace synthetic forms with analytic ones; also, prepositions may substitute for affixes (cf. Schmidt, this volume).

4   Theoretical aspects of first language attrition

The phenomenon of first language attrition can be seen as a natural continuation of a general language acquisition or learning strategy in which some rules are transferred between the existing grammars available to the speaker, while others appear to derive from innate or universal principles of language acquisition. The import of first language attrition for theories of language acquisition, both first and second, is of interest to several researchers in this volume: Sharwood Smith & van Buren; de Bot & Weltens; Maher; Turian & Altenberg; and Seliger. Here we would like to address two issues raised by first language attrition that impinge on current concerns in general linguistic theory. Sharwood Smith & van Buren (this volume) elaborate further on these, and other theoretically relevant attributes of the first language attrition process.

It is currently accepted in Chomskyan linguistic models (e.g. Chomsky 1981) that language abilities follow innate UG principles, which are then modified to suit the data to which the language learner, first or second, is exposed. Based on these modifications or parameter settings, a grammar for a specific language develops. Given the natural tendency of human language grammars to seek the most parsimonious system of rules, we are specifically interested in two questions: (a) What occurs when two languages with different arrays of parameter settings coexist in the same mind?; and (b) How are conflicts between language specific constraints and more universal rules resolved?

Within the Chomskyan model, a language grammar is comprised of two parts: a **core**, which consists of the rules a particular language has selected from UG, and a **periphery**, which consists of rules specific to that particular language and not to others. Since the core rules for any particular language are a subset of the UG, these rules are shared with other languages which may contain parts of the subset within their own core. The rules contained in the periphery part of the grammar are not shared since they are not part of the UG.

One definition of a theory of markedness in light of the core/periphery distinction is that rules from the core are considered **unmarked** ($_u$) while rules in the periphery are considered **marked** ($_m$). For example, in English verbs such as *give, send, make* allow either the prepositional phrase construction or the direct object + indirect object construction to express dative relationships; in contrast, verbs such as *donate, explain, construct* allow only prepositional phrase datives. Since of the two variant dative expressions only the prepositional phrase construction is found universally, verbs such as *give, make, send* are marked in the periphery grammar of English for allowing the language specific other option.

Within the parameter setting theoretical framework the following linguistic relationships might be hypothesized for cases of bilingualism that evidence some form of first language attrition:

(12)   a. $L2_u$ and $L1_u \rightarrow L1_u$
         b. $L2_m$ and $L1_u \rightarrow L1_u$
         c. $L2_m$ and $L1_m \rightarrow L1_m$
         d. $L2_u$ and $L1_m \rightarrow L1_u$

In the first relationship, (12a), both L2 and L1 contain the unmarked form of a rule, i.e. they share the same universal rule. An example of this relationship would be when both L1 and L2 express the dative through prepositional phrases. In a case such as this, first language attrition is not expected to obtain.[3]

In relationship (12b) we have the case of a marked form in L2 and an unmarked form in L1. Since the tendency is normally toward simplification, it would be predicted that a marked form in L2 would not displace an unmarked form in L1. As an example, consider the fact that pronoun copy is more common in relative clause constructions than pronoun deletion. If L2 contains a pronoun deletion rule, it is predicted that this rule will not displace a pronoun copy rule in L1.[4]

In relationship (12c) both L2 and L1 are matched for marked forms in a construction. It would be predicted that each language would maintain autonomy with regard to these rules so that the L1 construction would not be attrited. Of course, it is recognized that "equally marked" is a problematic collocation since markedness may be understood in the context of language attrition as both an interlingual and an intralingual designation. That is, while a form may be marked or unmarked **within** L1 or L2, the form or degree of markedness may be different across languages.

Relationship (12d) is the most likely to produce language attrition. In this case, an unmarked form will replace a marked form. Taking dative formation as an example, L1 attrition would be predicted if L1, but not L2, contained rules for dative alternation. In particular, the unmarked prepositional phrase construction is expected to be preferred over the marked double object construction. That is, simplification would tend toward the elimination of marked forms in favor of unmarked forms.

5   Conclusion

The scope of the contributions in this volume is both deep and wide. Each article is oriented toward relating the facts of L1 attrition to other areas of linguistic inquiry, such as L2 attrition, first and second language acquisition, language change, language use, language variation, and language organization. In Figure 1.2 we tabulate the language contact situations for which original L1 attrition data are presented, analyzed, and explained in Parts II and III of this text.

L1	L2	Author(s)
Dutch	French	de Bot, Rossing & Gommans
Breton	French	Dressler
Dyirbal	English	Schmidt
Pennsylvania German	English	Huffines
Spanish	English	Silva-Corvalán
Hebrew	English	Kaufman & Aronoff
German	English	Altenberg
Russian	English	Turian & Altenberg
English	Hebrew	Olshtain & Barzilay; Seliger
Hungarian	Hebrew	Vago

1.2   Group and case studies of this volume

It is sincerely hoped that this volume will be judged as a modest contribution toward providing an answer to the question: What is first language attrition, and why is it important to understand it?

Notes

1   Olshtain & Barzilay (this volume) show that attrition may affect a highly prestigious L1 as well.
2   We are indebted to George Bollag for information on the German data.
3   Of course, it must be kept in mind that if the same rule is involved in both languages, it might appear that when the speaker is using L1 he is utilizing the L1 rule, when in fact he may be utilizing the L2 rule. There would be no way of knowing which is the case from the performance of the speaker.
4   There may be other explanations for the retention of surface elements such as pronoun copy which are related to questions of psycholinguistic saliency or semantic transparency.

References

Chomsky, N. 1981. *Lectures on government and binding*. Dordrecht: Foris.
Cook, V. 1984. ''Chomsky's universal grammar and second language learning,'' *Applied Linguistics* 6: 1–18.

Corder, S. P. 1978. "Language learner language," in J. Richards (ed.), *Understanding second and foreign language learning*. Rowley, MA: Newbury House Publishers, 71–93.

Dorian, N. 1981. *Language death: The life cycle of a Scottish Gaelic dialect*. Philadelphia: University of Pennsylvania Press.

Fishman, J. 1972. *The sociology of language*. Rowley, MA: Newbury House Publishers.

Flynn, S. 1987. *A parameter-setting model of L2 acquisition*. Dordrecht: D. Reidel Publishing Company.

Gass, S. 1979. "Language transfer and universal grammatical relations," *Language Learning* 29: 327–344.

Hyltenstam, K. 1987. "Markedness, language universals, language typology, and second language acquisition," in C. Pfaff (ed.), *First and second language acquisition processes*. New York: Harper and Row, 55–80.

Schmidt, A. 1985. *Young people's Dyirbal: An example of language death from Australia*. Cambridge: Cambridge University Press.

Vago, R. M. 1976. "Theoretical implications of Hungarian vowel harmony," *Linguistic Inquiry* 7: 243–263.

1980. *The sound pattern of Hungarian*. Washington, DC: Georgetown University Press.

2 First language attrition and the parameter setting model

MICHAEL SHARWOOD SMITH AND PAUL VAN BUREN

1 Introduction

The focus of this paper, which is based on a reading of investigations into attrition reported in the literature, will be theoretical. It will consider the relevance of recent ideas in the learnability literature including the notions of "input" and "evidence" and their potential relevance for the analysis and explanation of attrition data. This means that the central concern will be the usefulness of such concepts as Universal Grammar (UG) as discussed within a Chomskyan framework, and related concepts such as markedness and parameter setting. In other words, the examples presented in the course of the discussion will serve to illustrate the appropriate theoretical problems raised by these concepts. It is, therefore, necessary to consider what kinds of questions an application of more recent versions of the Chomskyan perspective to attrition studies would raise with regard to the interpretation of attrition data.[1] It is also necessary to see what kinds of implication could be drawn as far as data elicitation techniques are concerned. Data reported in the literature will be used to illustrate both questions of interpretation raised by the theory as well as the need for special testing techniques for collecting data.

2 Competence and performance attrition

In Sharwood Smith (1983a and 1983b), attrition problems were examined in the light of, amongst other things, the basic Chomskyan distinction between competence and performance (see also Sharwood Smith 1989). It was suggested that, however satisfactorily situated attrition data were within current **sociolinguistic** models, they could not be properly understood without considering their **psycholinguistic** status. In particular, it seemed important to know whether a given subject has lost **or is even able to** lose those kinds of underlying mental representations of his or her first language that may be referred to as L1 competence.

It should be emphasized here that the notion of competence can be treated in two senses. The first, more specific sense, familiar from the Chomskyan literature, is grammatical competence, whose instantiation in a given mother tongue acquirer will be constrained by principles of Universal Grammar. The second, more extended sense includes pragmatic knowledge, also allowed for (but not discussed in any detail) by Chomsky (see Chomsky 1982). The important difference for the discussion that follows is not so much between grammatical competence and pragmatic competence (see Foster 1985), but rather between knowledge and the on-line processing of knowledge. In this case, it is the distinction that holds between linguistic knowledge of whatever kind resident in the mind of the language learner/loser[2] and those mechanisms which the learner/loser recruits to deploy that knowledge in given instances of language use, i.e. on-line performance mechanisms that are responsible for accessing and manipulating that knowledge millisecond by millisecond. In this way, language users may be said to know (or "cognize") something (see Chomsky 1975: 165), without this statement giving any information on the facility with which that knowledge may be deployed in the various mental operations necessary for speech production and speech recognition.

To rephrase the basic question to be asked of a language "loser" under investigation in terms of Bialystok & Sharwood Smith (1986), one may ask whether there has been a change in the subject's L1 "knowledge" or whether there has been a change in the subject's "control" of that knowledge. In this perspective, control has specifically to do with the nature of the on-line access (retrieval and integration) mechanisms and not with the available knowledge itself, be it syntactic, phonological, pragmatic or whatever. Hence a subject's intuitions about the first language (L1) may have remained intact even though the data show clear deviance from the native norms. One may note, in this context, Seliger's initial definition of attrition as "erosion in the linguistic **performance** [author's emphasis] of a first or primary language" (Seliger 1985).[3] If the subject's L1 intuitions were intact, then tests designed to probe L1 knowledge (typically via acceptability judgement tests) would indicate that the deviance was due to performance ("control") factors: in other words, the subject was no longer as fluent in L1 as we would expect a native speaker to be. This would also show up if the subject occasionally still produced the standard forms/structures in question (in the appropriate contexts with the same meaning intentions) in such a way as to allow us to conclude that neither the syntactic properties of the forms concerned nor their pragmatic properties had in fact been lost in any way, only the facility with which they were manipulated on-line.

One might, for example, propose as a working hypothesis that, in normal situations, that is, where there has been no physical damage to the brain, it is impossible to lose L1 competence. This would mean that all attrition amongst normals can be accounted for as loss of (fluent) access.[4] This, however, would seem to be an undesirable starting point since one can never probe competence without involving performance mechanisms, however light the processing load involved in the given experimental task. The hypothesis in question would reduce the status of "permanent competence" to a belief, and would place it beyond scientific enquiry (that is, until such time as physical correlates of competence are discovered and become accessible without recourse to elicitation tests). Hence it seems sensible to assume that attrition may occur at both levels, competence and performance. Furthermore, we should adopt the line that certain elicitation techniques can, in fact, make competence **relatively** transparent for language attrition research.

The elicitation of data probing competence may be effected in a manner uncomplicated by factors such as time pressure or the requirement to do many different things at once. As a consequence of this, theoretical questions such as the following may be asked: (a) Can competence change independently of changes in access and retrieval ability ("control changes")? (b) Does competence change typically follow a first stage characterized by a loss of accessibility and stagnate due to lack of use?

These questions relate to all types of competence, grammatical or otherwise. One might discover eventually that the various types of knowledge investigated, say grammatical and pragmatic competence, or subsystems within these competences, behaved differently such that one type was typically more permeable. That is to say, a certain type of knowledge might be more liable to attrition than another. Massive lexical loss might be accompanied by minor syntactic loss, surface morphology might change faster than more basic grammatical features, pragmatically conditioned aspects of word order may change before more purely syntactic aspects (see findings reported in Olshtain 1986), and so forth; these all seem to be interesting empirical questions.

If one looks at acquisition, it is certainly the case, given the framework appealed to here, that competence may, in principle, change for what are essentially competence reasons: if the language learner undergoes a shift in perception such that there is a **restructuring** of his or her current grammar, this does not have to be because Grammar 2 (or some subsystem of Grammar 2) is more "processible" than (an equivalent subsystem in) Grammar 1. For example, Japanese learners acquiring English may come to restructure their current developmental grammar ("interlanguage") from one in which English is treated as though it allows interruptions of verb and direct object, as in example (1), into one that observes strict adjacency in given contexts, as in (2) and (3), respectively (see, for example, Zobl 1988).

(1)   *He drove slowly the car.
(2)   He **drove the car** slowly.
(3)   Slowly, he **drove the car**.

   Looking at this from an attrition point of view, one might consider an English speaking immigrant immersed in a Japanese speaking community and apparently unable to maintain his or her L1 competence. Then one might predict that, under the pervasive influence of L2, the immigrant would begin to perceive the L1 in a new light and the result of this shift in perception at the level of competence is that the requirement for strict adjacency as exemplified above is relaxed and the L2 brought more into line with the L1. The immigrant would then accept sentences like the one illustrated (above) in (1) as "good" English. In actual fact, to establish clearly that such a shift in L1 was motivated by competence factors rather than processing ones, it would have to be shown how the move away from strict adjacency actually created complications at the processing level. If the psycholinguistic evidence were available that allowed the rating of a construction for ease of processability then one could test out whether perception of the basic structural make-up of a grammar outweighed processing considerations. To sum up, it does seem reasonable to suggest, at least as a working hypothesis, that the attrition of competence may be triggered by changes in the learner's perception of the basic structure of his or her L1 grammar and not just by a tendency to ease the processing burden of an underused L1.

   It has to be stressed that, until we have refined theories of processing, we will not be able to tell how important the processability of the L1 is: at face value it would indeed seem convenient, now looking at things from a processing point of view, if the loser can bring his or her L1 into line with L2 so that L1 in some sense becomes a dialect of L2. In this case the move from an L1 of type T_i to an L2 of type T_j will be epiphenomenal and hence not, as was suggested above, triggered by a change in perception.

   The fact that a given construction in L2, the influencing system, turns out to require **more** complex on-line processing than its equivalent in L1, the influenced system, does not of course imply that the L1 loser is ignoring processing considerations: even if L1 became more complex in this sense, it would still be a convenience to use the same processing routines for both languages. For example, it would be convenient when assembling an utterance for production to always employ the same routines for the linear placement of the main verb or adverbials in surface structure irrespective of whether L1 or L2 was being used.[5] If L1 requires, say, 7 processing operations for assembling a given construction where L2 would normally require 10, it will still be convenient to use 10 for both languages, especially as the loser may be more motivated to model everything along the lines of the dominant language (L2) in his or her immediate environment rather than the underused or unused L1 system.

3   Eliciting competence and control

It is important to keep in mind the fact that the competence/control distinction implies elicitation tests that probe **mainly** competence facts, the results of which can be matched against tests that focus on the tapping of **fluency**, i.e. control ability. The tests that probe competence have to be given a clear theoretical underpinning and this includes the question of whether **metalinguistic** knowledge, that is, explicit knowledge about language structure, is understood to have a different epistemological status than the status accorded to **tacit** knowledge in the Chomskyan sense.

If a test can be done using both modes of knowledge (tacit or explicit) then clearly the test results are going to be hard to interpret. Researchers can get around this obstacle by making the crucial experiments in the more subtle areas of language structure where the subject is not likely to have any explicit notions of what should or should not be the "correct" (native) solution. Also the use of various different techniques to probe intuitions can provide some kind of security against the application of irrelevant linguistic "prejudices" obscuring the subjects' gut feelings about forms offered for their judgement. In a language loss study carried out in Utrecht by Van Vlerken & Galbraith (see, for example, Van Vlerken 1980: 59ff), young English speaking immigrants were given words on cards to sort in order to make acceptable sentences as well as a straight acceptability judgement test. The results were compared with a structured spontaneous speech task in which they had to talk about a pair of pictures. In Van Buren & Sharwood Smith (1985), which reported an investigation into acquisition but this time using the Chomsky perspective to frame research questions, elicitation techniques were used that involved subjects selecting acceptable positions for prepositions that were placed in boxes above the test utterance. There was another test where they were asked to reconstruct the questions of a deaf man who missed a vital piece of information in a statement addressed to him and also a judgement test of sentences not taken in isolation but set inside a wider frame of discourse (see discussion in Bialystok & Sharwood Smith 1986).

Clearly, there has to be a great deal of care and further research connected with probing competence in order that processing control effects can be isolated and the right conclusions can be drawn about the theoretical status of the attrition (or acquisition) data.

4   "Input" in attrition and the notion of "evidence"

In attempting to align ideas and findings in acquisition research with those that are now appearing in the field of language attrition, one of the first theoretical problems that arises is what to make of the relevance of "input" in attrition studies. At first glance, it would seem that, in this respect, acquisition and attrition cannot be compared. An acquirer builds grammars, lexical systems, and so forth, on the basis of input data. The changes that occur in language attrition would seem rather to be accompanied by the **lack** of relevant data. This is interesting because it is usually assumed that mature native languages are typically stable as opposed to interlanguages or developing L1 systems, which are characterized as typically **unstable** (see Adjemian 1976, for example). It would appear from this assumption that once attained, the mature L1 is "fixed" and needs no further input either to disconfirm faulty learner hypotheses or to **maintain** its final state. The L1 data that served once as input is therefore no longer input except to the receptive system as a whole (cf. Sharwood Smith 1986 for a discussion of two types of input). Why then should attrition occur? There are two obvious candidates:

(a)   L1 deprivation
(b)   crosslinguistic influence from another language being acquired.

The purest attrition situation one can conceive of is clearly the "desert island" one: left alone with no opportunity to read or hear the L1, no opportunity to use it to communicate with other (present) native speakers, and finally, making no effort to write or speak aloud, the native speaker might or might not undergo some further development in his or her L1 which would diverge from the norms. The implied empirical question here could, as suggested above, be split up into two, namely, would the shipwrecked sailor:

(a)   progressively lose control over an unchanged L1 competence?
(b)   develop a new L1 competence?

The first possibility (a) – progressive loss of control – immediately seems feasible: on analogy with what happens with the motor skills due to lack of use (muscular weakness), one may conceive of that part of on-line processing ability which does not actually involve any actual muscular activity (as, for example, when using language while thinking and without any subvocalization) also to be prone to atrophy through disuse. The second possibility (b) – the development of a new competence – suggests that not only the on-line aspects of performance but also the relevant knowledge structures themselves do atrophy through lack of use. In this case, one would expect (a) as a first stage to be followed by (b) with a structurally and functionally reduced (possibly pidginized) system.

Another theoretical possibility is that the native speaker not only needs evidence for developing an L1 system but also needs evidence to maintain his or her L1: the L1 changes not because of lack of use but because of a lack of confirming evidence that the L1 is the way it is in a community of native speakers. As was mentioned above, this would make natural languages appear to be less fixed than they are normally assumed to be and less distinct from developing systems such as early versions of L1 or interlanguages created by second language learners (cf. Adjemian 1976).

The standard kind of situation discussed in the literature is more complex than is the case in the simple desert island situation outlined above, and it involves both lack of continuous exposure to L1 as well as exposure to L2 input, which is generally understood to have a marked effect on L1 behavior. It might seem that one could neatly mark off L2 influenced changes from L1 internal changes and attribute the first type to exposure of L2 and the second type to changes that would occur in the desert island situation and hence are peculiar to attrition. However there is a problem in this neat interpretation of language loss data since, in acquisition studies, people have often observed developmental processes that do not seem to be attributable to crosslinguistic influence.[6] Hence, if attrition data suggest changes which are **not** due to crosslinguistic influence (CLI),[7] we cannot earmark that data as evidence for processes that occur only in attrition. However, if these changes can be attributed to some process observed in acquisition research where learners simply cease to pay attention to the L2 and create their own structures, then the parallel with attrition becomes more evident. The difference between acquisition and attrition is then a fairly superficial one: in the one case the L1 is environmentally present but ignored (not treated as input) and in the other case the relevant L1 is simply environmentally absent. This in turn means that theories about acquisitional change that is **not** triggered by CLI may, after all, be applied to parallel changes in attrition.

Despite the fact that findings and theories in acquisition research have a close bearing on our understanding of attrition phenomena and that we can therefore consider applications of the Chomskyan approach to diverging competences (Sharwood Smith 1983b), there is a conceptual problem arising out of the term "evidence" when used to characterize input. While we may speak of the L2 affecting L1 as a kind of input from within, to what extent may we see L2 "input" in term of "evidence," an important concept in the Chomskyan approach? According to most researchers, negative evidence in the sense of overt corrections of syntactic errors and the detailing of what is **not** possible in the L1 is not normally available to the child and is typically ignored when it is available. In L2 acquisition, the question is more complicated and this may be the case for L1 attrition in the sense that it is happening in the context of another language being acquired. The L2 acquirer may have available much more negative evidence of the type discussed above; it is however another question as to whether he or she actually uses this evidence to reshape the current IL grammar. The L2 research pointing to similar patterns of development in L1 and L2 acquisition would suggest that this negative evidence, consciously perceived by the learner or not, does not filter through to the underlying developmental grammar. The onus thus falls on to:

(a)   the positive evidence in the input showing simply what **is** possible in L1

(b)   the constraints on possible natural grammars provided by UG.

What, however, is the "evidence" that would induce an L1 loser to shift from a current grammar (or area of grammar) to a new one? Certainly, it cannot be native speaker L1 input: this is no longer available. It could conceivably be exposure to L1 speakers who were already speaking an altered (attrited) L1, but the question then arises as to how they came to change their grammar. It might also (conceivably) be the L2 input which is by some "sleight of the brain" taken to be quasi-L1 input; but this gives us a rather convoluted notion of what is entailed by the concept of evidence. The only reasonable option remaining is to say that one might talk of "input" (in the sense of L2 input to the L1) but that there is no such thing as "evidence" in language attrition since there is no such thing as "hypothesizing."

5   Parameter resetting via input

If there is no such thing as evidence in language attrition, can one then say that the Chomskyan model in which this notion plays a crucial role is not applicable? To answer this, one needs to consider the basic idea of parameter setting and parameter resetting. L1 language learners[8] are supposed to infer from the evidence what grammatical parameters from the repertoire provided by UG, so to speak, are relevant for a particular L1 that they are exposed to. For example, there must be evidence in the input which signals that the grammar has to be configurational and contain movement rules for "move alpha" to be applied and bounding nodes to be set. This is in order that movement may be constrained according to UG. Furthermore, a characteristic of particular parameters is that they carry with them a certain preference structure: this is the domain of the theory of markedness, which says that some values will be preferred over others unless the evidence shows otherwise.

One implication that may be drawn from the theory of markedness in UG with regard to parameters that have different possible values is that if learners have evidence for certain parameters being relevant and if counter-evidence is not immediately available or if they are not immediately **sensitive** to evidence that actually **is** available, then the "unmarked" value is assumed. The reason for this, arguing from considerations of learnability, is that the learner only makes assumptions that can be disconfirmed by the input, i.e. does not require "negative evidence."[9] White has suggested (for example White, in press) that second language learners initially assume L1 settings for parameters such that they copy over any L1 marked values that exist for particular parameters leading to, for example, preposition stranding (see for example Liceras 1986; Van Buren & Sharwood Smith 1985) and, depending on the theoretical account used, null subjects (see White 1985; Hilles 1986), which would not automatically be the case for L1 learners. This means that Spanish learners of English will initially use and accept (4) as English, where (5) would be appropriate:

(4)   Is beautiful.
(5)   It is beautiful.

and they will not use, and reject, sentences like (6), where the preposition "to" has been stranded instead of "following" the *wh*-word to the initial position in the sentence:

(6)   Who are you talking to?

Kean has pointed out (Kean 1986) that L2 learners, if they have access to UG while developing their new grammar, have access to a different kind of UG, an already parameterized UG. She suggests further (Kean 1988) that this altered nature of the language capacity may have a clear neurolinguistic status. That is to say, the neural architecture will have physically developed in this way making it impossible for L2 learners to have recourse to the early stages of the language capacity (UG) which they experienced in mother tongue development. This means that they cannot learn the L2 in the same way as they would have learned it had it been their L1.[10] This also means that the resetting of parameters in L2 acquisition must follow various indirect routes (see Zobl 1988; Rutherford & Sharwood Smith 1986).

What, however, are the parameter setting implications for language attrition? If relevant evidence is lacking from primary language data, as was claimed above, then what might be called the "realignment" of L1 along, say, L2 lines, such that L1 parameters are reset to match any existing relevant equivalents in L2[11] is even more unlikely than in L2 acquisition. This implies, *ceteris paribus*, that the marked parameters of L1 will stay marked during attrition and that prepositions will continue to be stranded, and null subject will continue to occur (or be absent, depending on the theoretical interpretation of pro-drop).

It is instructive to look at examples from Seliger's (1989) data on preposition stranding. Seliger's subject, a child immigrant to Israel from the United States, demonstrates the loss of stranding in attrited L1 English apparently by aligning English with Hebrew which is unmarked in this respect and therefore does not tolerate stranding (see also Sharwood Smith 1989). The same observations were made by Berman, who reports typical constructions such as (7), which are correct, albeit formal standard English, but for the missing "m" (marking oblique case), as well as constructions such as (8), which are actually incorrect in English (Berman & Olshtain 1982):

(7)   He doesn't know to who it belongs.
(8)   He's thinking about with what they can play.

Finally, Seliger (1989) reports the reverse situation where attrited Hebrew contains normally unacceptable stranded prepositions as in (9) (see also the discussion in Sharwood Smith 1989):

(9)   *Ma at midaberet al?*

Taken at face value, this looks like the resetting of an L1 parameter via a crosslinguistic alignment of relevant parameters, i.e. without any evidence to trigger it but rather as a result of crosslinguistic input activating an "L2-to-L1" copying procedure. This would certainly seem to be the case if there were supporting evidence from acceptability judgement tests that showed a change in the child's perception of L1. Otherwise, apparent parameter setting would have to be recategorized as, for instance, the effect of preferred real time processing routines: an alignment of control mechanisms, in other words, rather than of grammatical competences.[12] Alternatively, it could be seen as the effect of change in the learner's perception not of the underlying grammar but rather of the pragmatic effects of stranding such that the responses in the metalinguistic tests excluded stranding for **stylistic** reasons alone.[13] This should underscore the necessity of using a battery of theoretically motivated tests rather than relying on production alone.

Finally, as has been pointed out elsewhere (see Kean 1988), if resetting during attrition occurs, it is important to find out whether this takes place within the confines of UG and whether this adherence to options provided by UG is simply the result of copying over L2 settings of L1, thus creating the possibilities of odd mixtures of parameter settings which, when taken together, could not occur in fully fledged, unattrited native languages, even though, when taken separately they **could** occur in one language or another.

6   Conclusion

Apart from the usefulness of applying a precise linguistic framework to attrition data, in this case Chomsky's Government and Binding theory, a number of interesting questions arise as a result of using this learnability oriented approach. These questions bear on the relationships between attrited systems on the one hand and non-attrited languages on the other. The questions actually parallel questions in acquisition studies concerning the theoretical status of learners' interlanguages, at least those parts of them that are relevant to Chomskyan accounts.[14] In particular, one may ask whether the attrited grammatical system is a "natural system" in that it can be classed as a possible human language within the constraints defined by UG. Clearly, whatever can be attributed to on-line borrowings can be discounted as relevant data to decide these issues. Carefully constructed acceptability judgements, however, may provide vital clues as to whether language losers undergo shifts in their underlying grammatical competence and whether the results demonstrate the ongoing applications of constraints on possible languages. At any event, the basic claim here is that, although applying the parameter setting model and its associated metatheory to attrition research may seem at first glance to release a Pandora's box of methodological problems, the gains in terms of linguistic precision and promised insights into the processes of attrition will far outweigh the disadvantages.

Notes

1 This in no way changes the approach adopted to such data in an earlier paper by Sharwood Smith (1983b) where it was claimed that a whole number of conspiring (for example) typological, semantic and processing effects would have to be taken into account.

2 Despite the misleading nature of the terms "loss" and "loser," they will be used here together with "attrition," for stylistic reasons.

3 In the paper cited here Seliger later refers to interlanguage (IL) grammars in attrition and would therefore appear to accept a competence dimension in attrition as well as a control dimension.

4 Loftus & Loftus (1980) critically discuss the "fallacy" that many people seem to have, namely the idea that everything is remembered deep down and that all memory problems are actually ones of recall. The evidence suggests that there is much more creativity in recall than subjects would care to admit to.

5 Note that convenience of processing here is a speaker oriented affair since it will be presumably more difficult for (non-attrited) native speakers to **receptively** process the new version of their L1 as produced by an L1 loser.

6 This is true whether the hypothesized processes are "general cognitive" in nature like simplification, overgeneralization, regularization or whatever one chooses to call it, or are specifically linguistic in nature such as the move to "demark" linguistic systems irrespective of the nature of the L1.

7 The term "crosslinguistic" was selected (see Sharwood Smith 1983a) to avoid implications of a behavioristic perspective implicit in "transfer" and also implications of monodirectionality (L1 to L2) to facilitate discussion of language attrition where the influence goes the other way (L2 to L1). See also Kellerman and Sharwood Smith (1986).

8 The term "learn" is used here in its informal sense without any implications concerning the information that is actually internalized and that which is innately given.

9 Negative evidence is explicit information that certain forms not in the input (and that the learner may have created for him or herself) are not permissible. This evidence is understood not to be regularly available to L1 learners (see Berwick 1985).

10 Few in fact have claimed such a very close parallel between L1 and L2 development (cf. Mazurkewich 1984).

11 L2 may, of course, have parameters selected from possible options

offered by UG that do not exist in L1 and can therefore provide no source of influence in developing other grammatical systems.

12 This effectively means it could be classified, following Seliger (1985), as code switching.

13 Stylistic effects can also occur in normal native-speaker behavior if it is the belief of the native speaker that the test is testing some prestige version of L1 in which stranded prepositions are taboo.

14 This of course means that a large area of what many would like to include under the terms "language" and "interlanguage" is still unaccounted for.

References

Adjemian, C. 1976. "On the nature of interlanguage systems," *Language Learning* 26: 297–320.

Berman, R., and E. Olshtain. 1982. "Language patterns affecting L2 attrition: data from Hebrew–English bilingual children." Paper presented at the Fifth International Conference on Contrastive Projects at the University of Jyväskylä, Finland.

Berwick, R. 1985. *The acquisition of syntactic knowledge.* Cambridge: MIT Press.

Bialystok, E., and M. Sharwood Smith. 1986. "Interlanguage is not a state of mind: an evaluation of the construct for second language acquisition," *Applied Linguistics* 6: 101–117.

Chomsky, N. 1975. *Reflections on language.* New York: Pantheon.

Chomsky, N. 1982. *Rules and representations.* Oxford: Blackwell.

Felix, S., and H. Wode (eds.). 1983. *Language development at the crossroads.* Tübingen: Gunter Narr.

Foster, S. 1985. "Divide and rule: taking a modular approach to universals of language acquisition." Paper presented at SLRF, Los Angeles, February 1985.

Gass, S., and L. Selinker (eds.). 1983. *Language transfer in language learning.* Rowley, MA: Newbury House Publishers.

Hilles, S. 1986. "Interlanguage and the pro-drop parameter," *Second Language Research* 2,1: 33–52.

Hyltenstam, K., and L. Obler (eds.). 1989. *Bilingualism across the lifespan.* Cambridge: Cambridge University Press.

Kean, M.-L. 1986. "Core issues in transfer," in Kellerman and Sharwood Smith (eds.).

Kean, M.-L. 1988. The shifting structural basis of second language acquisition. In Pankhurst, Sharwood Smith and Van Buren (eds.).

Kellerman, E., and M. Sharwood Smith (eds.). 1986. *Crosslinguistic influence in second language acquisition.* Oxford: Pergamon.

Liceras, J. 1986. *Linguistic theory and second language acquisition: The Spanish non-native grammar of English speakers.* Tübingen: Gunter Narr.

Loftus, E., and G. Loftus. 1980. "On the permanence of stored information in the human brain," *American Psychologist* 35: 409–40.

Mazurkewich, I. 1984. "The acquisition of the dative alternation by second language learners and linguistic theory," *Language Learning* 34: 91–110.

Olshtain, E. 1986. "The attrition of English as a second language: a case of Hebrew speaking children," MS, Tel-Aviv University.

Pankhurst, J., M. Sharwood Smith, and P. Van Buren (eds.) 1988. *Learnability and second languages*. Dordrecht: Foris.

Rutherford, W., and M. Sharwood Smith. 1986. "Consciousness-raising and universal grammar," *Applied Linguistics* 6: 274–282.

Seliger, H. 1985. "Primary language attrition in the context of other language loss and mixing," MS, Queens College.

Seliger, H. 1989. "Deterioration and creativity in childhood bilingualism," in Hyltenstam and Obler (eds.).

Sharwood Smith, M. 1983a. "On first language loss in the second language acquirer," in Gass and Selinker (eds.), 222–231.

Sharwood Smith, M. 1983b. "On explaining language loss," in Felix and Wode (eds.), 49–69.

Sharwood Smith, M. 1989. "Crosslinguistic influence in language loss," in Hyltenstam and Obler (eds.).

Van Buren, P., and M. Sharwood Smith. 1985. "The acquisition of preposition-stranding by Dutch learners of English," *Second Language Research* 1: 2. 18–46.

Van Vlerken, M. 1980. "Adverbial placement: a study of first language loss," unpublished MA dissertation, English Department, University of Utrecht.

White, L. 1985. "The pro-drop parameter in adult second language acquisition," *Language Learning* 35: 1. 47–62.

White, L. 1988. "Universal grammar and language transfer," in Pankhurst *et al.* (eds.).

Zobl, H. 1988. "Configurationality in Japanese–English interlanguage," in Pankhurst *et al.* (eds.).

3 Recapitulation, regression, and language loss

KEES DE BOT AND BERT WELTENS

1 Introduction

Roman Jakobson opens his monograph *Kindersprache, Aphasie und allgemeine Lautgesetze* with a quotation from Karl Bühler: "Die einzige Gelegenheit die wir haben, die menschliche Sprache in statu nascendi zu beobachten, bietet das Kind," and he himself adds: "Die einzige Gelegenheit die wir haben, die menschliche Sprache im Abbau zu beobachten, bieten die pathologischen Sprachstörungen zentraler Natur" (Jakobson 1941: 348).[1]

In his article Jakobson sketches parellels between three processes of language change: diachronic language change, first language acquisition, and language loss as a result of brain damage. He argues that parallels between these three processes suggest that there are universal mechanisms in language. He provides evidence to show that phonemes should be looked upon as bundles of features, and that in all three processes distinctive features rather than individual phonemes play a role. In his view, those features that are acquired late are also relatively uncommon in natural language, and early candidates for attrition. Although his evidence is largely phonological, Jakobson assumes that there are universals at other linguistic levels as well.

The supposed parallels between language history and first language acquisition (or second language acquisition, for that matter) are usually labelled as the **recapitulation hypothesis**; the supposed parallelism between language acquisition and language loss as the **regression hypothesis**.

Both hypotheses have been the object of some linguistic research. In this paper we will examine whether parallels between language acquisition and diachronic language change can indeed be interpreted as recapitulation. Furthermore, we will investigate the tenability of the regression hypothesis in Jakobson's sense, in particular for other types of language loss – i.e. with causes other than brain damage.

2   Ontogeny, phylogeny, and recapitulation

It is probably not fair to call Jakobson an avowed recapitulist. His main goal was to show parallels in language development, not to provide supportive evidence for the original recapitulation hypothesis. This hypothesis is based on Haeckel's biogenetic law of 1868: "Ontogeny is a concise recapitulation of phylogeny." According to this law, the individual in its development from an embryo to a fully grown organism goes through the same stages as the species in the course of evolution. Genetically determined traces of evolutionary stages can be identified particularly in the prenatal stages. Haeckel (1874: 5) saw this development as determining the development of the individual: "Die Phylogenese ist die mechanische Ursache der Ontogenese."[2]

Haeckel's biogenetic law was considered to be applicable in different scientific fields, but actual research into the comparability of stages in ontogeny and phylogeny was not carried out until much later. The results of these investigations show that a strict interpretation of the biogenetic law is untenable. Lamendella (1976: 397) outlines the main problems in the recapitulation hypothesis:

(1)   The supposition that ontogenetic stages would be a recapitulation of stages in the development of **adult** predecessors

(2)   The supposition that, as far as the course of development is concerned, the correspondence between ontogeny and phylogeny would be **perfect**

(3)   The supposition that recapitulation occurs **at the highest level**, i.e. at the level of the entire organism. It seems more plausible to look at functional subsystems in which recapitulation may or may not occur.

The strict version of the recapitulation hypothesis presupposes a continuous and gradual development of both individual and species, a development that is always headed in the same direction, namely from simple to complex and more specialized. Here, the Darwinistic character of Haeckel's opinions emerges. "*Natura non facit saltus,*" the dogma of the gradual development, is the foundation of the hypothesis. A second presupposition was that any stage at any given moment in evolution was an optimal adaptation to the environment, and therefore functional. More recent evolution research has shown both dogmas to be untenable: evolutionary jumps do occur, and so do non-adaptive changes, or at least changes that cannot be **explained** as adaptations. For a survey of the development of evolutionary theories, we refer to Leakey's (1979) introduction to a recent edition of Darwin's *On the origin of species*.

Applying the recapitulation hypothesis in the strict sense to language is less simple than people thought at the end of the nineteenth century (Stam 1976). Apart from the question whether language can be compared with a biological organism – although someone like Paul (1888) had no problem whatsoever with that – there are several aspects that are problematic. Validity of the recapitulation hypothesis would imply that both language acquisition and diachronic language change are continuous, gradual processes which are governed by the principle "from simplicity to increasing complexity." Whether or not the process of first language acquisition is continuous is one of the main matters of debate. Clark & Clark (1977: 298) opt for continuity as the main rule: "In language acquisition, it is continuity rather than discontinuity that appears to be the rule," but other child language researchers have struck a different note (Gleitman & Wanner 1982; Shatz 1982).

For diachronic change, there is no certainty either that continuity, gradualness and unidirectionality are the rule. In diachronic language research, the definitions of "complexity" and changes in complexity in the course of time are problematic. In this respect, **morphological** complexity seems to be relatively clear-cut, compared with syntactic or lexical complexity.

Givón (1979: 303–304) suggests a number of factors that might explain why man's linguistic communication system has become more complex, or – to use his own words – more syntacticized. Increasing diversity in physical environment and in sociocultural structure and context play an important role: the increasing diversity would call for a more detailed linguistic system with less ambiguity.

Kiparsky (1976: 98), on the other hand, argues that the position of a gradual development from a simple to a more complex language is not tenable. He makes the interesting suggestion that the degree of complexity of a linguistic system, in particular its morphology, is dependent on the nature of the speech community. He suggests a tendency towards complexity in smaller, closed communities, on the assumption that in closed communities language is a suitable means for individuals or groups of individuals to distinguish themselves from others. When speech communities are larger and especially when they frequently come into contact with others, this would, according to Kiparsky, lead to simplification and uniformity, because the speech community would want to demonstrate unity.[3]

The limitations that Lamendella (1976) set to the applicability of the recapitulation hypothesis have the following consequences as far as language change is concerned:

(1)   Not all stages found in child language are recapitulations of stages in adult predecessors. In other words, some stages may have occurred in the past, but were, in fact, never part of the adults' repertoire (e.g. expressions fashionable in subcultures)

(2)   Not all stages identifiable in language acquisition have occurred in the diachronic development, and vice versa

(3)   Recapitulation does not necessarily occur at the highest level of the hierarchy, and not in the same way within different subsystems. This means that, for example, finding a parallellism on the phonological level does not imply the existence of something similar on the syntactic or lexical levels.

Several investigators who have dealt with the relation between ontogeny and phylogeny are not very clear about what exactly they mean by "the" phylogeny that they want to compare with ontogeny. Jakobson (1941) and Baron (1977), for example, have limited their discussions to the more recent eras in the development of the Indo-European languages. Their diachronic data mainly come from older writings, rather than being reconstructions of proto-languages. This means that they only look for parallels in the last part of phylogeny; the many hundreds of thousands of years of development before that remain out of sight. However, as early as 1876, Friedrich Engels claimed that comparisons should indeed be made with this relatively short, later period: "The mental development of the human child is only a[n] ... abbreviated repetition of the intellectual development of [its] ancestors, at least the later ones" (Engels 1876/1954: 241).

By contrast, some of the contributors to the 1976 conference on "Origins and evolution of language and speech," organized by the New York Academy of Sciences (Harnad, Steklis & Lancaster 1976), do deal with the earliest, hypothetical forms of language. On the basis of (neuro-) anatomical reconstructions and comparisons with communication systems in other primates, they try to gain some insight into these early stages of language. The latter group of people might be regarded as most faithful to Darwinism: only the great changes in nature are important, not the minimal changes that occur in, say, a thousand years.

It seems useful here to distinguish between two episodes in the phylogeny of language: one in which the transition from primitive forms of communication as sexual signals and expressions of emotions into a syntacticized language system occurred, and a second episode in which this minimally syntacticized form developed into the languages as we know them today. Research into parallels between language acquisition and the **first** episode has in fact more right to be qualified as recapitulation research, given the fact that the major changes that took place during the earlier stages are more likely to be reflected in incipient language behavior of infants than the comparatively small changes that occurred more recently. Unfortunately, data from these earlier stages are beyond reach, so parallels – if found at all – will in general have to be largely hypothetical.

Researchers who compare language acquisition with the **second** episode in the phylogeny of language are looking for possible explanations for language change, rather than for fossils of a distant past (Baron 1977).

At the moment, parallels between ontogeny and phylogeny are acknowledged by most researchers. Theories on language change (Anderson 1973; Sturtevant 1917; Weinreich, Labov & Herzog 1968) in fact often regard the child as an important initiator of language change, and therefore as an important factor in diachronic language change. This does not mean that the idea that both processes progress gradually and unidirectionally is generally accepted, too. As indicated by Kiparsky (1976), it is most plausible that languages go through periods of becoming more complex and less complex, depending on the sociolinguistic context. As a consequence, a language may have gone through different periods in which it became more complex, rather than just **one**. In that case, parallels with language acquisition would apply to historically distant periods which do not form a continuum.

Language acquisition and diachronic language development are not two continuous processes in which the **order** and **timing** of the comparable stages run parallel, because the relation between successive stages can be radically different in phylogeny and ontogeny respectively. Child language can provide important indications of potential changes, and explain some of the diachronic data. It is obvious, however, that this kind of parallellism is essentially different from the one implied in Haeckel's original ideas about recapitulation, namely that the ontogenetic stages are hereditary, genetically conditioned remnants of earlier phylogenic manifestations.

Researchers who concentrate on the more recent episode of diachronic change adopt a point of view that is diametrically opposed to that of the researchers with a Darwinistic orientation: for the former, ontogeny is a determining factor in phylogeny; for the latter, phylogeny determines ontogeny. This brings us to the heart of the matter: the directionality of the causal relation between ontogeny and phylogeny. Lamendella (1976) proves himself a real recapitulist: "Most recently encoded genetic information tends to unfold later in ontogeny so as to preserve the temporal sequence in which the new components of the genetic information code were laid down" (398). By saying this he opts for a position that biologists gave up some fifty years ago. In his brilliant *Ontogeny and phylogeny*, Gould clearly shows that the recapitulation hypothesis in its strict sense is untenable: "The biogenetic law finally collapsed as Mendelian genetics repudiated the generality of its two necessary principles – terminal addition and condensation" (1977: 8). If biologists have given up the hypothesis for good reasons, there does not seem to be very much ground for preserving it in linguistics.

Abandoning the recapitulation hypothesis does not imply ruling out parallels between ontogeny and phylogeny. Koffka (1928, cited by Gould 1977: 144) rejected the recapitulation hypothesis and put forward a "correspondence theory," according to which ontogeny seems to parallel phylogeny because external constraints impose a similar order on both processes. In fact, the same ideas can be found in Piaget's work on epistemology.

For Jakobson (1941), a comparison of phylogeny and ontogeny was just a means to show the possibility of universal characteristics of language. If one rejects the determination of ontogeny by phylogeny, that does not imply the rejection of a genetically determined language ability: apparently children form the same hypotheses about language when acquiring it, some of which lead to permanent changes and some of which do not. In this respect, evidence for parallels between ontogeny and phylogeny is at the same time supportive evidence for the idea of universals, particularly for language acquisition universals, which have also been confirmed by crosslinguistic investigations (Slobin 1982).

Parallels between language change in individuals and changes in the language itself have only very recently attracted renewed interest in the context of language attrition research. Boyd & Andersson (1988) report on the loss of clitic elements in Finnish speakers in Finland and Sweden, and their pilot data seem to suggest that the tendency to drop clitic elements in possessive constructions is accelerated in immigrant Finns in Sweden as compared to a control group in Finland. In a sense, this can be interpreted as an "attrition variant" of recapitulation: language attrition as a condensed form of change processes in the language itself. Comparable findings are reported by Geelen & De Bot (1986) on individual dialect loss. They showed that processes of change that have been going on in the dialect for several decades are speeded up and finalized in dialect speakers that have left their region of origin and have, accordingly, had little contact with the dialect for a number of years.

The empirical research done so far is still too scarce to draw final conclusions, but it may be the case that with (first) language loss research the recapitulation hypothesis is given new life in linguistics, be it in a reversed version.

3   Regression and language loss

3.1   *Regression and language pathology*

As already mentioned, Jakobson also tried to find indications for the existence of universals in the language of aphasics, particularly in comparison with first language acquisition. The idea of loss as the mirror image of acquisition was not new when Jakobson proposed it in 1941. John Hughlings Jackson used the term "dissolution" to denote the course of certain diseases of the central nervous system: "It is a process of undevelopment, it is a 'taking to pieces' in order from the least organized, from the most complex and most voluntary, towards the most organized, most simple, and most automatic . . . Hence the statement 'to undergo dissolution', is rigidly the equivalent of the statement 'to be reduced to a lower level of evolution'" (Jackson 1958: 46). Dissolution in Hughlings Jackson's sense not only referred to aphasia, but also to muscular atrophy, hemiplegia and dementia causing diseases such as Huntington's chorea.

Kussmaul (1910) was the first to try and test the regression hypothesis on aphasic phenomena. As Spreen (1968: 467ff.) writes in his historical sketch, the interest in the regression hypothesis – as well as in the recapitulation hypothesis, for that matter – was typical of the "Zeitgeist" around 1880, in which the integration of different disciplines into one great concept formed an ideal. Ribot (1883) applied the hypothesis to aphasic multilinguals and on it he based his law that in aphasia the language learned last is affected most heavily and recovers slowest, while languages learned earlier are less subject to damage. Originally, Freud (1891) also used the term regression in connection with aphasia; it was not until later that he used it in connection with his psychoanalytic work.

In those days, the usefulness, especially the explanatory power of the regression hypothesis was not questioned. Parallels between acquisition, history and loss were readily accepted as proofs for universal mechanisms operative in language. Apparently, the existence of universals did not have to be explained.

Comrie (1981: 23–26) gives three possible explanations for their existence: monogeny, the development of all languages from one protolanguage; innate language ability; and functional/pragmatic causes. The choice one makes in explanations for language universals has immediate consequences for the value one attaches to the regression hypothesis. Obler (1981: 385) thinks that "elegance of symmetry" is in fact all it has to offer, but that appears to us to be too rash a rejection. Again, the question of causality arises: is loss a mirror image of acquisition because of external constraints, or does the process of acquisition **determine** the process of loss? For obvious reasons (species do not die out backwards) biology is not going to solve this dilemma as it did for recapitulation.

Symmetry in the construction and dissolution of language may tell us more about the structure and storage of language. In language acquisition, particularly in second language acquisition, the way something is acquired or learned can influence the way it is stored in memory (cf. Lambert & Fillenbaum 1959 for the compound–coordinate distinction; and Kerkman & de Bot 1989 for a similar effect at the lexical level).[4]

Also from a Chomskyan point of view, regression research can provide useful information. If one starts from the assumption that there is a neural substratum of language ability in the brain, as the Chomskyan tradition does, then parallels between phylogeny and ontogeny are feasible, but the likelihood of regression is very low: arbitrary damage done to the language associated parts of the brain will also affect the neural substratum just mentioned, which makes the occurrence of regression unlikely. The situation is different for diffuse brain damage as it occurs in dementia; in that case, we are dealing with a process of "dissolution" in Hughlings Jackson's sense, much more so than is the case in aphasia.

On the other hand, if one does not take the neural substratum too literally, a hierarchy of the rule system as proposed by Jakobson for the phonological component is not dissimilar to the hierarchical organization of sentence structure according to Transformational Grammar (TG). The psychological reality of this hierarchy would be much more founded if it could be shown to play a role in acquisition and loss processes. One of the few studies that did this is Myerson & Goodglass (1972).

The tenability of the regression hypothesis also depends on the hierarchical level at which it is applied:

(1)   between languages: with respect to the order of acquisition and loss of languages in multilinguals (Ribot's law)

(2)   within languages: in acquisition, perception precedes production, and spoken language precedes written language, in language loss, the sequence is reversed

(3)   within skills: as far as phonology, morphosyntax and lexicon are concerned.

Not so long ago, Wepman & Jones (1962) tried to add an extra dimension to the regression hypothesis: they tried to link up different kinds of aphasia with stages in child language development. The pointlessness of this enterprise may be demonstrated by the fact that the babbling phase in children was "equated" with jargon aphasia, in which patients have only a limited number of set expressions at their disposal.[5]

The tenability of the regression hypothesis as a basic principle for the processes mentioned under (1) and (2) above has not been really questioned until now, but things are quite different for the third level. As already mentioned, Jakobson's evidence was largely phonological. In addition, he himself admits that there were relatively few data available. The most important attempt at actually testing the tenability of the regression hypothesis is Caramazza & Zurif's (1978) collection of papers, *Language acquisition and language breakdown: parallels and divergencies*. They invited a number of – in their own words, all – researchers who had dealt with aphasia as well as child language to present their data on the relation between the two. Their general conclusion is that, except for segmental speech perception, the regression hypothesis is untenable. This outcome is, however, not surprising in our view. The situation in aphasia is fundamentally different from that of language acquisition or diachronic language change. In the first place, local brain damage does in general not lead to **global** deterioration of cognitive and linguistic skills, but to **specific** deficits of parts of the language system. Secondly the brain damage causes, in most cases, an **immediate** rather than a **gradual** deterioration.

A somewhat crude analogy would be that one would, in investigating the phenomenon of walking on two legs, compare children learning to walk, man's development from quadruped to *homo erectus*, and the way people walk who have suddenly lost the use of their right foot. The comparison of the first two processes is justifiable, that with the third is not. Yet some have tried to confirm or reject the regression hypothesis as formulated by Jakobson in such a way.

There are two elements in the quotation from Jackson (1958) given at the beginning of this section that deserve further discussion. Firstly, his reference to dissolution as making a step backwards in evolution. In doing so, he follows the Darwinistic tradition of a gradual transition to increasing complexity of the organism: in his view, aphasia is regarded as a gradual recurrence of earlier stages. This is interesting in the light of the second remarkable point in the quotation: in summing up the diseases of the central nervous system that are subject to "dissolution," he also includes Huntington's chorea. This disease, like the diseases of Alzheimer and Parkinson, involves dementia-like phenomena in its more progressive stages. Dementia is a general term for a number of behavioral characteristics occurring in combination, leading to a deterioration of personality, especially a gradual deterioration of memory and cognitive abilities. It is assumed that this behavior is caused by diffuse brain damage, e.g. by arteriosclerosis. Aphasia, in contrast, is usually caused by **local** brain damage.

Research into the language of the demented is relatively scarce. The most important study is the one by Irigaray (1973), but the fact that it is written in French has kept it from attracting the attention it deserves. In her review of the study, Obler (1981) points out that the regression hypothesis is probably much more valid for dementia than for aphasia. The results of Ajuriaguerra & Tissot (1975), Lahey & Feier (1982) and Martin & Fedio (1983) point in the same direction. Particularly in the area of the dissociation of word meaning, the parallels between demented persons and children are striking. In dementia the number of semantic features attached to a given concept gradually decreases, while in children the number of features increases over time. Both groups also tend to construct their language from an egocentric perspective in the Piagetian sense: a lot of knowledge is presupposed, also in front of strangers. Obler (1983) suggests that such similarities may be attributable to attention and memory processes, which are less efficient for both groups compared with healthy adults. On the other hand, it should be pointed out that the demented exhibit some types of behavior that do not occur in child speech, such as the tendency to use endless paraphrases ("circumlocution"), and vice versa: the morphosyntactic component appears to remain remarkably intact in dementia, and child-like overgeneralizations do not occur in the speech of the demented. Language in dementia may become an important test field for the regression hypothesis, but then the collection of more specific data is needed.

3.2   *Regression and non-pathological language loss*

3.2.1   *The language of the elderly*
While language loss in dementia can be subsumed under Jakobson's "pathologischen Sprachstörungen zentraler Art" (cf. Section 1 above), several other forms of language loss certainly cannot. Non-pathological forms of language loss are in fact more suitable for testing the regression hypothesis than pathological ones, because one cannot rule out the possibility that the pathology influences the organization of language in the brain; in other words, the organization that resulted from the acquisition process may be changed by the brain damage.

Recently, the language of the elderly and loss phenomena in it have attracted some attention (Beasley & Davis 1981; Clyne 1981; Obler & Albert 1982; De Bot & Lintsen 1986). Language loss in the elderly might be regarded as intermediate between pathological and non-pathological language loss – to aim at a real demarcation between the two would, of course, be futile.

In old age, certain behavioral changes occur that may be related to physiological changes, but a causal and necessary relation between the two is not certain: old age, even very old age, does not necessarily lead to language loss in all individuals, although one can observe a deterioration of certain aspects of language when measuring across larger groups.

Signs of regression in elderly speech have been mentioned by Warren & Warren (1966), Clyne (1981), and Emery (1986). In her research, Emery showed that elderly informants exhibit problems in interpreting sentences like "He told his son what to do" versus "He asked his son what to do." The misinterpretations of the elderly showed remarkable similarities with those of young children (Chomsky 1969).

Caporael & Culbertson (1986) suggest an explanation for the occurrence of regression in the elderly that is quite different from the traditional, neurological one: their research showed close parallels between the language spoken **to** children and **to** elderly people, especially when the latter are hospitalized. Sentences appear to be significantly shorter and less complex than in the language spoken to middle-aged adults. Ryan, Giles, Bartolucci & Henwood (1986) even suggest that language loss in the hospitalized elderly may be (partly) caused by the impoverished linguistic environment they are in. Parallels between acquisition and loss are thus explained by parallels in linguistic input. Such a functional/ pragmatic explanation for regression is of course totally different from explanations that are based on the working of innate mechanisms.

Regression on the level of languages (see Section 3.1 above) is suggested in research by Clyne (1981), who describes a number of Dutch and German immigrants in Australia, who show a tendency to revert to their first language and to lose their second language (English). In a recent follow-up study, De Bot & Clyne (1989) hypothesize that language reversion is not a simple regression phenomenon occurring in every individual, but is dependent on the level of proficiency acquired in L2. According to Neisser (1984), reaching a "critical threshold" makes language proficiency relatively immune to attrition. Apparently some of the informants tested by De Bot & Clyne did reach this level of proficiency in L2, making their skills immune to attrition, while others did not, making their skills much more vulnerable.

3.2.2   *Mother tongue shift*

A very common situation is that in which a group of speakers exhibit "mother tongue shift." Usually, this occurs in a situation with competing languages or language varieties, in a bilingual community in which the relative position of either language (variety) is unstable. Initially, a so-called domain shift occurs: language B is introduced into domains that were previously reserved for language A, with the ultimate result that, in subsequent generations, language B becomes dominant over language A. This development takes place with indigenous minorities (see e.g. Van Hout & Münstermann 1988; Trudgill 1983), but a comparable phenomenon also occurs with non-indigenous minorities, i.e. immigrants. Their original mother tongue (L1) is gradually replaced by the language of the host country in the course of two to three generations (see e.g. Gonzo & Saltarelli 1983). The domain shift, also called "functional loss," ultimately leads to "structural loss," i.e. changes in the structure of the linguistic system (Münstermann & Hagen 1986). This type of loss, however, does not occur so much **with individuals** as **across generations of speakers**. Therefore, we are also dealing with the phenomenon of "imperfect learning" (Trudgill 1983: 124–126): the mother tongue is transferred to the second generation in a mutilated form; to the third and following generations in an even more mutilated form, if transferred at all.

Research in this field is usually of the survey type: by means of questionnaires or interviews, different generations are questioned about their language preference in certain situations or domains, and sometimes global self-assessments are obtained with respect to the degree of proficiency in the "threatened" language. Research into the consequences of mother tongue shift for the structure of the language system of **individual speakers** is not very frequent (Geelen & De Bot 1986); investigations of the possibility of regression in this connection are scarce. Brewer-Bomar (1981) investigated the possibility of regression in two second generation Spanish immigrants in the United States. She found no regression, but rather the opposite: "Some of the most basic syntactic patterns were the most interfered with, while semantically and grammatically more complicated models were not only left untouched in the L1 [i.e. Spanish], they were still being perfected" (5105-A). This finding strongly suggests that loss patterns depend on the (limited) opportunities for using L1; a possible explanation for finding the reverse of regression could be that the "most basic syntactic patterns" are used daily in the second language (L2), the new mother tongue, replacing the original L1 structures, while more complex structures have not yet been formed in it, and are therefore still left intact in L1.

The phenomenon of imperfect learning has far-reaching consequences for the methodology of research into L1 loss. In order to be able to test the regression hypothesis, one needs acquisition data from the same, or at least highly comparable individuals; it is inadequate to compare, for example, loss data from second generation immigrants with acquisition data from monolingual children in the country of origin. However, if acquisition data from the "losing" informants are not available, the language of fully competent native speakers of comparable age and socioeconomic status will have to do as the point of reference for measuring language loss (cf. Jaspaert, Kroon & Van Hout 1986).

In a current project at the University of Nijmegen (Jordens, De Bot, Van Os & Schumans 1986) the regression hypothesis is investigated. The hypothesis is tested by comparing first language acquisition with first language loss and foreign language learning with foreign language loss. Case marking in German has been chosen as the linguistic variable, because it meets the conditions of gradualness and a more·or less fixed order of acquisition. Jordens (1983) has shown that factors such as cognitive load appear to play a role in the use and acquisition of the case marking system. Regression is expected to occur because these same factors may also play a role in language loss. In order to test the hypothesis, a closely defined linguistic element has been chosen, rather than a large set of phenomena on different linguistic levels.

In the case of L1 acquisition and loss, three groups of informants were compared: a group of monolingual German primary school children (mean age 8.5) and two groups of German emigrants. One group had been in the Netherlands for at least ten years and the other had been in Australia for at least twenty years. The results show that, in the first place, remarkably little is lost: the emigrants made very few case marking errors in their German. Furthermore, the factors that appear to play a role in their case marking behavior and, more importantly, explain their errors only partially overlap with those applying to the children acquiring German as L1. Apparently, cognitive factors are more important for the adult migrants, while these factors are still only developing in the children.

3.2.3   *Second/foreign language loss*

Second language loss may occur with people who have been staying in a foreign country for some time, have learned or perfected L2 there, but start losing it again after their return to the L1 community. Foreign language loss occurs with people who have learned a foreign language (FL) in an instructional setting, but use the FL to an insufficient degree after the course has finished, and consequently lose it again (for a survey of the literature, see Oxford 1982 and Weltens 1987).

Some research has already been carried out in both areas, but the attention paid to the possibility of regression has been minimal. Only Cohen (1975) explicitly looked for regression patterns in his data on the spontaneous speech of three English speaking learners of Spanish. He found that a period of non-use of three months leads to regression in some areas: two of the three informants clearly regressed to incorrect patterns they had used in the learning stages. Cohen adds, however, that at least two other phenomena occur: "residual learning," the elimination of incorrect hypotheses about the language, and "new incorrect patterns," i.e. incorrect patterns that had **not** occurred at some point in the learning process.

Godsall-Myers (1981) also claims some evidence for regression in her investigation of FL loss with American students of German, but this appears to be based on the fact that tests that measure simple phenomena, which were taught relatively early, show less loss than tests that measure more complex phenomena, which were taught relatively late. We feel, however, that actual learning data about the degree of mastery of these phenomena in the course of the learning period would be needed in order to be able to decide whether this indeed reflects regression (cf. note 4 below). An additional complication is that establishing the point of reference is problematic in this kind of research, too.

An interesting contribution in this respect is the one by Andersen (1982). He claims that linguistic factors to a certain extent determine the process of language loss.[6] On the lexical level, for example, frequency and degree of similarity between L1 and FL words would be relevant factors: high frequency elements would be retained better than low frequency ones; words which are closely related to their L1 equivalents, so-called cognates, would be retained better than non-related words.

Interestingly enough, some of these "linguistic attributes" run parallel to the order of presentation in FL teaching: usually, words of high frequency are presented first, and the frequency of the subsequent words gradually decreases. On the grammatical level we also find a clear parallel: the simplest structures are taught first, and gradually they become more complex and less functional (in the sense of "functional load"). As far as these linguistic attributes indeed run parallel to orders of presentation, they do not lead to predictions different from the regression hypothesis, but in some cases the two can predict conflicting results. We will try to demonstrate this by means of a concrete example. Let us consider the case of English speaking learners of French. They will most probably learn the common French words first; their English equivalents typically are **Germanic** in origin, and therefore not related to the French words. Later on the less frequent French words are taught, but they are, in many cases, English–French cognates, because about 50 percent of the words in the English lexicon are of Romance origin, namely the less usual, more formal words. When we apply Andersen's hypothesis to this case, the result might be an interaction between the two, e.g. in the sense that low-frequency words are only lost earlier if they are non-cognates, or even a result opposite to one of the two, e.g. in the sense that similarity between L1 and FL overrules the effect of frequency.

Another interfering variable is the fact that certain phrases and sets of words are overlearned, and therefore enjoy a special status in terms of memory storage. One could think of greeting routines and closed set items such as the days of the week, the months of the year and the numbers one to ten. Berko-Gleason (1982: 21) adds, rightly so, "songs and emotionally laden words like curses and body parts," but she notes that there are important differences between L1 and L2/FL learners, especially on this point. She gives the example of the use of registers, stylistic variation in speech dependent on the listener(s): four-year-old children already exhibit characteristics of baby talk when addressing two-year-olds, while many L2/FL learners never get to the point where they can productively distinguish between registers. Berko-Gleason (1982: 21–22) therefore concludes that, if we accept Pitres' (1895) interpretation of regression ("Those things learned best will be retained longest"), method of instruction and "what one tends to rehearse" become essential factors (Berko-Gleason 1982: 21–22). Data from studies by Berman & Olshtain (1983) and one of our own pilot studies (Aertssen, Van de Berg, Buursen & Claassen 1985) on the loss of a second language in children seem to support this suggestion. In both studies, considerable loss on the lexical and grammatical levels was found, but some pragmatic elements appeared to be well retained. In particular, idiomatic expressions ("it's kinda hot") and social fillers ("let me see," "for that matter") are used fluently. Berman & Olshtain's (1983: 233) explanation is in line with Berko-Gleason's conclusions: "With respect to the special kind of interlanguage that emerges in the course of language attrition, we found, then, that there are certain types of knowledge which are deeply entrenched through the original learning experience, where English was acquired to the point of native-like proficiency in a naturalistic setting at school, with friends, in the neighbourhood, and often at home with siblings even though not with parents. Such knowledge seems very resistant to loss, especially among the older children."

4   Conclusion

Surprisingly little research has been carried out in order to actually test a hypothesis that has attracted the attention of many (psycho-) linguists over the last forty years. Caramazza & Zurif's (1978) book is a compilation of research notes on the comparison of child language data and data from aphasic patients. Their conclusion is that, for aphasia, the regression hypothesis does not bear close scrutiny. For reasons mentioned earlier, this finding is not really surprising. Furthermore, it does not mean that therefore the idea of regression should be rejected.

The tenability of the hypothesis for other types of language loss has not been investigated thoroughly so far. Several researchers (Cohen 1975; Ervin-Tripp 1974; Godsall-Myers 1981; Knapp 1980) found some attraction in it for the explanation of their data, but their research was not aimed at testing the regression hypothesis as such.

One of the problems that has not been solved satisfactorily in L1 and L2 acquisition research, and that is also of major importance in research into language loss, is how to establish actual orders of acquisition. There are no objective criteria for deciding **when** something has been acquired (or lost). What is considered to be an "order of acquisition," may depend on the percentage correct that is chosen as a yardstick (Van Els, Bongaerts, Extra, Van Os & Janssen-van Dieten 1984:89), or on the aspects under investigation. Like Jakobson's distinctive features in phonology, it may be features of linguistic elements, rather than the elements proper, that are central in the explanation of acquisition and loss.

Research aiming at either corroboration or falsification of the regression hypothesis has to meet certain conditions. Regression presupposes gradualness and a more or less fixed sequence/order in acquisition and loss. Therefore, only those linguistic phenomena that appear to develop gradually and in a fixed sequence can be used. Accordingly, the number of suitable linguistic phenomena is rather small. Only those phenomena that are clearly rule governed in the sense that we know what the rules look like and how they develop over time are in fact relevant. This means that the lexicon is much less suitable than morphosyntax or phonology.

There are a number of other conditions that have to be met. Extra-linguistic factors may influence the patterns of loss considerably. The influence of factors such as frequency of use or differences between informants in acquisitional setting and use patterns has to be eliminated as much as possible; this is particularly relevant in the investigation of FL loss: FL learners use the FL in a way which is radically different from the way L1 acquirers do; already during the learning period, selective rehearsal and, as a consequence, selective retention occur, and they most probably will not follow the "natural" patterns of L1 acquisition. Finally, in research on L2/FL loss, interference has to be taken into account.

To conclude, it may not be possible to settle the discussion about the regression hypothesis once and for all. At the same time, it has become important enough to warrant research in which regression is more than just a digression.

Notes

This research was partly sponsored by the Dutch Linguistics Foundation, which is funded by the Netherlands Organization for Scientific Research (NWO). The authors would like to thank Theo Bongaerts and Theo van Els for their inspiring comments.

1   "The only opportunity we have for observing human language *in statu nascendi* is offered by the child"; "The only opportunity we have for observing human language in a state of dissolution is offered by pathological speech defects of a central nature" (our translation).
2   "Phylogeny is the mechanical cause of ontogeny" (our translation).
3   An interesting aspect here is that functional explanations can confirm two totally contradictory opinions.
4   Of course, we do **not** wish to imply here or anywhere else that a **teaching** strategy automatically leads to a corresponding **learning** strategy.
5   Incidentally, this is a nice example of how one can score high on a citation index by means of questionable research.
6   Note that Andersen's "linguistic attributes" can be looked upon as "features" in Jakobson's sense, i.e. they can be applied not only to phonology but also to other linguistic levels.

References

Aertssen, J., M. van de Berg, R. Buursen, and T. Claassen. 1985. "Tweedetaalverlies. Verlies van het Engels bij Nederlandse kinderen," MA thesis, Department of Applied Linguistics, Nijmegen.

Ajuriaguerra, J., and R. Tissot. 1975. "Some aspects of language in various forms of senile dementia," in E. H. Lenneberg and E. Lenneberg (eds.), *Foundations of language development, 1*. New York: Academic Press, 323–329.

Andersen, R. 1982. "Determining the linguistic attributes of language attrition," in Lambert and Freed (eds.), 83–118.

Anderson, J. 1973. *Structural aspects of language change*. London: Longman.

Baron, N. 1977. *Language acquisition and historical change*. Amsterdam: North-Holland.

Beasley, D., and G. Davis. 1981. *Aging, communication processes and disorders*. New York: Grune & Stratton.

Berko-Gleason, J. 1982. "Insights from child language acquisition for second language loss," in Lambert and Freed (eds.), 13–23.

Berman, R., and E. Olshtain. 1983. "Features of first language transfer in second language attrition," *Applied Linguistics* 4: 222–234.

Boyd, S., and P. Andersson. 1988. "Linguistic change among bilingual speakers of Finnish and American English in Sweden – background and some tentative findings." Paper presented at the Workshop on Maintenance and Loss of Ethnic Minority Languages, Noordwijkerhout, the Netherlands, August 28–30, 1988.

Brewer-Bomar, K. 1981. "Second language lexical and syntactical interference in the first language of two four year old Spanish speakers," *Dissertation Abstracts International* 42: 5105-A.

Caporael, L., and G. Culbertson. 1986. "Verbal response modes of baby talk and other speech at institutions for the aged," *Language and Communication* 6: 99–112.

Caramazza, A., and E. Zurif. 1978 (eds.). *Language acquisition and language breakdown: parallels and divergencies.* Baltimore: The Johns Hopkins University Press.

Chomsky, C. (1969) *The acquisition of syntax in children from 5 to 10.* Cambridge, MA: MIT Press.

Clark, H., and E. Clark. 1977. *Psychology and language.* New York: Harcourt, Brace, Jovanovich.

Clyne, M. 1981. "Second language attrition and first language reversion among elderly bilinguals in Australia," in W. Meid and K. Heller (eds.), *Sprachkontakt als Ursache von Veränderungen der Sprach- und Bewußtseinsstruktur: eine Sammlung von Studien zur sprachlichen Interferenz.* Innsbruck: Institut für Sprachwissenschaft, 25–32.

Cohen, A. 1975. "Forgetting a second language," *Language Learning* 25: 127–138.

Comrie, B. 1981. *Language universals and linguistic typology, syntax and morphology.* Oxford: Blackwell.

De Bot, K., and M. Clyne. 1989. "Language reversion revisited," *Studies in Second Language Acquisition* 11: 167–177.

De Bot, K., and T. Lintsen. 1986. "Foreign-language proficiency in the elderly," in Weltens *et al.* (eds.), 131–141.

Emery, O. 1986. "Linguistic decrement in normal aging," *Language and Communication* 6: 47–64.

Engels, F. 1954. *Dialectics of nature.* Moscow: Foreign Languages Publishing House (originally published in 1876).

Ervin-Tripp, S. 1974. "Is second language learning like the first?" *Tesol Quarterly* 8: 111–127.

Freud, S. 1891. *On aphasia, a critical study.* New York: International University Press (reprinted 1953).

Geelen, E., and K. De Bot. 1986. "Dialectverlies op individueel niveau," *Taal en Tongval* 38: 172–184.

Givón, T. 1979. *On understanding grammar.* New York: Academic Press.

Gleitman, L., and E. Wanner. 1982. "Language acquisition: the state of the art," in Wanner and Gleitman (eds.), 3–48.

Godsall-Myers, J. 1981. "The attrition of language skills in German classroom bilinguals – a case study," *Dissertation Abstracts International* 43: 157-A.

Gonzo, S., and M. Saltarelli. 1983. "Pidginization and linguistic change in emigrant languages," in R. Andersen (ed.), *Pidginization and creolization as language acquisition*. Rowley, MA: Newbury House Publishers, 181–197.

Gould, S. 1977. *Ontogeny and phylogeny*. Cambridge, MA: Belknap Press.

Haeckel, E. 1868. *Natürliche Schöpfungsgeschichte*. Berlin: Georg Reimer.

Haeckel, E. 1874. *Anthropogenie: Keimes- und Stammes-Geschichte des Menschen*. Leipzig: Engelmann.

Harnad, S., H. Steklis, and J. Lancaster. 1976 (eds.). *Origins and evolution of language and speech*. New York: New York Academy of Sciences.

Irigaray, L. 1973. *Le langage des déments*. Den Haag: Mouton.

Jackson, J. H. 1958. *Selected writings of John Hughlings Jackson*. London: Staples Press.

Jakobson, R. 1941. *Kindersprache, Aphasie und allgemeine Lautgesetze*. Uppsala: Almqvist & Wiksell. (Also in R. Jakobson, *Selected writings, 1, phonological studies*. Den Haag: Mouton, 1962.)

Jaspaert, K., S. Kroon, and R. Van Hout. 1986. "Points of reference in first-language loss research," in Weltens *et al.* (eds.), 91–100.

Jordens, P. 1983. *Das deutsche Kasussystem im Fremdspracherwerb*. Tübingen: Gunter Narr.

Jordens, P., K. De Bot, Ch. Van Os, and J. Schumans. 1986. "Regression in German case marking," in Weltens *et al.* (eds.), 159–176.

Kerkman, H., and K. de Bot. 1989. "De organisatie van het tweetalige lexicon," *Toegeposte Taalwetenschap in Artikelen* 34: 115–121.

Kiparsky, P. 1976. "Historical linguistics and the origin of language," in Harnad *et al.* (eds.), 97–103.

Knapp, K. 1980. *Lehrsequenzen für den Zweitsprachenerwerb. Ein komparatives Experiment*. Braunschweig: Vieweg.

Kussmaul, A. 1910. *Die Störungen der Sprache. Versuch einer Pathologie der Sprache*. Leipzig: Vogel.

Lahey, M., and C. Feier. 1982. "The semantics of verbs in the dissolution and development of language," *Journal of Speech and Hearing Research* 25: 81–95.

Lambert, R., and B. Freed. 1982 (eds.). *The loss of language skills*. Rowley, MA: Newbury House Publishers.

Lambert, W., and S. Fillenbaum. 1959. "A pilot study of aphasia among bilinguals," *Canadian Journal of Psychology* 13: 28–34.

Lamendella, J. 1976. "Relations between the ontogeny and phylogeny of language: a neorecapitulationist view," in Harnad *et al.* (eds.), 396–412.

Leakey, R. 1979. *Introduction to Darwin's The origin of species*. London: Rainbird.

Martin, A., and P. Fedio. 1983. "Word production and comprehension in Alzheimer's disease: the breakdown of semantic knowledge," *Brain and Language* 19: 124–141.

Münstermann, H., and A. Hagen. 1986. "Functional and structural aspects of dialect loss: A research plan and some first results," in Weltens *et al.* (eds.), 75–96.

Myerson, R., and H. Goodglass. 1972. "Transformational grammars of three agrammatic patients," *Language and Speech* 15: 40–50.

Neisser, U. 1984. "Interpreting Harry Bahrick's discovery: what confers immunity against forgetting?" *Journal of Experimental Psychology: General* 113: 32–35.

Obler, L. 1981. "Review of: L. Irigaray, *Le langage des déments*," *Brain and Language* 12: 375–386.

Obler, L. 1983. "Language and brain dysfunction in dementia," in S. Segalowitz (ed.), *Language functions and brain organization*. New York: Academic Press, 267–281.

Obler, L., and M. Albert. 1982. "Language in aging," in M. Albert (ed.), *Clinical neurology of aging*. New York: Oxford University Press, 245–253.

Oxford, R. 1982. "Research on language loss – a review with implications for foreign-language teaching," *Modern Language Journal* 66: 160–169.

Paul, H. 1888. *Prinzipien der Sprachgeschichte*. Halle: Max Niemeyer (reprinted 1920).

Pitres, A. 1895. "Etude sur l'aphasie chez les polyglottes," *Revue de Médecine* 15: 873–899.

Ribot, T. 1883. *Les maladies de la mémoire*. Paris: Librairie Germer Bailliere.

Ryan, E., H. Giles, G. Bartolucci, and K. Henwood. 1986. "Psycholinguistic and social psychological components of communication by and with the elderly," *Language and Communication* 6: 1–24.

Shatz, M. 1982. "On mechanisms of language acquisition: can features of the communicative environment account for development?" in Wanner and Gleitman (eds.), 102–127.

Slobin, D. (1982) "Universal and particular in the acquisition of language," in Wanner and Gleitman (eds.), 128–170.

Spreen, O. 1968. "Psycholinguistic aspects of aphasia," *Journal of Speech and Hearing Research* 11: 453–466.

Stam, J. 1976. *Inquiries into the origin of language. The fate of a question*. New York: Harper & Row.

Sturtevant, E. (1917) *Linguistic change. An introduction to the historical study of language*. Chicago: The University of Chicago Press (Reprinted 1965).

Trudgill, P. 1983. *On dialect. Social and geographical perspectives*. Oxford: Blackwell.

Van Els, T., T. Bongaerts, G. Extra, Ch. van Os, and A. Janssen-van Dieten. 1984. *Applied linguistics and the learning and teaching of foreign languages*. London: Arnold.

Van Hout, R., and H. Münstermann. 1988. "The multidimensionality of domain configurations," *International Journal of the Sociology of Language* 74: 107–124.

Wanner, E., and L. Gleitman. 1982 (eds.). *Language acquisition. The state of the art*. Cambridge: Cambridge University Press.

Warren, R. M., and R. P. Warren. 1966. "A comparison of speech perception in childhood, maturity and old age by means of the verbal transformation effect," *Journal of Verbal Learning and Verbal Behavior* 5: 142–146.

Weinreich, U., W. Labov, and W. Herzog. 1968. "Empirical foundations for a theory of language change," in W. Lehman and Y. Malkiel (eds.), *Directions for historical linguistics*. London: Austin, 95–195.

Weltens, B. 1987. "The attrition of foreign-language skills: a literature review," *Applied Linguistics* 8: 22–38.

Weltens, B., K. De Bot, and T. Van Els. 1986 (eds.). *Language attrition in progress*. Dordrecht/Providence: Foris.

Wepman, J., and L. Jones. 1962. "Five aphasias: a commentary on aphasia as a regressive linguistic phenomenon," in D. Rioch and E. Weinstein (eds.), *Disorders of communication. Vol. 17.* Baltimore: Williams & Wilkins, 190–203.

4 First language loss in bilingual and polyglot aphasics

LORAINE K. OBLER AND NANCY R. MAHECHA

1 Introduction

It is generally understood that one will lose facility even in one's first language if it is not used for a long enough period. As the Russian–French bilingual writer Triolet[1] puts it vividly, "You cannot keep [a language] safe deep within you, it must get some exercise. You must use it, or else it gets rusty, atrophies and dies." To complement the growing literature on second language (L2) attrition, a literature on first language (L1) attrition is developing. Several populations are of interest in considering the question of first language loss or diminishment: healthy bilingual individuals with reduced practice in their L1 (e.g. the study of Olshtain & Barzilay 1987), demented bilinguals (as in Hyltenstam & Stroud 1989; DeSanti, Obler, Abramson, & Goldberger 1989) and aphasics.

Indeed, the primary source of data in neurolinguistics has been the study of aphasics, individuals with brain damage resulting in language disturbance. Thus it is to bilingual and polyglot aphasics that we turn for converging evidence on loss of the first language. In previous work we have discussed the phenomena that predict various of the differential recovery patterns in aphasia (Albert & Obler 1978; Obler & Albert 1977; also see Paradis 1977 for a classification of differential recovery patterns). In particular we determined that for the group of polyglot aphasics as a whole, it is the rule proposed by Pitres in 1895 that holds: in the event that only one language returns, it is most likely to be the language that was being used around the time of the accident, rather than, for example, always being the first learned language. Of course for a substantial number of individual bilingual aphasics, the language used around the time of the aphasia producing incident is the same as the first language. In this paper we focus particularly on those patients for whom the first language does **not** return after the aphasia. Our primary question, then, is: What characterizes this group, as compared with those for whom the first language does return first, or at the same time as the second language?

This question is closely linked to the question of what factors influence the brain in learning and maintaining both first and later languages. For the neurolinguist, the questions of interest are determining the neuro-physiological systems that are involved in this real or apparent loss, and the neuroanatomical and neurophysiological ramifications resulting from learning a language in different ways, or from ceasing to use it at different ages. It is conceivable, for example, that being literate in one's first language makes a difference in how an L2 is registered in the brain, and it is even conceivable that how one learns a second language influences how the first one is organized within the brain. For example, there have been some hints in the literature to suggest that bilinguals are more bilaterally organized for both their first and second language than are monolinguals for their only language (e.g. Albanese 1985; Albert & Obler 1978; Gordon 1980; Silverberg *et al.*, 1979; Sussman *et al.* 1982).

In the current study, we are limited by the data provided in the case histories of polyglot aphasics with differential recovery published over the past century. Thus we can ask questions about gross type of aphasia, etiology of the aphasia, and gender, but we cannot, strictly speaking, ask questions about literacy *per se*, or about the specific age and manner of acquisition or learning of the second language. We can, however, indirectly estimate education levels. With the material that Paradis' (1987) major study promises, we should be able to return to these questions again in some years, since the bilingual language history questionnaire he has developed will provide markedly more detailed information than has been available for the subjects included in this study. What follows is intended to provide the first approximation to what we can learn from aphasia studies about the apparent sudden loss of a first language.

2   Methodology

The corpus of 156 cases used for the present first language attrition study in aphasics was drawn from two main sources: Albert & Obler 1978, and Paradis 1983. Whenever possible, any conflicts of information were checked against the original source or its translation. In a few cases, when neither the original nor a translation could be obtained, several sources which described the case in question were used to clarify specific points (e.g. age of subject). In addition, articles concerning this study published within the last five years were added to the corpus. Case studies for which a recovery pattern could not be assigned, that were vague, and/or had little information were not included (e.g. Trousseau, cited in Paradis 1983).

3   Coding of information

3.1   *Recovery patterns*

All types of recovery patterns were based on the individual's verbal production skills. A total of seven recovery patterns were determined. They were:

> **+ Ribot (+ R)**: recovery followed the rule of Ribot, that is, the first language (mother tongue) was recovered first or was the only one recovered
>
> **+ Ribot + Pitres (+ R + P)**: recovery followed both the rule of Ribot and the rule of Pitres, that is, the language recovered was both the mother tongue and the one used most at the time preceding the onset of aphasia
>
> **+ Ribot − Pitres (+ R − P)**: recovery followed the rule of Ribot but the mother tongue was not the one used most frequently prior to the onset of aphasia
>
> **− Ribot (− R)**: recovery did not follow the rule of Ribot, that is, the first language was not recovered first or was lost entirely
>
> **− Ribot + Pitres (− R + P)**: recovery followed the rule of Pitres, that is, the language recovered was not the mother tongue but the one most used during the period prior to the onset of aphasia
>
> **− Ribot − Pitres (− R − P)**: recovery did not follow either rule, that is, the language recovered was neither the mother tongue nor the one most used, yet it was differential recovery
>
> **Equal/Parallel**: all languages were lost and recovered to a similar extent.

3.2   *Criteria established*

The following criteria were established:

Gender

If gender was not mentioned it was classified as male based on the assumption that the author(s) usually mention whether an individual is female as it is the marked case (fewer female aphasics). Gender was thus determined for all 156 cases.

Age

If the age was stated to be within a specific decade (e.g. ''in the 30s''), a midpoint was used (i.e. 35). If age was stated as being towards the end of a specific decade (e.g. in the "late 50s"), then the digit 7 was used (i.e. 57). If the term "approximately" preceded a stated age, just the age was coded (e.g. "approximately 40" was coded as 40). If an individual suffered several instances of brain damage at different ages then only the age concerning the aphasia and recovery being discussed was used (usually the age of the first etiology). No age was recorded for analysis if vague terms, such as "old," "middle aged," were used. Age was determined for 139 cases.

Other languages

Languages were coded as either being used proficiently or being partially known. Individuals were classified as "polyglot" if they were proficient in more than two languages (i.e. able to understand, speak, and use the other languages), or if they were proficient in two languages and had considerable knowledge of one or two additional languages. Individuals were classified as "bilingual" if they were proficient in two languages or if their knowledge of additional languages was minimal. This category was determined for all 156 cases.

Manner of acquisition

This was classified in three ways:

Compound: if two or more languages were learned simultaneously before the age of five years (McLaughlin 1984).

Coordinate: if language(s) were learned after the age of five years.

Compound/coordinate: this was assigned if the languages were learned simultaneously before the age of five years but later were used in different situations, if two languages were learned simultaneously before the age of five years and other languages were added after this age and were used in different situations (this category included primarily adult immigrants), and finally, if languages that were learned in a coordinate fashion were used in a compound way, that is, used with the same frequency within the same daily contexts.

Manner of acquisition could be determined for 145 cases.

Etiology

This was classified as cerebral vascular accident (CVA), trauma, tumor, and miscellaneous. The term "apoplectic attack" was classified as a CVA. A CVA etiology was assumed for one case (De Menasce 1962) who had a left sided injury, right hand dominance, and an expressive aphasia. A total of 112 cases were classified as either CVA, trauma, or tumor. The miscellaneous category included encephalitis, seizures, meningitis, sickness, syphilis, aging, softening of brain tissue, atrophy of brain tissue, severe recurrent migraine headaches, terminal illnesses, removal of epileptogenic tissue, cerebral vascular disease, subdural hematoma, surgery of Heschl's gyri, and unreported etiology. Forty-four cases were classified as miscellaneous.

Handedness

This was classified as dextral, sinistral, or ambidextrous. The ambidextrous category included a few individuals who were forced to become dextral during their childhood. If handedness was not reported it was coded as "dextral" **only if** there was also a left hemispheric lesion which caused a significant aphasia, on the assumption that the case represented the prototypical right handed, left sided dominant individual. A total of 85 cases were assigned right handedness based on this criterion. No assumptions were made as to left handedness or ambidextrality even when the evidence was strong (e.g. expressive aphasia following a right hemispheric lesion) since an unreported crossed aphasia could have existed. Handedness could be determined for 122 cases.

Hemispheric involvement

The hemispheric damage was classified as being left, right, or bilateral. If hemispheric damage was not reported it was assumed to be left **if** the person was right handed, had incurred a CVA resulting in aphasia, and exhibited some form of right sided paresis or paralysis. If the patient had a CVA resulting in left sided paralysis, and no right sided signs, the patient was included in the right hemisphere damaged group. It was assumed to be bilateral for all aphasics who had incurred a severe head injury and thus must have had contrecoup damage. Hemispheric damage could be determined for 127 cases.

Aphasia

Aphasia was classified as being either expressive, receptive, mixed (i.e. expressive and receptive), or miscellaneous (e.g. anomia, conduction aphasia, etc.). The terms "dysphasia" and "executive aphasia" were classified as expressive aphasias. The term "central aphasia" was classified as conduction aphasia. Type of aphasia could not be determined for only one case in our corpus. This involved a twenty-one-year-old male who suffered a trauma (Smirnov & Faktorovich 1949) who was placed in the miscellaneous category. Thus, type of aphasia was classified for all 156 cases.

Education

After much consideration, the category of education was divided into the following levels: minimum, minimum-to-moderate, moderate, and advanced. Each individual was categorized according to the information that was provided or that could be reliably inferred from the case history. Criteria used were as follows:

Minimum education: a grade school education or less was reported. If it was not reported, the subject was placed within this level if she/he held a job requiring little education (e.g. maid, baker, gardener), if the subject was a female born in the 1800s of whom nothing else was known, if the individual resided in a country where education was not obligatory (e.g. some South American countries), and if there was no mention of reading/writing abilities during the recovery process.

Minimum-to-moderate education: a subject was placed at this level if "schooling", however vague, was mentioned, if it was strongly suspected that the subject had more than a grade school education but the extent was unclear, if the person's knowledge of a set of languages indicated a population that as a rule is educated (e.g. knowledge of Hebrew besides Yiddish), and if difficulties with reading/writing skills were mentioned within the recovery history.

Moderate education: at least some high school education was reported. If unreported, subjects were classified as moderate if they had a white collar job (e.g. stenographer, travel agent, merchant), belonged to a religious order, especially towards the end of the last century and the beginning of this one, and if reading/writing disturbances were mentioned within the recovery history.

Advanced education: a subject was placed in the advanced level if a profession was reported (e.g. physician, professor, lawyer), and/or if some college education was mentioned. It was inferred for those individuals described as being "educated" if they also had a considerable knowledge of classical languages such as Greek and Latin.

In order to explore the effects of education further, the above categories were also grouped into low (minimum), medium (minimum-to-moderate and moderate), and high (advanced), low versus non-low (medium and high), and non-advanced (minimum and minimum-to-moderate) versus advanced.

Note

A more in-depth study was not done on the following observed factors due to insufficient number of cases: inability to translate at all or on command, inability to switch at all or on command, presence of inappropriate mixing of languages during recovery, regression of one language as other(s) recovered, influence of the written knowledge of a language on its recovery, affective factors influencing recovery, amount of speech therapy provided, and the influence of environmental factors on the recovery process (e.g. language used at the hospital). In addition, the category of mother tongue could not be analyzed as it contained too much variation.

4   Statistical analyses

All data (recovery type, gender, age, manner of acquisition, etiology, hemispheric damage, handedness, aphasia type, level of education, and whether the individual was a polyglot or a bilingual) were treated categorically except for age, which was also treated as a continuous variable (i.e. specific age was coded for each subject).

Pearson Chi-squares were performed on each of the categories. Significance is reported if the Chi-square probability value (p) or the Yates corrected Chi-square value (p*) was < .05. All cases in the "Equal/Parallel" recovery category were eliminated since they did not directly address the question of this study. In addition, all of the cases where information was not specified (e.g. unknown handedness, miscellaneous etiology, etc.) were eliminated from those specific analyses. A comparison was then made within the −Ribot group to see if any factors differentiated the −Ribot +Pitres group (N = 35) from the −Ribot −Pitres group (N = 12), and, within the + Ribot group to see if any factors differentiated the +Ribot +Pitres group (N = 24) from the +Ribot −Pitres group (N = 8). Both analyses were significant for the presence/absence of polyglotism. An increased incidence of polyglotism was to have been expected for the −Ribot group as it contains −R−P, which by definition implies polyglotism. It is unclear at this time why the +R+P group also has an increased number of polyglots. In addition, the −R group obtained a significant age effect (p = .005) whereas the +Ribot did not (p = .75). Since all of the other factors were non-significant (p > .05), and since the age category would be subjected to a series of analyses, we collapsed the two −Ribot categories to form a single −Ribot group (N = 63) and the two +Ribot categories to form a single +Ribot group (N = 64). Comparisons between these two categories (i.e. +R versus −R) more directly addressed the principal question of this study, that is, what factors are related to individuals who do not recover their native/first language (i.e. −R) following a brain insult as compared with those individuals who do recover it (i.e. +R). This total of 127 cases was used for all remaining Pearson Chi-square analyses involving recovery (i.e. −R versus +R). In addition, a discriminant analysis of the age factor was performed.

5   Results

Two factors were found to be significant in predicting whether or not the first language is lost completely or recovered after other languages have been recovering. These were: hemispheric damage (p = .03) and handedness (p = .05). In terms of hemisphere damaged (see Table 4.1), many more individuals with a unilateral right hemispheric lesion did not recover their first language than did (10/1), whereas for individuals with left sided or bilateral lesions, equal numbers of subjects either recovered their L1 or did not.

Table 4.1 *Hemispheric lesion × recovery type*

	+ Ribot		− Ribot	
	%	(N)	%	(N)
Left	81.2	(39)	69.6	(39)
Right	2.1	(1)	17.9	(10)
Bilateral	16.7	(8)	12.5	(7)
Totals	100	(48)	100	(56)
p = .03				

Table 4.2 *Handedness × recovery type*

	+ Ribot		− Ribot	
	%	(N)	%	(N)
Dextral	92.2	(47)	90.0	(45)
Sinistral	0.0	(0)	8.0	(4)
Ambidextrous	7.8	(4)	2.0	(1)
Totals	100	(51)	100	(50)
p = .05				

As to handedness, all four left handers in this study exhibited a − Ribot recovery pattern, hence left handedness would seem to predict the loss of the mother tongue following a brain insult[2] (see Table 4.2).

Trends for predicting the loss of the mother tongue fell within the categories of education and etiology. Individuals with minimum or minimum-to-moderate education (i.e. those with less than a high school education) are more likely not to recover the first language than to recover it; those with moderate to advanced levels of education, by contrast, were more likely to follow the rule of Ribot than not (see Table 4.3). Other groupings of education, however, revealed no significant differences.

In terms of etiology, it appears that individuals suffering traumatic lesions would less likely recover their mother tongue. This is noted, for example, when the two largest groups, CVAs and trauma cases, are compared (see Table 4.4).

The following categories were non-significant in predicting the loss of the mother tongue: gender ($p^* = .87$), degree of bilingualism or polyglotism ($p^* = .53$), whether or not languages were learned in a co-ordinate, compound, or coordinate/compound manner ($p = .29$), age

Table 4.3 *Four educational levels × recovery type*

	+ Ribot		− Ribot	
	%	(N)	%	(N)
Minimum	13.7	(7)	23.2	(13)
Min.-to-mod.	19.6	(10)	32.1	(18)
Moderate	25.5	(13)	14.3	(8)
Advanced	41.2	(21)	30.4	(17)
Totals	100	(51)	100	(56)
$p = .14$				

Table 4.4 *Etiology × recovery type*

	+ Ribot		− Ribot	
	%	(N)	%	(N)
CVA	74.3	(26)	55.3	(26)
Trauma	25.7	(9)	44.7	(21)
Totals	100	(35)	100	(47)
$p^* = .12$				

whether divided into four (p = .21) or three (p = .28) categories, and type of aphasia (p = .44). Interactions found to be non-significant were those of manner (coordinate versus compound) × education (p = .46), gender × aphasia (p = .21), gender × etiology (p = .27), and gender × education. This last interaction was non-significant regardless of whether there were four levels of education (p = .45), three (p = .37), or two, non-advanced versus advanced (p* = .25), and low versus non-low (p* = .81).

Additional analyses were performed on the age factor as it was considered a potentially significant variable involved with the recovery or loss of the first language. Although a discriminant analysis was non-significant, some clustering effects were obtained. Specifically, aphasics who recovered their first language tended to cluster between the ages of fifty-four and sixty-four years (N = 27 out of 51) whereas less of a clustering within this age region was noted for those who did not recover or were delayed in recovering their first language (N = 16 out of 60). Hence, aphasics who do not recover their first language can be of any age.

6   Discussion

Despite beliefs that type of bilingualism can influence organization of both the L1 and the L2, this study suggests that it does not make a difference in whether L1 is recoverable or not after aphasia. In particular, the manner of acquisition of the L2 was seen not to influence access after brain damage.

It appears, rather, that lateral organization for language, apparently apart from manner or mode of learning the L2, interacts with the recovery of L1 post-morbidly. The evidence from this study suggests that individuals with reversed dominance are most likely not to recover their L1 – shown by the loss of the L1 by all of the left handers in this study and by the majority of individuals who were aphasic with a right unilateral lesion. These individuals could fall within the familial clusters that Geschwind has reported (1983; Geschwind & Galaburda 1985), which include relatively poor verbal abilities from early in life. This could be linked to the trend that individuals with less than a high school education were more likely not to recover their L1 than individuals with a high school education or more. It seems clear, however, from studies of monolinguals, that literacy *per se* does not affect lateral dominance for language (see, for example, Castro & Morais 1987). Thus we assume that within the low education population there exists a subpopulation which was unable to achieve a higher education because of existing minimal language deficits to begin with.

7 Conclusion

To summarize our results, the permanent or temporary loss of a first language following a brain insult was significantly predicted by a unilateral right hemispheric lesion and left handedness. In fact, all left handers in the corpus (N = 4) had unilateral right hemispheric lesions but 5 out of 6 additional cases with right sided lesions contradicted the rule of Ribot as well. Less than a high school education and the presence of a traumatic lesion also point to the relative likelihood of a − Ribot recovery pattern. Age was not a significant factor regardless of how it was grouped or analyzed.

The other major trend, that individuals with trauma would most likely not recover their first language, provides weak converging evidence on the question of laterality. Even though 19 lesions labelled bilateral did not tend to result in lack of recovery of L1, this may be because they were relatively underreported. Trauma was reported for 30 lesions; even if it was reported as resulting in unilateral lesions, we should suspect that some bilateral damage was present.

So rather than factors of bilingual history *per se*, it would appear to be brain based factors that determine recovery from aphasia in the L1. In particular, it would seem that individuals with an unusual brain organization are most likely to lose their L1. Such a phenomenon might also be expected to similarly affect language attrition in individuals who are not brain damaged.

One question we cannot address, but that should be brought up, is whether the first language is truly lost in the −Ribot cases, or simply difficult to access. What is unclear from much of the literature is the extent to which it was determined that the L1 was lost because the patient did not respond to L1 in conversation and/or when she/he was tested in the L1. Of course it is possible that the patient understood the tests or questions well, but did not have access to the L1 for production, only for comprehension. In a number of the early reported cases this possibility simply was not considered.

One further point that bears relevance, but cannot be resolved, is the extent to which the individuals who lost their L1 had been using it before their aphasia producing incident. It is certainly possible that as a group they were more likely to have been transplanted to an area where they had not been using it, hence, some attrition may have already been in process. It is simply impossible, however, to glean this information from the case histories reviewed for this study.

Notes

1 Elsa Triolet's *Collected Works*, volume 1, page 26, cited in Beaujour (1989).
2 These results should be replicated with a larger sample because they become non-significant when the non-dominant categories are collapsed. Specifically, non-significant results were obtained when non-dextrals (sinistral + ambidextrous) were compared with dextrals ($p^* = .97$) and when non-left hemispheric lesions (right + bilateral) were compared with left-sided lesions ($p^* = .26$). Note that out of the 5 ambidextrous subjects, 4 recovered their L1 first.

References

Albanese, J.-F. 1985. "Language lateralization in English–French bilinguals," *Brain and Language* 24: 284–296.
Albert, M. L., and L. K. Obler. 1978. *The bilingual brain: neuropsychological aspects of bilingualism.* New York: Academic Press.
Beaujour, E. K. 1989. *Alien tongues: bilingual Russian writers of the "first" emigration.* Ithaca: Cornell.
Castro, S., and J. Morais. 1987. "Ear differences in illiterates," *Neuropsychologia* 25: 409–418.
DeSanti, S., L. K. Obler, H. Abramson, and J. Goldberger. 1989. "Discourse abilities and deficits in multilingual dementia," in Y. Joanette and H. Brownell (eds.), *Discourse abilities in brain damage.* New York: Springer Verlag.
Geschwind, N. 1983. "Genetics: fate, chance, and environmental control," in C. Ludlow and J. Cooper (eds.), *Genetic aspects of speech and language disorder.* New York: Academic Press, 21–36.
Geschwind, N., and A. Galaburda. 1985. "Cerebral lateralization: biological mechanisms, associations and pathology: a hypothesis and a program for research," *Archives of Neurology* 42: 428–459, 521–552, 634–654.
Gordon, H. W. 1980. "Cerebral organization in bilinguals: I. Lateralization," *Brain and Language* 9: 255–268.
Hyltenstam, K., and C. Stroud. 1989. "Bilingualism in Alzheimer's dementia," in K. Hyltenstam and L. K. Obler (eds), *Bilingualism across the lifespan.* Cambridge: Cambridge University Press.
McLaughlin, B. 1984. "Individual differences in language learning strategies," in B. McLaughlin, *Second language acquisition in childhood,* Vol. 1. Hillsdale, NJ: Erlbaum Associates, 136–176.
Menasce, J. de (translation in Paradis, 1983). "Observations d'un dysarthrique sur ses moyens de communication," *Journal de Psychologie,* 70, 209–220.
Obler, L. K., and M. L. Albert. 1977. "Influence of aging on recovery from aphasia in polyglots," *Brain and Language* 4: 460–463.
Olshtain, E., and M. Barzilay. 1987. "Attrition of English in adult native speakers of English living in a Hebrew speaking environment in Israel." Paper presented at the Variation in Second Language Acquisition Conference, held at the University of Michigan, Ann Arbor.

Paradis, M. 1977. "Bilingualism and aphasia," in H. Whitaker and H. Whitaker (eds.), *Studies in neurolinguistics,* Vol. 3. New York: Academic Press.

Paradis, M. 1983 (ed.). *Readings on aphasia in bilinguals and polyglots.* Canada: Didier.

Paradis, M. 1987. *The assessment of bilingual aphasia.* Hillsdale, NJ: Erlbaum.

Pitres, A. 1895. "Etude sur l'aphasie chez les polyglottes," *Revue de Médecine* 15: 873–899.

Ribot, T. 1882. *Diseases of memory: an essay in the positive psychology.* London: Paul.

Silverberg, R., S. Bentin, T. Gaziel, L. Obler, and M. L. Albert. 1979. "Shift of visual field preference for English words in native Hebrew speakers," *Brain and Language* 8: 184–190.

Smirnov, B. L., and N. Y. Faktorovich. 1949. "Kvoprosu ob afazii u poliglotov," *Neuropatologiia Psikhiatria* 18: 26–28 (translation in Paradis 1983).

Sussman, H. M., F. Franklin, and T. Simon. 1982. "Bilingual speech: bilateral control?," *Brain and Language* 15: 125–142.

5 A crosslinguistic study of language contact and language attrition

JULIANNE MAHER

1 Introduction

Most treatments of language contact presuppose one or more of the following conceptual models: (1) language contact as borrowing, or an additive model, such as Bloomfield (1933); (2) contact as opposing forces, or a resistance-to-mixture model, such as Sapir (1921); or (3) contact as selective blending, or the interference model, such as Weinreich (1953). Recent studies, however, provide empirical data which contradict the neat logic of these concepts. While it is clear that borrowing, interference, and autonomous change may and do occur in language contact situations, other linguistic effects are discernible as well. And these effects, in many cases, overshadow both borrowing and interference in shaping the language forms which result from the contact situation.

As Einar Haugen (1978: 37) points out:

> As the learner builds new systems in the language he acquires, he dismantles and reorders the systems of the language he already knows.

It is this dismantling and reordering process which is the subject of this article. One of the best places to study this process is in the enclave speech community. Enclaves, for this purpose, are communities where speakers of one language, A, are surrounded and/or dominated by speakers of a different language, B, in a defined political or geographic area. The essential characteristics of the enclave community are: (1) that it is multilingual in the broadest sense; (2) that language A is natively spoken by a significant number of speakers; (3) speakers of A constitute a minority of the polity, either numerically or politically/socially; and (4) the A speaking community has generally existed in relative isolation from other A speakers for approximately one hundred to four hundred years.

An illustrative but not exhaustive list of enclave speech communities comprises two general categories. The first are immigrant, or transplanted, communities such as the Finnish in Minnesota (as described in Larmouth 1974); Slavic communities in the American midwest (as in Henzl 1981); French communities in Louisiana (Conwell & Juilland 1963;

Whatley and Jannise 1982), Missouri (Dorrance 1935; Thogmartin 1970), New England (Locke 1949; Valdman 1979), and the Virgin Islands (High-field 1979); Albanian in Greece (Trudgill 1983); Hindi in Trinidad (Bhatia 1982, Mohan 1978), Guyana (Gambhir 1983), Fiji (Moag 1984) and Maur-itius (Domingue 1980); German in Iowa (Kehlenbeck 1948), Texas (Eikel 1949), and Pennsylvania (Haag 1982). The second general category is indigenous communities where the encroachment of B speakers, though more gradual, is no less real: Scots Gaelic in northern Scotland (Dorian 1973, 1978, 1981); Breton in France (Dressler 1972; Timm 1980); numerous Amerindian communities (Hill 1973; Miller 1971; Voeglin & Voeglin 1977); Nahuatl in Mexico (Hill & Hill 1978, 1980); Urdu in Kupwar, India (Gumperz & Wilson 1971); Konkani (Nadkarni 1975); and Hun-garian in Austria (Gal 1979, 1984).

Despite their diversity and despite the various B languages with which they are in contact, languages spoken in these sociolinguistic circum-stances reveal a restructuring or reconfiguration of morphological and syntactic structures which display the following characteristics:

(a) Reduction in the number of allomorphs (i.e. more invariable forms, or fewer context sensitive rules). Increased paradigmatic regularity.
(b) Replacement of synthetic forms by analytic ones or by periphras-tic constructions.
(c) Progressive reduction in inflectional morphology, entailing less flexible word order.
(d) Preference for coordinate rather than embedded constructions.
(e) Distinctive aspectual constructions in verbal systems.

Data reflecting these general trends from three immigrant (Finnish, Hindi, and French) and three indigenous communities (Scots Gaelic, Dyirbal, and Urdu) are presented in the following two sections. (For more extensive examples from a larger number of enclaves, see Maher 1985.) While the sociolinguistic character of immigrant communities may differ from those indigenous ones, it will become evident that the restructuring process evident in the A language in both communities is substantially the same. Possible explanations for this restructuring are discussed in the final section.

2   Immigrant enclave communities

Larmouth (1974) studies immigrant Finnish speakers in northern Minnesota across four generations, focusing particularly upon the change in the use of case endings and concord devices from G1 (the first generation of immigrants) through G4 (fourth generation) speakers. In general, he finds that case endings are close to standard among first generation speakers, optional in the second and third generation and inconsistently evident in the fourth. As in (1) below, the accusative marked -*n* is obligatory on the noun *huone*, optional on the determiner, *se*, *sen*, in G1; both are optional in G2, and disappear completely in G3 and G4. (Determiners themselves become optional in G3 and G4.)

(1)   G1: *Mies osti se(n) huonen*
        G2: *Se mies osti se(n) huone(n)*
        G3: *Se mies osti (se) huone*
        G4: *Mies osti (se) huone*
            "(The) man bought (the) house"

        (1974: 357)

Predictably, word order becomes fixed in G4, as the result of the loss of inflections. Thus in (2) G1 maintains two variants, while G4 has only one.

(2)   G1: *Mieheltä kuoli äiti*
            "From (the) man (ablative) died (the) mother"
        OR
            Miehan äiti kuoli
            "(The) man's (genitive) mother died"
        G2: *Mieheltä kuoli äiti. Miehen aiti kuoli*
        G3: *Miehen äiti kuoli*
        G4: *Miehen äiti kuoli* (genitive construction only)

        (1974: 359)

In addition, adjective–noun concord disappears in G4, such that case and number, when they are marked at all, are marked only on the noun: in (3) *vanha* "old" in G3 and G4 no longer carries ablative case ending -*lta*. (Accusative ending on *kirjeen* also disappears.)

(3)   G1: *Minä sain kirjeen vanhalta mieheltä*
                    "I got (a) letter (accusative) from (the) old man (ablative)"
                G2: *Minä sain kirjee siltä vanhalta mieheltä*
                    "I got (a) letter from that old man (ablative)"
                G3 & G4: *Minä sain kirjee vanha mieheltä*
                    "I got (a) letter from old (no inflection) man (ablative)"

Number agreement endings on the adjective and verb disappear, or become optional (-*t* and -*vat*):

(4)   G1: *Vanhat miehet syövat omenia*
               "(The) old men are eating (plural) apples (partitive)"
          G2: *Vanha(t) miehet syövat omenia*
               "(The) old men are eating apples"
     G3 & G4: *Vanha miehet syö(vat) omenat*
               "(The) old (no inflection) men is (are) eating (the) apples" (note that partitive is replaced by accusative in G3 and G4)

Another change evident in this generational study is the replacement of case endings by periphrastic forms, as in (5).

(5)   G1: *Jussi ajaa kaupungista*
             "John is driving out of town (elative case)"
        G2: *Jussi ajaa kaupungista ulos*
             "John is driving town (elative) out"
        G3: *Jussi ajaa taunia ulos*
             "John is driving town (partitive) out" (note English loan)
        G4: *Jussi ajaa ulos tauni*
             "John is driving out town"
        (1974: 360)

In (5) the postposition *ulos* gradually replaces the elative case ending and becomes, finally, a preposition. The influence from the English model is evident. However, English influence does not explain all developments. For example, in enclave Finnish the genitive case is quite weak overall, while the genitive is the only remaining case ending in English, the B language. Thus, English influence would predict genitive case tenacity. In fact, of all cases in American Finnish, the ablative is the most resistant to loss; the partitive and accusative are the least resistant. Interference from English does not explain these developments.

Larmouth (1974: 363) describes another morphological change: "the interrogative pronouns in later-generation American Finnish have broadened their range at the expense of the relative pronouns", as in (6):

(6)   G1: *Minä näin (sen) miehen joka osti se(n) huone(n)*
             "I saw (the) man who bought the house"
        G2: *Minä näin se mies joka osti (sen) huone(n)*
        G3: *Minä näin se mies kuku osti (se) huone*
        G4: *Minä näin (se) mies kuka osti (se) huone*

The interrogative pronoun *kuka* replaces the relative pronoun *joka*. Case marking remains strong on interrogative pronouns throughout the fourth generation, but the substitution of interrogative for relative forms is "system-wide," according to Larmouth. The replacement of interrogative for relative pronoun forms is a very common pattern in enclave languages.

The structures noted in enclave Finnish are similar to those found in transplanted South Asian languages. Gambhir's (1983) analysis of the Bhojpuri of Guyana notes the loss of inflectional categories in comparison with standard forms. These observations are echoed by Bhatia (1982) in reference to Trinidad Hindi. Bhatia conducted a three-generational analysis of Hindi speakers in Trinidad which revealed a loss of gender, number and case distinctions in the NP among younger speakers. Example (7) illustrates the loss of adjective–noun gender agreement:

(7)   a. *baṛā*   *xarab ciz*
           big (masc. sing.)   bad thing (fem. sing.)
           "a very bad thing"
        b. *chotā*   *chorī*
           little (masc. sing.)   girl (fem. sing.)
           "a little girl"
        (Bhatia 1982)

In addition, he notes loss of the oblique case, regularization of irregular verbs, and loss of pronominal forms. He cites, as an example, the future of the verb "to come," which in Trinidad Bhojpuri has only three forms, stating:

> When we compare this paradigm with the Indian Bhojpuri paradigm which has eighteen inflexional forms, it becomes clear that there has been a substantial reduction. This reduction involves factors such as elimination of honorific inflection in the 2nd and 3rd person, loss of the singular vs. plural distinction and loss of feminine inflexional forms (1982: 143).

Durbin (1973) notes similar reductions in morphology in Trinidad Bhojpuri and remarks upon a development in syntax as well. Where traditional Bhojpuri has embedded constructions for causatives, relatives and antitheticals, Trinidad Hindi tends to juxtapose independent clauses, avoiding the embedded structures.

In Mauritius, where the contact is now with French Creole, Bhojpuri speakers follow similar patterns. Domingue (1980, 1981) compares Traditional Bhojpuri speakers (those who use Bhojpuri primarily) with Innovative Bhojpuri speakers (those who use Creole primarily). Her findings indicate a tendency among Innovative Bhojpuri speakers to erase distinctions and to generalize optional rules. Allomorphs are reduced in nominal case endings, for plural markers and copular verbs; these changes, she claims, are independent of the contact with Creole. Domingue contrasts the morphological alternations in the verbal system of Mauritian Bhojpuri (MB) with the source language, Continental Bhojpuri (CB), with respect to honorifics:

(8)   "See," past, plural

	Continental Bhojpuri (CB)	Mauritian Bhojpuri (MB)
1st	*dēkhalijã* (unmarked)	*dēkhalisa* (ordinary)
		dēkhalijã (honorific)
2nd	*dēkhalasa* (contemptuous)	*dēkhalasa* (ordinary)
	dēkhala (ordinary)	*dēkhalijã* (honorific)
	dēkhalī (honorific)	
3rd	*dēkhalesa* (contemptuous)	*dēkhalansa* (ordinary)
	dēkhal (ordinary)	*dēkhalanjã* (honorific)
	dēkhalī (honorific)	

(Domingue 1981: 156)

The paradigm in (8) reveals: (a) that the traditional rather asymmetrical system becomes symmetrical, (b) that the six distinctive CB forms are reduced to five in MB and the three honorific levels are reduced to two; (c) that the CB "contemptuous" -*sa* weakens to MB "ordinary" and (d) that the CB unmarked first person suffix -*jã* is extended to all MB honorific environments. Certain of these developments may be sociolinguistically motivated (a general leveling of caste distinctions, for example) but the change is interesting from a purely linguistic perspective as well. MB gradually eliminates distinctions and creates a more regular paradigm.

Numerous examples of French speaking enclave communities are found in North America. Without detailing the differences among such communities in Louisiana (LaF), Missouri (MiF), the Virgin Islands (VIF), New England and parts of Canada (CaF), one can observe certain common characteristics. Generally speaking, French enclaves, as compared with Standard French (SF), tend to avoid allomorphic variation in verb paradigms. The linguistic strategies used, however, vary from one enclave to another.

In LaF there is a trend to invariant verb forms by eliminating inflectional endings. The indefinite pronoun *on* with a third singular verb form replaces first person plural subject *nous* with *-ons*. The second plural *-ez* suffix is rarely used; the second singular subject pronoun *tu* is strongly favored over formal *vous*, and when plurality is stressed the *vous-autre(s)* form is used with the third person singular form of the verb. Thus:

(9)   LaF: *On a nuzot . . .*
        SF: *Nous avons . . .*
          "We have . . ."

      (Morgan 1970)

(10)   LaF: *Vous-autres, ça va à l'école*
        SF: *Vous allez à l'école*
          "You go to school"

      (Conwell & Juilland 1963: 143)

On the other hand, Missouri French has maintained inflectional endings but has affixed these endings to regularized stems, usually formed from the present, as in (11):

(11)

MiF Fut./Imp.	Suppletive SF forms	Gloss
vadrai	*irai*	"I will go"
ontais	*avais*	"I had"
sontais	*étais*	"I was"
fontais	*faisais*	"I made"

      (Dorrance 1935)

This tendency to regularize on the basis of present stems extends to past participles as well:

(12)

MiF present	MiF past part.	SF past part.	Gloss
lis	/li/	*lu*	"read"
responds	/repo/	*repondu*	"answered"
suis	/syi/	*suivi*	"followed"
tais	/te/	*tu*	"quieted"
vis	/vi/	*vecu*	"lived"

      (Thogmartin 1970: 35)

Thus, some French enclaves regularize verb stems; others regularize by eliminating verbal endings. In addition, most French enclaves use a single auxiliary verb, *avoir*, for transitive, intransitive and reflexive verbs, avoiding the SF *avoir/être* alternation. The inflected future tense is moribund, replaced by the use of the periphrastic *aller* "to go" plus infinitive. Hull (1956) reports this periphrastic form replacing the inflected present tense as well in certain Canadian French dialects.

Reduced numbers of allomorphs and paradigmatic uniformity are evident not only in the verb but also in pronominal systems. Generally, the Standard French gender distinctions are not maintained and the Standard distinctive pronoun forms for subject, object, indirect object and disjunctive are collapsed to two. In addition there is a tendency to collapse relative and interrogative pronoun forms as well. Hull (1956: 51), for example, states "*Quoi* is widely used in both relative and interrogative situations." Locke (1949: 159) finds a substitution of interrogative *qu'est-ce qui* for relative *ce qui* in the French of Brunswick, Maine:

(13)   *Tout qu'est-ce qui monte, il faut descendre*
    SF: *Tout ce qui monte doit redescendre*
    "Everything that goes up must come down"

As in transplanted Finnish and Bhojpuri, adjective–noun concord gradually disappears in French enclaves. Determiners become either invariant or phonetically determined; forms of the demonstrative adjective for example become *st* before a vowel and *sta* before a consonant:

(14)   **Standard French   Enclave varieties   Gloss**
    ce
    ces   "this/these"
    cette   [st]/ _V
    cettes
    cet   [sta]/ _C
    (Valdman 1979)

While the loss of concord processes varies in degree from enclave to enclave, the tendency to invariable forms, or to phonologically rather than grammatically determined variants, is common to all of them.

The movement away from inflectional devices and allomorphic alternation toward more regularized or analytic forms is accompanied by a preference for periphrastic constructions over synthetic ones and for lexemes over bound morphemes to express grammatical relations. One finds in enclave varieties numerous examples of distinct lexical entities expressing genitive, negation, sequencing of events, interrogatives, and, particularly, aspect in the verbal system. We have already noted the virtual loss of inflected futures, replaced by the periphrastic *va*. In addition, French enclaves report novel aspectual constructions. In MiF, LaF, and CaF progressive or continuous aspect is expressed by *être* "to be" plus the preposition *après* "after" plus the infinitive.

(15)   *Il est après travailler*
         "He is after to work = He is working"
         Il était après travailler
         "He was working"

In Virgin Islands French the same semantic effect is achieved with a different device: *être* plus a relative pronoun (*qui*) plus a finite verb.

(16)   VIF: *t'e ki vey*
         SF: *tu regardes (veilles)*
             "you are watching"
         (Highfield 1979: 95)

Although the form looks like a SF relative clause, it has apparently lost the force of a relative and is used to indicate progressive aspect. In these instances the B language (English) has a highly productive progressive form, *-ing*. One might suppose that contact motivates these novel progressives. However, these forms are not bound morphemes like the English inflected progressive. Moreover, the past forms with *après* and *ki* are difficult to explain from a functional perspective since they overlap with the SF imperfect which has the same semantic value. However, if we recall that the SF imperfect combines both past tense and continuous aspect, it is clear that SF provides no means for distinguishing progressive aspect in the verb. Thus, we might conclude that in these enclave structures, the internal resources of the language have been exploited to factor aspect out of the verbal morphology and render it a more distinct and salient feature of the predicate phrase. This factoring process results in morphology that, as in Creole languages, expresses tense and aspect separately.

It is this factoring process or decomposition of complex structures that is the most striking feature of the enclave language. As Highfield (1979: 92) puts it:

> In general the simple and the periphrastic tenses are the most frequently and consistently used. St. Thomas French [VIF] Dialect speakers show a disinclination towards using composite structures, replacing them most usually with periphrastic devices.

Enclave languages rely on coordinating elements, simple juxtaposition, and contextual clues to express complex syntactic relations and to avoid embedded constructions. Conwell & Juilland (1963), for instance, comment frequently on the LaF tendency to reduce or eliminate connectives.

(17)   LaF: *J'ai longtemps j'ai pas passé*
            I have long time I have not passed
            "It's been a long time since I passed by"
        SF: *Il y a longtemps que je n'ai pas passé*

Likewise Valdman (1979: 172) reports "relativization by parataxis" and possession by juxtaposition in Missouri French:

(18)   MiF: *la fille roue-la*
        SF: *la fille de ce roi*
            "the daughter of this king"
        MiF: *i'portrait princesse-la*
        SF: *le portrait de cette princesse*
            "the picture of this princess"

Note that while ellipsis is common in English, the B language, elimination of connectives in these cases produces ungrammatical results in English. To project English models for these French forms does not, therefore, seem reasonable. As Thogmartin (1970: 71) states:

> The influence of English on phonology and morphology of OMF [Old Mines French, here MiF] has been negligible, despite almost 150 years of constant contact between the two languages and the overwhelming dominance of English in matters of prestige and utility.

3   Indigenous enclaves

Thus far we have been looking at examples of transplanted enclave communities. The indigenous enclave community demonstrates many of the same features, albeit to a lesser degree. Dorian's (1973, 1978, 1981) studies of Scots Gaelic speakers, bilingual in Gaelic and English, in northern Scotland provide good examples of this latter type of enclave. Since Gaelic has been ceding to English in this area over a period of centuries, it is possible to study an erosion process through the gradual loss of fluency among its last speakers, the categories she terms Young Fluent Speakers (YFS) and Semi-speakers (SS), compared with older, more fluent Conservative Speakers.

Scottish Gaelic has two morphemes with an exceptionally large number of allomorphs, the noun plural and the gerund. The highly complex system of older speakers, which involves eleven different inflectional devices, both mutational and suffixed, is modified by less fluent speakers to one strongly productive allomorph, the suffix -*an* for plurals and -*al* for gerunds. Dorian notes also that where there are competing structures that have the same semantic value, there is movement toward a single favored structure. Thus, for example, older speakers use two different structures to indicate personal possession: a preposed possessive pronoun used with inalienables, and postposed forms of the conjugating preposition *aig* "at" for all other contexts. Semi-speakers use the latter form in almost all contexts. Semi-speakers also avoid complex verb morphology and eliminate synthetic forms by substituting transparent analytic forms as in (19), where the Gaelic so-called "conjugating" prepositions are replaced by free-standing prepositions and pronouns.

(19) | **Conservative speaker** | **Semi-speaker** | **Gloss** |
|---|---|---|
| *dhomh* | orn mis' | "for me" |
| *rium* | ri mis' | "to me" |
| *bhuatha* | bho aid | "from them" |

Dorian (1981: 15) is careful to point out that many complex aspects of the language are not lost by the SS or YFS, that mutational patterns are surprisingly consistent with conservative norms, and that complex morphology is retained better in certain categories. Thus, while simplification is not generalized in the language:

> One of the more suggestive findings of my Gaelic language death studies ... is that the imperfect speakers in my sample show certain kinds of reductive phenomena in common in their Gaelic, regardless of acquisitional history. For example, a greater or lesser use of analogically regularized allomorphs in place of irregular allomorphs; complete loss of morphemes that are already showing weakness in the fully fluent population's Gaelic; loss of "inventory" ... and also in loss of vocabulary from both open and closed classes.
>
> (1982:56)

Another example of morphological change in an indigenous community is Gumperz and Wilson's (1971) study of three languages used in Kupwar Village near Karnataka, India. Kannada, Marathi and Urdu are the primary languages in this traditionally multilingual community, with Kannada the majority language in the village and Marathi the dominant language of the district. Not surprisingly, it is Kupwar Urdu, the non-dominant language, which demonstrates the greatest variation from standard forms. Gumperz and Wilson's study describes changes as syntactic convergence among the three languages, but in fact their data reveal fewer examples of convergence than of the restructuring of Kupwar Urdu in a number of ways.

In terms of noun gender, Hindi/Urdu (HU) nouns display two gender classes, M and F, with animates classed by sex, inanimates assigned to either category. In Kupwar Urdu (KuU) all non-human nouns are merged into the masculine such that only human females remain as a special gender category, as in (20).

(20)   "There was a flood"
        HU: *wəhā nədii a-ii* (fem.)
        KuU: *hwa   nədi   ay-a* (unmarked masc.)
               there river came

        (Gumperz & Wilson 1971: 156)

Verbal agreement markers are greatly reduced in Kupwar Urdu. Where HU has agreement markers on V and AUX, Kupwar Urdu has only one at the end of the VP. Where HU has two instances of gender agreement marking in the VP, Kupwar Urdu has only one form which agrees for person not gender as in (21).

(21)   "Where did you go?"
        HU: *kəha   gə-ya th-a   tu* (masc.)
                         gə-ii th-ii tu (fem.)
        KuU: *khā   gəe   te   tu*
        where   gone were you

        (Gumperz & Wilson 1971: 157)

NP–VP agreement in HU is complex: in the structure NP1 NP2 VP, when NP2 is not human the VP shows agreement with NP2. In Kupwar Urdu the VP agrees uniformly with NP1. Where HU has a paradigm for the future tense marker varying with person/number/gender, Kupwar Urdu has one invariable future marker *-ēg-*.

Word order differences are evident as well. While HU has the normal order subject–complement–VP, Kupwar Urdu has normal order subject–VP–complement. HU allows the interrogative marker *kya* to appear in several places in the verb construction, in Kupwar *kya* can only appear in final position.

Gumperz and Wilson (1971: 162) conclude about Kupwar Urdu:

> It has adapted its gender system and radically restructured its system of agreement markers, in some cases even to the point of reshaping gender agreement markers. It has further given up such typical HU features as verb compounding and has also undergone a number of semantic changes including the creation of a new distinction between exclusive and inclusive personal pronouns.

The last development is probably influenced by the contact languages, Kannada and Marathi, which both make that distinction. While the influence of the B language(s) makes itself felt in certain constructions, borrowing cannot account for the evolution of all divergent forms.

Lest we assume that these patterns of morphological change reflect forces that lie hidden in Indo-European languages, it is helpful to look briefly at the data presented by Schmidt (1985a, b) from enclave Dyirbal speakers in North Queensland, Australia. Schmidt studies the speech of a 100-member aboriginal tribal community assembled on federally donated land at Jambun, the last of an original 3,000 Dyirbal speakers. In this relic community only those over the age of thirty-five speak traditional Dyirbal (TD): fifteen- to thirty-five-year-olds speak "imperfect" Dyirbal (YD) and those under fifteen have no fluency in the language at all, having become monolingual English speakers. Schmidt (1985b: 381) states:

> At first my impression of "imperfect" Dyirbal was of a dismal patchwork of inconsistencies and (from the point of view of TD) mistakes, haphazardly distributed over speakers and situations. It was easy to suppose that such a picture reflected a sporadically disrupted stage in the decay of TD. However, I gradually became aware that the apparent "mistakes" of the YD speakers were not random errors: rather, each individual had his own grammatical system for Dyirbal communication, involving simplification of the traditional grammatical norm to a greater or lesser degree.

The patterns evident in this simplification are remarkably similar to what we have already seen: allomorphic reduction; radical simplification and regularization of certain paradigms; generalization of a single case affix to cover various peripheral case functions; a tendency to eliminate verbal inflectional affixes; a breakdown in agreement rules; and diminished frequency of clause subordination; change from free to rigid word order (1985a: 229–232).

In addition, Schmidt's detailed analysis of the allomorphic reduction in ergative case marking, preceding complete loss of the category, reveals five distinct stages of change, reflected in the speech of a continuum of YD speakers. According to Schmidt, the six phonologically conditioned allomorphs of TD are gradually reduced to four, then to two, and then to one, before, for the youngest speakers, disappearing altogether. The process begins with the use of two allomorphs, *-gu* and *-ŋgu*, in free variation; continues with the extension of this *-(ŋ)gu* allomorph into new environments; then with the loss of morphophonemic rules operating over morpheme boundaries, creating more agglutinative morphological structures with each morpheme retaining its own form; and finally, the emergence of a single morpheme *-gu* for ergative case in all stems. Ultimately, the ergative case ending is eliminated altogether and syntactic function is marked by word order alone. Schmidt's very close analysis provides a unique insight into the attrition process as it unfolds.

4   Conclusion

It is clear from the preceding examples that the development noted in enclave Indo-European languages is paralleled in non-Indo-European languages such as Dyirbal and Finnish; the phenomenon is evidently not, as Sapir and others have suggested, a characteristic development of the Indo-European language family. Moreover, while English may be seen as exerting an influence in some cases, the examples from Kupwar Urdu and Mauritian Bhojpuri reflect similar tendencies with differing contact languages. The restructuring cannot be explained wholly in terms of borrowing or interference. The question, therefore, remains: If neither borrowing nor internal change can account for these effects, how can we explain this ''dismantling and reordering'' process, to use Haugen's term?

One is tempted to look to the discussions of the so-called ''language death'' phenomenon for explanations of these types of change. The restructuring that occurs in ''language death'' has been explained in functional terms. As language A dies out, speakers use it in fewer and fewer sociolinguistic contexts; it is suggested, therefore, that the need for stylistic variants in language A is reduced. Moreover, among intimates, context predetermines much of the message. The need for more formal, elaborated or context-independent speech varieties is, therefore, limited. It is supposed that elaborate language forms gradually die out, leaving only those informal variants used in the intimate setting. While this description oversimplifies the actual situation, there is no question that functional diglossia characterizes many ''language death'' situations. However, ''language death'' is not the overriding process in every enclave situation; there are stable diglossic communities, such as Kupwar Urdu, where the restructuring process is nonetheless evident. Moreover, morphosyntactic restructuring is also evident in other bilingual situations which do not involve attrition: second language Swahili as spoken in Nairobi and Kumpala (Scotton 1979); Bozal (Africanized) Spanish (Lipski 1986); Nagamese (Ferguson 1983); Afrikaans and other ''creoloids'' or creole-like languages. It is not clear, therefore, that the phenomena under review are unique to ''language death'' or to the language attrition process.

An alternative explanation based on bilingualism can be proposed as follows: bilingualism creates a need for communicative efficiency which promotes certain reduced linguistic forms over other more complex ones. Mohan and Zador (1986) suggest that it is the optional or redundant elements that are lost in these situations. Vago (this volume) and Maher (1985) describe the process as an elimination of opaque constructions in favor of greater morphosyntactic transparency. In both cases bilingualism is seen as favoring strategies which render communication in the less frequently used language more efficient and less ambiguous. Bi- or trilingualism is a factor in all the enclave communities under review here. However, it would be impossible to maintain that multilingual situations generally produce morphosyntactic restructuring in the less dominant language; thus multilingualism cannot be taken as an explanatory factor in and of itself.

An alternative explanation disregards issues concerning language use in the adult community, and focuses rather on how language A is acquired in the multilingual setting. Intergenerational language change in bilingual communities is seen in these terms as the result of inadequate exposure to language A for latter-generation children. While these children are exposed to language B and learn it easily, exposure to A gradually diminishes, resulting in "partially replicated grammars." The regularized forms typical in child language seem sufficiently similar to restructured forms to suggest, as in Jakobson (1972), a strong relationship between acquisition and loss. (A review of relevant crosslinguistic data on partially replicated grammars and their theoretical implications is found in Maher 1985: 229–277.) This explanation has an additional appeal in that it may provide a principled relationship between the restructuring in enclaves and pidgin/creole languages. If restructuring occurs in enclaves due to inadequate exposure to language A, then the similar structures in pidgins and creoles may also be explained in terms of inadequate exposure to the target language. However, since no detailed studies of language acquisition in an enclave community have been done, all theories about language acquisition in these situations are mere conjecture. Such studies are feasible, however, and would yield interesting results.

It would be difficult at this point to rule out any of these possible explanations. Language use, language acquisition, and bilingualism may all play a role in determining the evolution of language A structures. Haugen's suggestion that the learner of a new language dismantles and reorders the language he already knows seems to be born out in enclave situations in the larger community context. In extending Haugen's observation, we can see that this reordering process is far more systematic and more general than earlier studies of bilingualism and language contact have indicated. A broader and more thorough analysis of these systematic reordering processes, as evidenced in individuals as well as in speech communities, will enrich our understanding of fundamental human linguistic processes and may also provide evidence for the structure of Universal Grammar.

References

Andersen, Roger W. 1982. "Determining the linguistic attributes of language attrition," in Richard D. Lambert *et al.* (eds.), *The loss of language skills.* Rowley, MA: Newbury House Publishers, 83–118.

Bhatia, Tej K. 1982. "Trinidad Hindi: three generations of a transplanted variety," *Studies in the Linguistic Sciences* 11: 135–150.

Bloomfield, Leonard. 1933. *Language.* New York: Holt, Rinehart and Winston.

Conwell, Marily J., and Alphonse Juilland. 1963. *Louisiana French grammar.* The Hague: Mouton.

Domingue, Nicole. 1980. "Syntactic innovations in Mauritian Bhojpuri," MS, McGill University.

    1981. "Internal change in a transplanted language," *Studies in Linguistic Sciences* 4: 151–159.

Dorian, Nancy. 1973. "Grammatical change in a dying dialect," *Language* 49: 411–438.

    1978. "The fate of morphological complexity in language death: evidence from East Sutherland Gaelic," *Language* 54: 590–609.

    1981. *Language death.* Philadelphia: University of Pennsylvania Press.

Dorrance, W. A. 1935. *The survival of French in the old district of Sainte Geneviève.* Columbia, MO: University of Missouri.

Dressler, Wolfgang. 1972. "On the phonology of language death," *Chicago Linguistic Society* 8: 448–457.

Durbin, Mridula Adenwala. 1973. "Formal changes in Trinidad Hindi as a result of language adaptation," *American Anthropologist* 75: 1290–1304.

Eikel, Jr., Fred. 1949. "The use of cases in New Braunfels German," *American Speech* 24: 278–281.

Ferguson, Charles A. 1983. "Is Nagamese a creoloid?" MS, Stanford University.

Gal, Susan. 1979. *Language shift.* New York: Academic Press.

    1984. "Phonological style in bilingualism: the interaction of structure and use," in D. Schiffrin (ed.), *Meaning, form and use in context.* GURT 84, Georgetown University Press, Washington, DC.

Gambhir, Surendra K. 1983. "Diglossia in dying languages: a case study of Guyanese Bhojpuri and Standard Hindi," *Anthropological Linguistics* 25: 25–28.

Givon, Talmy. 1979. "Prolegomena to any same creology," in Ian Hancock (ed.), *Readings in Creole studies.* Ghent: Story-Scientia, 3–36.

Gumperz, John J., and Robert Wilson. 1971. "Convergence and creolization," in

Dell Hymes (ed.), *Pidginization and creolization of languages*. Cambridge: Cambridge University Press, 151–168.

Haag, Earl C. 1982. *A Pennsylvania German reader and grammar*. University Park, PA: Penn State University Press.

Haugen, Einar. 1978. "Bilingualism, language contact, and immigrant languages in the United States: a research report 1956–1970," in Joshua Fishman (ed.), *Advances in the study of societal multilingualism*. The Hague: Mouton, 1–112.

Henzl, Vera. 1981. "Slavic languages in the new environment," in Charles A. Ferguson and Shirley B. Heath (eds.), *Language in the USA*. Cambridge: Cambridge University Press, 293–321.

Highfield, Arnold R. 1979. *The French dialect of St. Thomas, US Virgin Islands*. Ann Arbor: Karoma.

Hill, Jane H. 1973. "Subordinate clause density and language function," in Corun, Smith-Stark and Geiser (eds.), *You take the high node and I'll take the low node*. Chicago Linguistic Society, 33–52.

and Kenneth C. Hill. 1978. "Honorific usage in Modern Nahuatl," *Language* 54: 123–155.

and Kenneth C. Hill. 1980. "Mixed grammar, purist grammar, and language attitudes in Modern Nahuatl," *Language and Society* 9: 321–348.

Hull, Alexlander. 1956. "The Franco-Canadian dialect of Windsor, Ontario: a preliminary study," *Orbis* 5: 35–60.

Jakobson, R. 1972. *Child language, aphasia and phonological universals*. The Hague: Mouton.

Kehlenbeck, Alfred P. 1948. "An Iowa Low German dialect," *American Dialect Society* 10. Greensboro, NC.

Larmouth, Donald W. 1974. "Differential interference in American Finnish cases," *Language* 50: 356–366.

Lipski, John M. 1986. "Convergence and divergence in Bozal Spanish: a comparative study," *Journal of Pidgin and Creole Languages* 1:2.

Locke, William N. 1949. "Pronunciation of the French spoken at Brunswick, Maine," *American Dialect Society* 12. Greensboro, NC.

Maher, Julianne. 1985. *Contact linguistics: The language enclave phenomena*. PhD dissertation, New York University.

Miller, Wick R. 1971. "The death of language or serendipity among the Shoshoni," *Anthropological Linguistics* 13: 114–120.

Moag, Rodney. 1984. "Factors in language attrition: Taniel in Fiji, 1945–75." Paper at Sixth SALA Roundtable. Austin, TX.

Mohan, Peggy R. 1978. "Trinidad Bhojpuri: a morphological study," PhD dissertation, University of Michigan.

and Paul Zador. 1986. "Discontinuity in a life cycle: The death of Trinidad Bhojpuri," *Language* 62: 291–319.

Morgan, Jr, Raleigh. 1970. "Dialect leveling in non-English speech of Southwest Louisiana," in Glenn G. Gilbert (ed.), *Texas Studies in Bilingualism*. Berlin: Walter de Gruyter, 50–62.

Nadkarni, Mangesh V. 1975. "Bilingualism and syntactic change in Konkani," *Language* 51: 672–683.

Rickford, John R. 1986. "The need for new approaches to social class analysis in sociolinguistics," *Language and Communication* 6:3.

Rickford, John R. 1986. "Social contact and linguistic diffusion," *Language* 62: 245–289.

Sapir, Edward. 1921. *Language*. New York: Harcourt Brace.

Schmidt, Annette. 1985a. *Young people's Dyirbal*. Cambridge: Cambridge University Press.

1985b. "The fate of ergativity in dying Dyirbal," *Language* 61: 378–396.

Scotton, Carol Myers. 1979. "The context is the message: morphological, syntactic and semantic reduction and deletion in Nairobi and Kampala varieties of Swahili," in Ian Hancock (ed.), *Readings in Creole studies*. Ghent: Story-Scientia, 111–128.

Thogmartin, Jr, Clyde O. 1970. "The French dialect of Old Mines, Missouri," PhD dissertation, University of Michigan.

Timm, Lenora A. 1980. "Bilingualism, diglossia and language shift in Brittany," *International Journal of Sociology of Language* 25: 29–49.

Trudgill, Peter. 1983. *On dialect*. New York: New York University Press.

Valdman, Albert. 1979. "Créolisation, Français populaire et le parler des isolats francophones d'Amérique du Nord," in A. Valdman (ed.), *Le Français hors de France*. Paris: Honoré Champion, 181–197.

Voegelin, C. F., and F. M. Voegelin. 1977. "Is Tubatulabal de-acquisition relevant to theories of language acquisition?" *International Journal of American Linguistics* 43: 333–338.

Weinreich, Uriel. 1953. *Languages in contact* (reprinted 1964). The Hague: Mouton.

Whatley, Randall P., and Harry Jannise. 1982. *Conversational Cajun French I*. Gretna, LA: Pelican Publishing Co.

Part II
Group studies

6   L1 loss in an L2 environment: Dutch immigrants in France

KEES DE BOT, PAUL GOMMANS, AND CAROLA ROSSING

1   Introduction

In his typology of non-pathological language attrition, Van Els (1986) distinguishes four different types, taking as points of reference **what** is lost – either the first or the second language – and the environment **in which** it is lost – either in an L1 environment or an L2 environment:

(1)   Loss of L1 in an L1 environment, e.g. first language loss by aging people;

(2)   Loss of L1 in an L2 environment, e.g. loss of native languages by immigrants;

(3)   Loss of L2 in an L1 environment, e.g. foreign language loss;

(4)   Loss of L2 in an L2 environment, e.g. second language loss by aging migrants.

An overview of research in this area is to be found in Weltens (1987).

The present investigation falls within the second category: L1 loss in an L2 environment. Most research in this category has been concerned with migrant groups rather than with individuals (see for instance Fishman 1966; Jamieson 1980; Clyne 1980). In the migrant studies sociological characteristics of the different ethnic groups are compared with each other in order to find the cluster of factors that determine either language maintenance or loss. Excellent examples of this approach are Clyne (1982) and Fishman *et al.* (1985).

Empirical research on individual L1 loss in an L2 environment has started only recently. In the investigation described below we tried to find within-group characteristics that might influence language maintenance and loss in such a setting. The focus was on two factors that tend to be mentioned in the language loss literature: amount of contact with L1 and time elapsed since emigration. The design was such that these two factors could be treated independently.

Another aspect we were interested in was the maintenance or loss of metalinguistic abilities. It could be hypothesized that metalinguistic skills are the first skills to be endangered in the attrition process. On the other hand, it is not inconceivable that these skills are well maintained because they have a monitoring function in the language production process.

2   Set-up of the investigation

2.1   *Informants*

Dutch immigrants in France were contacted using various methods: through embassies and consulates in France and in the Netherlands, Dutch emigration services, and advertisements in a number of Dutch and (regional) French newspapers. The response was sufficiently high to allow the application of a number of selection criteria:

(1)   Emigration after age seventeen. At this age the acquisition of the first language has been completed both through formal and informal input.
(2)   Lived in France for at least ten years.
(3)   Variation in the amount of contact with the Dutch language since emigration.

For the third criterion it appeared to be very difficult to define and quantify more than two levels: many contacts versus few contacts. Informants in the former group had a Dutch partner and had contact with other Dutchmen at least once a week, while informants in the latter group had a French partner or no partner, and had contact with other Dutchmen less than once a week. Accordingly, the factor "amount of contact" (henceforth: "contact") had two levels: many and few.

The factor "time elapsed since emigration" (henceforth: "time") had seven levels: 11–15/16–20/21–25/26–30/31–35/36+ years.

The number of informants in each category is listed in Table 6.1.

Table 6.1 *Number of informants per category*

	Time in years					
	11–15	16–20	21–25	26–30	31–35	36+
Many contacts	3	3	3	2	4	3
Few contacts	3	4	2	0	2	1

2.2   The tests

In order to test general proficiency in Dutch, two tests were administered: an editing test and the Foreign Service Interview (FSI). The editing test consisted of a short story in which words were added at random. The task here is to find the words added. The test we used was developed by the Dutch Central Institute for Test Development (CITO 1981) as a global proficiency test for learners of Dutch as a second language of different ages. The editing test can be described as a global/ indirect test. Since this test had not been used previously in this kind of research, we had no data on its validity and reliability. Therefore it was decided not to rely on this test only.

The FSI was chosen because its reliability and validity have been established sufficiently (Clark 1979; Jones 1979). A major advantage of the FSI is that it is an informal interview in which a well trained interviewer can disguise even the impression that language proficiency is being tested. The interview consists of three parts or stages. In the first stage, the interviewer establishes the global level of proficiency (low, medium, high). In the second stage the interviewer accommodates his language and the topics to the level of proficiency of the interviewee. In the third stage, the interviewer increases the complexity of language and topics to the point that the upper limit of the interviewee's proficiency becomes perceptible. The interview forms the basis for a scaling of the interviewee on a ten-point scale (0, 1, 1+, 2, 2+ ...4+, 5) on five different aspects of language proficiency: pronunciation, grammar, vocabulary, fluency, and comprehension. The five aspects are used to establish the general level of proficiency (for a detailed description of this procedure, see Jones 1979: 111). In order to assess interjudge reliability scores, the interviews were recorded on tape and scored independently by two trained judges. The FSI can be described as a direct/discrete point test.

The grammaticality judgement test used was an adapted version of a test developed by Koster *et al.* (1985) for the assessment of metalinguistic abilities in different types of aphasic patients. Thirty-six non-aphasic informants served as controls in the Koster *et al.* study, and, accordingly, in the present study. The test consists of seventy sentences covering ten different types of grammatical constructions that appear to be difficult for both aphasic and, to a lesser degree, non-aphasic speakers of Dutch. (See the Appendix at the end of this chapter for a list of the types of constructions used.) The task is to indicate for each sentence whether it is grammatical or not. The test is structured in such a way that the combined reactions to the set of sentences for a given construction reveal the nature of the problem an informant may have with this construction. Through this test the "vulnerability" of different grammatical structures could be assessed. A comparison between different types of pathological loss and non-pathological loss could not be made, since Koster *et al.* didn't find a difference between types of aphasia.

2.3   Procedure

All informants were tested at home in May 1986. The test sessions lasted about two hours. After a short introduction, the cassette recorder was started for the first and second part of the FSI. Then the two formal tests were administered, the editing test always preceding the judgement test. As will become clear in the next paragraph, the editing test appeared to be (too) easy for most informants. This was a problem from a statistical point of view, but it certainly increased the informants' linguistic self-confidence. The third part of the FSI concluded the test session. All interviews and tests took place within the first two hours of the visit in order to avoid differential retraining effects for proficiency on Dutch. In the third part of the FSI, it appeared to be difficult to get some of the informants to discuss more abstract and difficult topics, which often had to do with private opinions. This was due to the limited time available for the tests and to the fact that the interviewers were strangers to the in-formants.

3   Results

3.1   The editing test

The maximum score, i.e. the total number of words added/to be found was 49. The mean score was 46.4 with a SD of 2.2 and a range of 42–49. The split half reliability (Spearman-Brown) was .68, KR-20 was .65. The low reliability scores are probably accounted for by the apparent ceiling effect.

Analyses of variance showed no significant effects of "time" and "con-tact" factors, nor a significant interaction.

3.2   The FSI

The taped interviews were rated by two trained judges. Signifi-cant interrater correlations (Spearman, $p < 0.10$) for overall score and subscores are presented overleaf in Table 6.2.

Table 6.2 *FSI interrater reliability*

Pronunciation	.77
Grammar	.58
Vocabulary	.80
Fluency	ns
Comprehension	.52
Overall score	.72

The correlations between the two judges are fair for pronunciation, vocabulary and overall score, but on the low side for grammar and comprehension. Apparently, the judges' concept of fluency differed considerably. Judge 1's scores for fluency correlated .94 with the (shared) overall score, while judge 2's scores correlated only .45 with this overall score. After extensive discussions the judges decided on joint scores, both overall and for the different aspects mentioned in Table 6.2. It is these scores that were used in the rest of the investigation.

Although the range of scores on the FSI was not very large (between 3 and 5), the analyses of variance showed significant effects for "contact" ($F = 23.26$, $p < .01$), "time" ($F = 4.16$, $p < .02$), and a significant interaction between these two factors ($F = 3.99$, $p < .02$). Further analyses showed that for both "contact" groups "time" was a significant factor. The correlation between the FSI scores and the "contact" factor was .50 ($p < .10$), while the correlation between FSI scores and the "time" factor was not significant. Partial correlations between FSI scores and "time," eliminating the effect of "contact", were significant for the "few contacts" group ($r = .84$, $p < .01$), but not for the "many contacts" group. In other words: proficiency in Dutch does not change over time when there are many contacts with Dutch, but it deteriorates linearly over time in the case of few contacts.

3.3   The grammaticality judgement test

The data from the judgement test were compared with both the aphasic and the non-aphasic groups in the Koster *et al.* (1985) study. Given the fact that their non-aphasic control group did not differ too much from ours on age, education and social class stratification, it seemed justified to use this group as a reference for our data as well. These reference data can be used in two ways: as an absolute norm and as a relative norm. In the former case, those sentences that were judged correct by the **majority** of the reference group were labelled "correct,"

Table 6.3 *Significant correlations with sentence types (p < .10)*

Sentence types	"time"	"contact"
Statives	−.33	
Middles		.40
Subcat. plus extra argument	.30	
Anaphora/definite	.31	
Anaphora/disjoint reference	−.35	

Table 6.4 *Percentages correct for control group and emigrant group per sentence type*

Sentence type	Control group	Emigrant group	Difference
I	0	0	0
II	61.1	60.0	1.1
III	72.2	75.0	2.8
IV	72.2	66.7	5.5
V	27.8	26.7	1.1
VI	47.2	25.0	22.2
VIIa	50.7	53.3	2.6
VIIb	41.2	45.6	4.4
VII ($\bar{x}$)	45.0	48.7	3.7
VIIIa	44.4	43.3	1.1
VIIIb	31.3	30.8	0.5
VIIIc	59.7	57.5	2.2
VIIId	50.7	47.5	3.2
VIII ($\bar{x}$)	46.5	44.8	1.7
IX	29.2	32.5	3.3
Xa	61.1	62.5	1.4
Xb	80.6	95.0	14.4
Xc	90.3	90.0	0.3
Xd	60.4	68.3	7.9
Xe	62.5	61.7	0.8
Xf	91.7	98.3	6.6
X ($\bar{x}$)	71.0	75.8	4.8

Note: $\bar{x}$ indicates the mean of the scores on all sentences and subtypes of sentences.

while sentences judged incorrect by the **majority** were labelled "incorrect." In the latter case the **percentage** correct of the reference group is used for the comparison with our data. Here, a given sentence is not labelled "correct" or "incorrect," but placed somewhere on a continuum, between these two extremes.

Table 6.5 *Significant F ratios for sentence types*

Sentence type	"Time"		"Contact"	
	F	p <	F	p <
II	4.03	0.01		
IV			10.62	0.01
X (x)	3.54	0.02	3.11	0.09
Xc	2.97	0.04		
Xd	2.65	0.06		

3.3.1 Comparison with an absolute norm

An analysis of variance with percentage correct as the dependent variable showed no significant effects of the "time" and "contact" factors, nor a significant interaction. Further analysis showed that the scores for **certain** sentence types correlated with the two main factors, as shown on the previous page in Table 6.3.

It should be noted, however, that the number of sentences per type was small and not equal for all types. Therefore it is hard to draw firm conclusions from the correlations in Table 6.3.

3.3.2 Comparison with a relative norm

By comparing the percentages of correct scores of both the control group and our emigrant group we would get some more detailed information about changes in acceptability of sentence types. Table 6.4 on the previous page lists these percentages for each sentence type. (See the Appendix at the end of this chapter for the sentence types corresponding to the figures.)

Overall, the control group accepted 50.8 percent of the sentences presented, and the emigrant group 50.6 percent, the difference not being significant. The correlation between the two groups is .97 (p < .01). Not surprisingly, no significant effects were found in the analysis of variance over all sentence types. Further analyses, however, produced significant F ratios for the sentence types listed in Table 6.5.

The data in Table 6.5 should be interpreted as follows: a significant F ratio for "time" means that the deviation from the control group increases with the amount of time elapsed since emigration, and for "contact" that the "few contacts" group deviated more from the control group than the "many contacts" group.

4   **Conclusion**

The present investigation was set up to provide data on two different questions:

(a)   What is the role of amount of contact and time elapsed since emigration in the maintenance or loss of a first language in a second language environment?
(b)   To what extent does the loss of metalinguistic skills precede or follow the loss of linguistic skills?

As to the first question, significant effects were found on the FSI only. The data show a significant effect of both "amount of contact" and "time elapsed since emigration," and a significant interaction. Further analyses showed that the relation between FSI scores, "contact," and "time" is a complex one: there is only a linear relation between "time" and attrition when there are few contacts with the first language. This effect is not extremely strong, but significant. An implication from this finding is that in measures of language contact as used in language loss research, "time elapsed since emigration" and "amount of contact" should not be used as independent measures: "time" only becomes relevant when there is not much contact with the language.

Our data show no significant relations between metalinguistic skills and "time" or "contact." This may be due to the fact that there is hardly any attrition of this type of skills.

As mentioned in Section 1, there are two contrasting hypotheses about metalinguistic and linguistic skills in the attrition process: metalinguistic skills are lost earlier because they are less automatized and the tests deal with "sensitive" areas that are avoided in normal language use, or the linguistic skills are lost first because without adequate metalinguistic "monitoring" language use as such is hampered. Our data suggest that the latter is the case: hardly any attrition of metalinguistic skills could be evidenced, while there was significant attrition of linguistic skills as measured in the FSI. We see no reason to doubt the validity of the test used: the data on non-attrited controls show that the sentence types used really are in sensitive areas.

Some types of sentences appear to be influenced by "time" and "contact," but it is not clear which general underlying principle can explain the attrition of these types only. For one of the sentence types, "Middles" (*Sportwagens verkopen snel*, "Sportcars sell quickly"), the difference between the control group and the emigrant group can be explained as a cohort effect: this type of sentence is fairly new in Dutch, and the informants who emigrated thirty years earlier simply missed this development in the Dutch language.

The present data can hardly be compared with other, more socio-linguistic, research on Dutch emigrants (Clyne 1980; Pauwels 1987; De Bot *et al.*, in preparation), since the Dutch in France do not in any sense constitute an ethnic group: they are not organized, do not act as one group and do not consider themselves as part of such a group. From a linguistic point of view such a comparison might be more fruitful: it will give us an opportunity to compare a language in attrition in L2 environments that differ considerably. It may provide us with some insight into the role of interference in the attrition process.

Appendix: Types of sentences in the Koster *et al.* (1985) grammaticality judgement test

I   Syntactic prose (2 sentences)
De late fietsen zongen bijna in waterige stenen.
"The late bicycles sang almost in watery stones."

II   Statives (4 sentences)
Ik ben mijn broer aan het kennen.
"I am knowing my brother."

III   Nesting (2 sentences)
De dochter van de buurvrouw van de boerin ging naar Amersfoort.
"The daughter of the neighbour of the farmer's wife went to Amersfoort."

IV   Middles (4 sentences)
Sportwagens verkopen snel.
"Sportcars sell quickly."

V   Prepositions (4 sentences)
Deze koekjes waren gemaakt aan kleine kinderen.
"These biscuits were made on small children."

VI   Definiteness (4 sentences)
Er wacht man bij het tuinhek.
"There waits man by the garden gate."

VII   (a) Selection restrictions/semantic category (4 sentences)
Ik denk dat mijn broer tennis speelt.
"I think that my brother tennis plays."

    (b) Selection restrictions/particles (6 sentences)
De inbreker gluurde het sleutelgat door.
"The burglar pierced the keyhole through."

VIII   (a) Subcategorization/extra argument (4 sentences)
Wat denkt Pieter dat Anna is?
"What thinks Pieter that Anna is?"

    (b) Subcategorization/missing argument (4 sentences)
Gerard legde het boek.
"Gerard put the book."

    (c) Subcategorization/missing embedded argument (4 sentences)
Wie dacht je dat zou uitnodigen?
"Who did you think would invite?"

    (d) Subcategorization/missing reflexive argument (4 sentences)
Het kleine meisje verkleedde voor het verjaardagspartijtje.
"The little girl changed clothes for the birthday party."

IX   Complements (8 sentences)
    Zij zegt dat mevrouw Janssen vanmiddag op bezoek te komen.
    "She says that Mrs. Janssen to come and visit this afternoon."

X   (a) Anaphora/definite (4 sentences)
      Ik zag meneer Smit en jij zag er een.
      "I saw Mr. Smit and you saw one."

    (b) Anaphora/control and reflexives (2 sentences)
      Hans beloofde Thomas niet over zichzelf te praten.
      "Hans promised Thomas not to talk about himself."

    (c) Anaphora/reflexives (2 sentences)
      De zus van Mieke kleedt zich aan's ochtends voor het ontbijt.
      "Mieke's sister dresses in the morning before breakfast."

    (d) Anaphora/control (4 sentences)
      Joost vroeg Sylvia de deur te sluiten en hij deed het.
      "Joost asked Sylvia to close the door and he did it."

    (e) Anaphora/disjoint reference (2 sentences)
      Mijn zus houdt van mijn zus.
      "My sister loves my sister."

    (f) Anaphora/scope (2 sentences)
      Iedereen zag zijn leraar.
      "Everyone saw his teacher."

Note

The authors wish to thank Jane Bennett for her comments on an earlier version of this article.

References

CITO (Centraal Instituut voor Toetsontwikkeling). 1981. *Instaptoets Anderstaligen.* Arnhem.

Clark, J. 1979. "Direct vs. semi-direct tests of speaking ability," in E. Briere and F. Hinofotis (eds.), *Concepts of language testing. Some recent studies.* Washington: TESOL, 35–49.

Clyne, M. 1980. "Typology and grammatical convergence among related languages in contact," *ITL-Review of Applied Linguistics*, 43; 23–36.

Clyne, M. 1982. *Multilingual Australia: Resources, needs, policies.* Melbourne: River Seine Publishers.

De Bot, K., M. Clyne, and I. Naber (in preparation). "Language maintenance and language loss among Dutch immigrants in Australia: a 15 year longitudinal study."

Fishman, J. (Ed.) 1966. *Language loyalty in the United States*. The Hague: Mouton.

Fishman, J., M. H. Gertner, E. G. Lowry, and W. G. Milan. 1985. *The rise and fall of the ethnic revival: perspectives on language and ethnicity*. The Hague: Mouton.

Jamieson, P. 1980. "The pattern of urban language loss," *Australian and New Zealand Journal of Sociology* 16: 102–109.

Jones, R. 1979. "Performance testing of second language proficiency," in E. Briere and F. Hinofotis (eds.), *Concepts in language testing. Some recent studies*. Washington: TESOL.

Koster, C., L. Blomert, H. van Mier, and M. L. Kean. 1985. "Taalstoornissen bij corticale and subcorticale letsels." Paper conferentie Ned. Ver. voor Neuropsychologie, December 1985, Nijmegen.

Pauwels, A. 1987. *Immigrant dialects and language maintenance in Australia*. Dordrecht: Foris.

Van Els, T. 1986. "An overview of European research on language attrition," in B. Weltens, K. de Bot and T. van Els (eds.), *Language attrition in progress*. Dordrecht: Foris, 3–18.

Weltens, B. 1987. "The attrition of foreign-language skills. A literature review," *Applied Linguistics* 8: 22–38.

7 The sociolinguistic and patholinguistic attrition of Breton phonology, morphology, and morphonology

WOLFGANG U. DRESSLER

1 Introduction

This contribution is based on empirical field research in two areas of Celtic Lower Britanny in western France:

(1) in the local Trégorrois (Trég.) dialect of Buhulien south-east of Lannion (western fringe of the Département Côtes du Nord), cf. Dressler (1972a, b),

(2) in the South Bigouden (Big.) subdialect of the Cornouaillais dialect, south-west of Quimper (southwesternmost part of the Département Finistère), cf. Dressler & Hufgard (1980).

Similar to Dorian (1981), I distinguish six groups of speakers according to qualitative and quantitative criteria of their competence in Breton (birth dates are only approximate):

(I) Healthy Breton speakers corresponding to Dorian's "older fluent speakers," born between 1892 and 1932 (with clusters around 1896–1900 and 1912–1920). My descriptions of dialects (Dressler 1972a; Dressler & Hufgard 1980) are based on these speakers.

(II) Weaker Breton speakers, approximately corresponding to Dorian's "younger fluent speakers," born between 1911 and 1942. The only reduction they show are consequences of a certain shrinkage of their Breton lexicon.

(III) Preterminal speakers, born between 1938 and 1951, show reductions and generalizations also in grammar.

(IV) Better terminal speakers, born between 1936 and 1952, exhibit even more reductions and generalizations.

(V) Worse terminal speakers, born between 1933 and 1962, have a severely reduced lexicon and a still more reduced grammar.

(VI) Rememberers recall only isolated items (they are not considered in the present study).

In Sections 2–4 I am going to deal with sociolinguistic attrition in the phonology, morphology, and morphonology of the two dialects of Breton mentioned above – not with literary Breton, which has experienced a certain renaissance since the early 1970s – and in Section 5 with patholinguistic, i.e. aphasic, attrition.

2   Phonology

2.1   *Interference*

As to phonology, the decay of recessive Breton is partially influenced by dominant French in the pronunciation of terminal speakers:

(1)   They may take over French final stress instead of Breton pre-final stress similar to secondary speakers of Breton, which is derided as *roazhonek* [rwazo'nɛk] (from Roazhon, the Breton name of Rennes, the former capital and main city of francophone Upper Brittany).

(2)   Many use French allophones instead of Breton ones, e.g. the French uvular vibrant instead of the apical vibrant of Trég. and the majority of Breton dialects.

(3)   If there are similar and diverse allophones, then allophones which are similar to French ones are maintained, those which are diverse are lost within terminal speakers, e.g. Big. terminal speakers maintain the allophones [ɑ(ː), a(ː)], but not [æ(ː), ɛ(ː),ɒː, ɒːw, ɒwː, ɑwː] of /a(ː)/ (cf. Dressler and Hufgard 1980: 48ff).

(4)   The Breton phoneme /h/ may be pronounced unsystematically or not at all.

Older healthy speakers who have incomplete French competence did exactly the reverse. Thus their Breton "accent" of French contrasts with the French "accent" in the Breton of terminal speakers. This asymmetric interference in terminal speakers reflects the sociological asymmetry between French and Breton. That is, economic, cultural, and social subordination of the Breton speech community results in subordination of Breton to French and thus in structural realignment of the recessive language to structures of the dominant language.

However, other phenomena of phonological decay cannot be attributed to French interference. Two general cases are discussed below.

2.2   *Innovation*

Terminal speakers (especially worse terminal speakers) may use new allophones which are neither Breton nor French. Thus, in terminal Trég., the vibrant phoneme has, in addition to the Breton apical and to the

French uvular trill, apical tap and approximant allophones in free variation, and fricative [ɾ] after (aspirated) stops, e.g. in [pɾa] as fast speech variant of [pə'raː] "what." Great variation among free allophones has been observed in other decaying languages as well (Jackson 1955; Miller 1971; Dressler 1972b: 454, 1982a: 326; Dressler and Wodak-Leodolter 1977a: 9, 1977b: 37; Kieffer 1977: 75f; Denison 1979; Dorian 1982b: 56f, 1982c: 44; Giacalone Ramat 1983). Cf. Trudgill's (1977: 35) general statement about Greek Albanian: "Arvanitika . . . is in a state of considerable flux, with no real norms of language" (cf. Dorian 1982c: 46). This insecurity is due to (1) decreasing use of the recessive language (i.e. lack of performance, cf. Section 6); (2) decay or, first, relaxation of sociolinguistic norms in general.

This means, in terms of Natural Phonology (cf. Stampe 1969; Donegan & Stampe 1979; Dressler 1984), that all these natural allophonic processes are at the disposal of small children, who in the normal course of language acquisition usually suppress all processes which are not used by adults. However, future terminal speakers are not subjected to enough sociolinguistic control in the recessive language during language acquisition so that they do not suppress all "deviant" processes.

2.3   *Monostylism*

Terminal language decay shows a tendency towards monostylism (Dressler 1972b: 454ff; Dressler & Wodak-Leodolter 1977a: 8, 1977b: 36ff; Dorian 1977: 27; Giacalone Ramat 1983), i.e. recessive languages are more and more used in casual styles, those which are appropriate for intimate routine interactions at home among close friends, etc. Thus the whole style repertoire shrinks to a very narrow one of casual styles both in phonology and in syntax. For example, in Breton the present "I sing/I'm singing" is normally expressed by *kan+añ a ra+n* "sing + inf. /particle/ do + I," if the subject is stressed/emphasized, by *me a gan* "I /particle/ sing" (with lenition after the particle *a*). In casual speech the particle is dropped (but lenition still applies): ['kaːnə rã = 'kan rã, 'meː gan]. Most terminal speakers use only the second construction and always drop the particle *a*.

Or in very casual speech the final *t* of the nominal plural and the past participle suffix [ət] is dropped. This deletion is generalized by terminal speakers, e.g. Trég. ['gweːlə] "seen" = *gwel+et*.

This stylistic shrinkage is a dysfunctional change insofar as the recessive language becomes inadequate for certain speech situations, domains, and functions. Moreover it implies loss of sociolinguistic norms governing stylistic choice (for Breton phonology cf. Dressler 1974, in general Dressler & Wodak-Leodolter 1982).

Monostylism is also a property of pidgin languages, as is reduced grammar (including inflectional and derivational morphology, and morphonology; see Sections 3.2, 3.3, 4). Moreover, pidgins are clearly dysfunctional languages insofar as they are only adequate for certain speech situations, domains and functions. Can one therefore say that language death is the reverse of language birth in the sense of the genesis of "normal" languages originating in pidgins? Despite many parallels it must be noted (cf. Dressler 1981: 13; Schmidt 1985: 391ff) that (1) the speech situations, domains and functions of dying languages are not identical with those of pidgins, neither are the attitudes of speakers; (2) the acquisition of pidgins is most often quite different from the modes of acquisition of dying languages (cf. Trudgill 1977: 49; Dorian 1981; 1982b: 51ff; Szemerényi 1981: 294; Dressler 1981: 6, 32; Williamson *et al.* 1983: 71f, 83); (3) pidgins do not show free allophonic variation, as discussed in Section 2.2.

3   Morphology

An early symptom of language attrition is represented by word formation rules ceasing to be productive (cf. Dressler 1977b). The main function of word formation rules, lexical enrichment, has been given up within Breton dialects and transferred to massive borrowing from French.

3.1   Borrowing

For any purist, massive interference by another language is a sure sign of language decay. But this is a reversible phenomenon because borrowing (e.g. loanwords) is a means of enrichment of language. For example, English, the most dominant language of today, even now freely borrows words from other languages, although many more words are loaned in the other direction. But there are properties of interference which are probably symptoms of moribundity:

(1) Massive lexical loans from the dominant into the recessive language, when loans in the other direction are sporadic (at best, cf. Dorian 1982b: 56; Fasold 1984: 241) and comprise only "folklore" words, i.e. words designating cultural items of folkloric interest which do not exist outside the culture identified with the recessive minority language. Examples are Fr. *menhir, dolmen,* from Br. *maen hir* "long stone," *taol mein*

"table of stones" (or rather with definite article: *an daol mein*). This asymmetry of interference reflects the hierarchical social, sociopsychological and (generally) socioeconomic and political difference between the two speech communities, i.e. the recessive speech community is subordinated to the dominant speech community, cf. Calvet's (1974) notion of linguistic colonialism.

(2) Borrowed lexical material tends not to be integrated morphologically and phonologically. Of course this is sometimes not easy to distinguish in running text from code switching (cf. Trudgill 1977: 38; Gal 1979: 173; Dorian 1981: 96ff; Williamson *et al.* 1983: 81ff).

(3) These borrowed words do not enrich the recessive language (and how could they, if they are not integrated?), but simply replace indigenous words. This substitution has been called relexification by Hill & Hill (1977; cf. Giacalone Ramat 1979; 137; Tsitsipis 1984) and reflects another property of linguistic colonialism: substitution of indigenous by non-indigenous concepts. In Breton, this has occurred e.g. with most names of diseases even among today's healthy speakers; none are left among the other categories of speakers.

(4) Another symptom of the terminal decay is the lack of puristic reactions against this massive interference (cf. Denison 1982: 11, 14). (Pre)terminal speakers fail to notice such "corruptions," and healthy speakers seem to have given up correcting them. This reflects a change in language attitude (cf. Ryan 1979): the recessive, decaying language is considered as worthless, not worthy of being properly transmitted. Such attitudinal change produces a relaxation of social, sociolinguistic and linguistic norms and thus permits non-integration of loans (cf. (2) above).

(5) An early sign of language decay is the cessation of giving and using proper names in the recessive language (Dressler & Wodak-Leodolter 1977b: 41 n. 16; Dressler 1982a: 325; Williamson *et al.* 1983: 78). Here several qualifications are in order.

First, Priestly (1984: §3.5) "wonder[s] how easy it is to distinguish the two layers in the Carinthian context" (of a recessive Slovene dialect and dominant German) and cites names of Latin origin. This objection confuses the prehistory of single proper names with systematic or at least massive replacement a few generations before language death.

Second, central political authorities and/or laws may prescribe proper names of the dominant language and proscribe those of the recessive language in domains of official documents etc. Therefore my claim concerns only oral in-group interactions in the recessive language, and thus particularly first names (or their equivalents). For example, Bretons who were officially named *François* earlier were still called *Fañch* or Trég. [feĩʃ] in oral in-group interactions; however, nowadays, even low class Bretons may be always called *François*.

Third, my claim does not hold for upper classes, where foreign fashions of naming may easily penetrate and where revivalists may easily resuscitate indigenous proper names. Both can be observed in Breton.

3.2   Word formation

Lexical creativity as represented by word formation rules (WFRs) also passed over from receding Breton to dominant French (see Dressler 1977b, 1981: 10, 1982a: 325; cf. Schlieben-Lange 1977: 103; Hill & Hill 1978; Knab & Hasson de Knab 1979: 474f; Williamson *et al*. 1983: 74). The two main functions of WFRs are (1) lexical enrichment (creation of neologisms), serving (via the lexicon) the communicative and cognitive functions of language, (2) morphosemantic and morphotactic motivation of existing complex word forms (cf. Dressler 1985: 315ff), thus economizing memory load.

In the nineteenth century, Bretons translated literally the newly invented Fr. *batt + euse* "threshing machine" with *dorn + erez* from *dorn + añ* "battre." However, in the twentieth century the newly invented Fr. *moissoneuse batteuse* "combined harvester" was taken over as such. Or in the nineteenth century "bicycle" was rendered as *marc'h-houarn*, literally "horse (of) iron," besides *belo*, definite *ar velo* from Fr. *vélo*. In contrast, after the Second World War, the popular car make *Deux Chevaux*, literally "two horses," was taken over as such whereas its literal translation *daou a gezek* is derided similar to other neologisms of standard literary Breton such as the loan translations *pellwel* "television" (lit. "far see") and *pellgomz* "telephone" (lit. "far speak"). These are examples for the shift from indigenous neologisms (via word formation rules) of the recessive language to systematic loaning of all neologisms from the dominant language (cf. Section 3.1). This is a consequence of the following changes: (1) communication in domains of progress (in technology, culture, fashions, etc.) has shifted from the recessive to the dominant language, at least in the vanguard of speakers who are most likely to be responsible for creating, adapting and sanctioning neologisms (according to sociological diffusion theory, cf. Cooper 1982b). So much for the communicative function. (2) As to the cognitive function, it is clear that at least with semi-speakers, thinking about the areas of progress is supported by the dominant language, and not by the recessive language (cf. Denison 1982). In this way form follows function.

In Lower Brittany this turning point seems to have occurred in the wake of the First World War when Breton men returned from service among non-Breton speaking Frenchmen. For example, a popular agricultural pamphlet (Lerot-Becot 1932) for Breton peasants contains very few Breton neologisms, but many French neologisms printed in italics as citation forms.

Thus today creative production of morphological neologisms is lost even with healthy dialect speakers. However, they have retained the passive competence of processing neologisms and understanding morphosemantically transparent ones as well as the competence of evaluating neologisms. On the other hand, in a test (see Dressler 1977b: 65ff), terminal and pre-terminal speakers were unable to evaluate complex words unknown to them. For example, worse terminal speakers did not recognize the rare deverbal instrument noun *dis + kell + er* ''cradle'' as a noun. Or no terminal and only three pre-terminal speakers recognized the difference between *kalz* ''much'' and its diminutive *kalz + ig* (with the productive diminutive suffix *-ig*). Thus terminal speakers lost the ability to motivate complex word forms from their bases/roots via word formation rules, i.e. the second function of word formation, morphosemantic and morphotactic motivation, was affected by language attrition.

Priestly's (1984: §4.4) counter-evidence from the Slovene Carinthian dialect of Sele Fara/Zell Pfarre cannot falsify our claims on the importance of lost productivity of word formation rules: (1) his data consist of existing complex words gathered in field work and do not include productivity tests (based on neologisms or nonce words); (2) the Slovene dialect of Sele Fara is clearly a recessive one, but Sele Fara is known as the most consistently Slovene speaking community of Carinthia. Thus its local dialect can hardly be called a dying dialect (in our sense), and there is no evidence of this in his material.

3.3 Inflection

There are reductions of Breton inflectional morphology which can be accounted for by assuming acculturation to French morphology. For example, the Breton verb has, in addition to the usual Indo-European three person endings of singular and plural, an impersonal form which has no correspondence in French, e.g. *bez + er* ''one is.'' Terminal speakers never used such forms, pre-terminal speakers only sometimes in the present, but not in other tenses.

Or Breton has preserved some special responsive forms (cf. Dressler 1971: 190f) such as *N'eo ket brav?* – *Geo!* ''Isn't it beautiful? – It is!,'' *(Ne) wel + ez ket an dra-ze?* – *Gwel + an* ''Don't you see that? – Oh yes, I see it!''

French has nothing comparable (except responsive *si!*), and pre-terminal speakers used only forms of the verb *bez + an* "to be," such as *Geo!, Geus!* (mostly in the present); worse terminal speakers have lost them completely.

However, often here as well the direction and hierarchy of decay cannot be attributed directly to interfering structures of the dominant language (cf. a striking Gaelic example in Dorian 1981: 148). A case in point is the decay of Breton plural formation (see Dressler 1981: 7–9). Whereas French always has article inflection (definite article *le, la* → *les*) and very rarely modification (*cheval* "horse" → *chevaux*), Breton generally has suffixation in the noun but uninflected articles. Thus French influence might result in greater decay of suffixation than in umlaut modifications such as in *maen* "stone" → *mein*. However, in terms of Natural Morphology (cf. Dressler, Mayerthaler, Panagl, & Wurzel 1987), the category of plural adds the meaning of plurality to the singular in the case of countable nouns, and this semantic addition is diagrammatically best reflected in the addition of a plural suffix; umlaut is less diagrammatic. Diagrammaticity as a parameter of morphological naturalness explains why suffixation is better preserved than umlaut among pre-terminal and terminal speakers, and why umlaut is often replaced by suffixation but never vice versa, e.g. Big. [miːn] "stone" → [miːnʊ] (with the plural suffix *-où*).

On another naturalness parameter, universal preference for bi-uniqueness (one meaning – one form) explains reduction of plural suffix allomorphy: *-(i)où, -ed, -(i)er, -(i)en, -i, -on*. Pre-terminal and terminal speakers of Breton come closer to this natural solution insofar as they replace many instances of other suffixes with suffixation by only two suffixes: *-ed, -(i)où*.

4   Morphonology

Passing over to morphonology and morphophonemics (cf. Dressler 1985) we find the interesting case of the decay and loss of Breton initial consonant mutations (cf. Jackson 1967: 308ff; Oftedal 1985) which have no counterpart in French. Now if we claimed that dying Breton dialects acculturated to French, we could account for the decay and loss of these mutations, but not for the hierarchy and order of decay. Let us briefly compare the fate of the three mutations in terminal speakers: spirantization, fortition, lenition (cf. Dressler 1972b):

(i)   Spirantization changes – after certain grammatical words – word-initial /p,t,k/ to /f,z,h/, e.g. *penn* "head" → *va/ma fenn* "my head."

(ii)   Fortition changes /b,d,g/ to /p,t,k/, e.g. *belo* "bike" → *o pelo* "your bike."

(iii) Lenition changes /p,t,k,b,d,g,m/ to /b,d,g,v,z,h,v/, e.g. *e benn, e velo* "his head/bike."

The main direction of decay is (a) decay of spirantization precedes decay of fortition or lenition, and spirantization is largely replaced by lenition, e.g. *va fenn* > *va benn*; (b) the consonants subject to lenition are reduced to /p,t,k/ thus *e benn, e belo*; (c) fortition is lost before and largely replaced by lenition, thus *o benn, o belo*; (d) the number of grammatical and lexical words triggering mutations is slowly reduced (called "lexical fading" by Dressler 1972b).

I interpret this hierarchy of decay in the following way:

(1)   Lenition is best preserved (as it was in closely cognate Cornish right before its death), because it is triggered by the largest number of grammatical words, by compounding, and by syntactic conditions, and applies to the largest number of consonants. It is, so to speak, the "default" mutation on which semi-speakers fall back. The notion "default" has found its place in Natural Morphology (cf. Dressler 1981: 16, 1985: 137ff).

(2)   The phonologically most natural (parts of) mutation rules are best preserved, i.e. the most regular ones which change only one phonological feature: (ii) fortition: /b,d,g → p,t,k/ and (iii) reduced lenition: /p,t,k → b,d,g/ (cf. Dressler 1985: 65ff, 120ff).

(3)   Of course, (cf. Dressler 1985: 67, 81f, 85f, 90f, etc., with references) such morphophonemic rules are simplified and subject to "lexical fading" in "normal change" as well (Priestly 1980, 1984 §4.2 versus Dorian 1981: 121ff), but there is the question whether this is a simplification or a reduction (loss without compensation, cf. Trudgill 1977; Dorian 1981: 153ff, 1982c: 44; Dressler 1982a: 315f; Giacalone Ramat 1983: 38). In normal language change, simplifications (however these are defined within the respective linguistic model) in some part of a linguistic system are compensated by complications/elaborations/enrichments in other parts. In contrast, reduction means simplification by structural loss without compensation. This point can be illustrated with case systems: in the development of Latin/Protoromance and English the case systems of Latin and Old English were simplified by loss of case forms, case categories and finally of the whole case systems, but in compensation prepositional constructions

flourished, word order became more rigid, and obligatory articles were introduced.

However, here as in morphology we have examples of structural loss without compensation, and the recessive language has become partially dysfunctional, because lack of compensation through structural enrichment etc. of the recessive language was compensated by functional shifts towards the dominant language. Clearly there is an interdependency (not a unidirectional causation) between gradual functional shift and gradual structural decay – a gradual interdependent change which could be cybernetically modeled as a self-regulating system. Such a model would also fit the mutually feeding factors of functional shift and structural decay.

5   Aphasia

As an appendix I want to compare aphasic data from two male Wernicke patients (L.T., sixty-five years, South Eastern Cornouaille; J.G., sixty-one years, Léon dialect, close to standard Breton). Both were healthy Breton speakers before their stroke, according to their neighbours.

Initial consonant mutations (see Dressler 1977a), on the one hand, were disturbed in the same way as in language decay (Section 4). On the other hand, mutations were produced where no mutation should have occurred at all, e.g. ['labm 'viən] (L.T.) "small rabbit" with wrong lenition $b \rightarrow v$ instead of *lapin bihan* (*lapin* is masculine; only a feminine singular triggers initial consonant lenition in the following adjective).

In phonology, disturbances were not similar to phonological decay (Section 2) but to aphasic disturbances in other languages (cf. Nespoulous *et al*. 1984; Dressler 1982b). As to morphology, the patients were unable to perform word formation tests, but showed no erroneous forms in spontaneous speech (similar to other languages). Plural formation tests were run together with naming tests: a single object was shown; after identifying it, the patients had to form the plural. The main results were:

(1)   The more severely disturbed patient L.T. (as well as three other severe cases not considered here) was rarely capable of forming a plural, i.e. the morphosemantically unmarked singular was easier to retrieve.

(2)   If the object normally does not occur as a single unit, all patients preferred to produce the plural in the naming test. This occurred typically with words denoting *leaf, potato, pear, cow, horse, shoe,*

tooth, lip, finger (but not *thumb*). This is a case of markedness reversal, i.e. the plural is cognitively unmarked (cf. Shapiro 1983).

(3)   Breton has a set of "dual" forms used for body parts (originating from fusions with prefixed *daou* (masc.), *diw* (fem.) "two"). Here markedness reversal occurred as well in naming tests. For example, I pointed to my left ear, but the response was almost invariably the respective dialect form of *divskouarn* "ears" (dual), instead of sing. *skouarn* (similar for "hand" and "eye").

(4)   Patient J.G. produced a few wrong plurals: similar to what has been observed in language decay (Section 3.3), he formed four wrong plurals in *-où*, three in *-et*, but only one in *-ien*.

(5)   Similar to worse terminal speakers (Section 3.3), patients produced some bizarre forms which are totally deviant from the point of view of Breton morphology, e.g. pl. *skournen* "ears."

6   Conclusion

If we try to compare sociolinguistic language decay (Sections 2–4) with aphasic disturbances (Section 5), then we can find the following common points:

(1)   Both types of attrition present examples of reduction but not of simplification (compensated by elaboration elsewhere).

(2)   Unmarked categories are better preserved than marked ones and unmarked ones may substitute marked ones rather than the reverse. (This has been a major concern of Natural Phonology and Natural Morphology.)

(3)   Both types of attrition present dysfunctional language production.

(4)   Both types of attrition show signs of insecurity in performance.

This is a well known phenomenon in aphasia. As to sociolinguistic language attrition I want to add the following concept to the model presented in Dressler (1981, 1982a). Language decay accompanies a shift from compact to diffuse performance of a recessive minority language. In the Breton case the following steps can be distinguished: geographically, the Breton speaking area became less compact through debretonization of towns such as Brest, Vannes, Douarnenez, etc. until it became a fragmented rural area. Massive emigration to Paris increased diffuseness, and then debretonized emigrants returned; socially, compact Breton speaking communities were reduced to lower classes, then rural lower classes, etc; sociolinguistically, compact domains of Breton became more and more "diffuse" due to always more subjective factors determining language choice (including code switching). Now, loss of compactness diminished the quantity and quality of Breton performance and thus resulted in insecurity of performance with all its negative consequences for language attitudes and thus language choice.

References

Calvet, L.-J. 1974. *Linguistique et colonialisme*. Paris: Payot.

Cooper, R. (ed.). 1982a. *Language spread*. New York: Academic Press.

1982b. "A framework for the study of language spread," in Cooper (ed.), 5–36.

Denison, N. 1979. "Zur Triglossie in der Zahre," in P. Ureland (ed.), *Standard-sprache und Dialekte in mehrsprachigen Gebieten Europas*. Tübingen: Niemeyer, 27–36.

1982. "A linguistic ecology for Europe?," *Folia Linguistica* 16: 5–16.

Donegan, P. and D. Stampe. 1979. "The study of Natural Phonology," in D. A. Dinnsen (ed.), *Current approaches to phonological theory*. Bloomington: Indiana University Press, 126–173.

Dorian, N. 1977. "The problem of the semi-speaker in language death," *International Journal of the Sociology of Language* 12: 23–32.

1981. *Language death: the life cycle of a Scottish Gaelic dialect*. Philadelphia: University of Philadelphia Press.

1982a. "Defining the speech community to include its working margins," in S. Romaine (ed.), *Sociolinguistic variation in speech communities*. London: Arnold, 25–33.

1982b. "Language loss and maintenance in language contact situations," in R. Lambert and B. Freed (eds.), *The loss of language skills*. Rowley, MA: Newbury House Publishers, 44–59.

1982c. "Linguistic models and language death evidence," in L. Obler and L. Menn (eds.), *Exceptional language and linguistics*. New York: Academic Press, 31–48.

Dressler, W. 1971. "Skizze einer bretonischen Textsyntax," in *Donum Indogermanicum, Fs. A. Scherer*. Heidelberg: Winter, 187–197.

1972a. *Allegroregeln rechtfertigen Lentoregeln: sekundäre Phoneme des Bretonischen*. Innsbruck: Institut für Sprachwissenschaft.

1972b. "On the phonology of language death," *Proceedings of the Chicago Linguistic Society* 8: 448–457.

1974a. "Minderheitssprachen als Spannungsfaktoren," *Wissenschaft und Weltbild* 27, 4: 234–252.

1974b. "Essai sur la stylistique phonologique du breton: les débits rapides," *Études Celtiques* 14: 99–120.

1977a. "Morphonological disturbances in aphasia," *Wiener linguistische Gazette* 14: 3–11.

1977b. "Wortbildung bei Sprachverfall," in H. Brekle and D. Kastovsky (eds.), *Perspektiven der Wortbildungsforschung*. Bonn: Bouvier, 62–69.

Dressler, W. 1981. "Language shift and language death – a Protean challenge for the linguist," *Folia Linguistica* 15: 5–28.

1982a. "Acceleration, retardation and reversal in language decay?," in Cooper (1982a), 321–336.

1982b. "A classification of phonological paraphasias," *Wiener linguistische Gazette* 29: 3–16.

1984. "Explaining Natural Phonology," *Phonology Yearbook* 1: 29–51.

1985. *Morphonology*. Ann Arbor: Karoma Press.

Dressler, W., and J. Hufgard. 1980. *Etudes phonologiques sur le breton sudbigouden*. Vienna: Akademie der Wissenschaften.

Dressler, W., W. Mayerthaler, O. Panagl, and W. Wurzel. 1987. *Leitmotifs in natural morphology*. Amsterdam: Benjamins.

Dressler, W., and R. Wodak-Leodolter (eds.). 1977a. "Language death," *International Journal of the Sociology of Language* 12 (= *Linguistics* 19, 1).

1977b. "Language preservation and language death in Brittany," in Dressler and Wodak-Leodolter (1977a), 33–44.

1982. "Sociophonological methods in the study of sociolinguistic variation in Viennese German," *Language in Society* 11: 339–370.

Fasold, R. 1984. *The sociolinguistics of society*. Oxford: Blackwell.

Gal, S. 1979. *Language shift*. New York: Academic Press.

Giacalone Ramat, A. 1979. *Lingua, dialetto e comportamento linguistico: La situazione di Gressoney*. Florence: Licosa.

1983. "Language shift and language death," *Folia Linguistica* 17: 495–507.

Hill, J., and K. Hill. 1977. "Language death and relexification in Tlaxcalan Nahuatl," *International Journal of the Sociology of Language* 12: 55–69.

1978. "Honorific usage in Modern Nahuatl," *Language* 54: 123–155.

Jackson, K. 1955. *Contributions to the study of Manx phonology*. Edinburgh: Nelson.

1967. *A historical phonology of Breton*. Dublin Institute for Advanced Studies.

Kieffer, Ch. 1977. "The approaching end of the relict Southeast Iranian languages *Ormuṛi* and *Parāči* in Afghanistan," *International Journal of the Sociology of Language* 12: 71–100.

Knab, T., and L. Hasson de Knab. 1979. "Language death in the valley of Puebla: a socio-geographic approach," *Proceedings Berkeley Linguistic Society* 5: 471–483.

Lerot-Becot, Y. 1932. *Kentelioù war al Labour-Douar*. Landerne.

Miller, W. 1971. "The death of language or serendipity among the Shoshoni," *Anthropological Linguistics* 13: 114–120.

Nespoulous, J.-L. *et al.* 1984. "Phonologic disturbances in aphasia: is there a 'markedness effect in phonemic errors'?," in Rose (ed.), *Advances in neurology* 42: 203–214.

Oftedal, M. 1985. *Lenition in Celtic and in Insular Spanish*. Oslo: Universitetsforlaget.

Priestly, T. M. S. 1980. "Variation on an alternation: the fate of the kasna palatalizacija in Sele Fara, Carinthia," *Slovene Studies* 2: 62–77.

1984. "Symptoms of 'language death' in Carinthian Slovene," MS, South Slavic Linguistic Conference, University of Chicago.

Ryan, E. B. 1979. "Why do low-prestige language varieties persist?," in H. Giles and R. St. Clair (eds.), *Language and social psychology*. Oxford: Blackwell.

Schlieben-Lange, B. 1977. "The language situation in southern France," *International Journal of the Sociology of Language* 12: 101–108.

Schmidt, A. 1985. "The fate of ergativity in dying Dyirbal," *Language* 61: 378–396.

Shapiro, M. 1983. *The sense of grammar*. Bloomington: Indiana University Press.

Stampe, D. 1969. "The acquisition of phonetic representation," *Proceedings of the Chicago Linguistic Society* 5: 443–454.

Szemerényi, O. 1981. "Sprachverfall und Sprachtod besonders im Lichte indogermanischer Sprachen," in Y. Arbeitman and A. Bomhard (eds.), *Bono homini donum: essays in historical linguistics, in memory of J. A. Kerns*, 281–310.

Trudgill, P. 1977. "Creolization in reverse: reduction and simplification in the Albanian dialects of Greece," *Transactions of the Philological Society* 1976/77: 32–50.

Tsitsipis, L. 1984. "Functional restriction and grammatical reduction in Albanian language in Greece," *Zeitschrift für Balkanologie* 20: 122–131.

Williamson, R. C., J. van Erde, and V. Williamson. 1983. "Language maintenance and shift in a Breton and Welsh sample," *Word* 34, 2: 67–88.

8 Language attrition in Boumaa Fijian and Dyirbal

ANNETTE SCHMIDT

1 Introduction

Language attrition is a common linguistic phenomenon evident in virtually every part of the world, as languages of great cultural and political potency spread at the expense of less prestigious indigenous codes. While language/dialect death is a global process, there is striking diversity in the **types** of language situation included in this general category. For example, in the Australian continent alone, where approximately only fifty of an estimated two hundred languages will survive the decade, one can recognize at least three distinct types of language death situation. Aboriginal languages are being replaced by:

(1)   a variety of English (e.g. Guugu Yimidhirr language of North Queensland);

(2)   one of the two newly evolved creole languages which function as lingua francas within and between Aboriginal communities: Kriol (spoken in northern Western Australia and the Northern Territory), and Cape York Creole (spoken in Cape York peninsula and Torres Strait islands);

(3)   another Aboriginal language. In multitribal communities, there is a tendency for one Aboriginal language to emerge as lingua franca at the expense of other Aboriginal languages in the region, e.g. Wik-Mungkan in Queensland, Murrinh Patha in Northern Territory.

In light of the diversity of the language loss phenomenon, the aim of this paper is to compare two very different cases of language attrition: dialect leveling in Boumaa Fijian, and language death of Dyirbal, a North Australian language.

First I will give a brief sketch of each sociolinguistic situation, the factors causing language attrition, and a summary of the linguistic changes occurring in each. Then, focusing on the resultant linguistic codes, it is shown that although contrasting in various respects, both Dyirbal and

Boumaa Fijian communities illustrate a sociolinguistic principle common to many cases of language attrition, namely the economy of distinctions, i.e. in the final stages of the language leveling process in Dyirbal and Boumaa Fijian, speakers do not adopt the encroaching form of Standard Australian English and Standard Fijian (although they have mastered these codes). Rather, they retain just a few salient markers of the traditional language/dialect in order to mark their language as distinct from the encroaching code. Finally, the semi-speaker perception of "language" is dealt with, with focus on how a modicum of features is used to symbolize the declining language variety.

2   Dialect leveling in Boumaa Fijian

In the Fijian village of Waitabu, Taveuni Island, dialect leveling is apparent as the local dialect, Boumaa Fijian, is gradually infiltrated by Standard Fijian, lingua franca of the archipelago. As a language variety of great political and social prestige, Standard Fijian is constantly promoted at the expense of local linguistic varieties. Consequently, Boumaa Fijian, as observed in Waitabu village, is under threat. Many distinguishing features of the Boumaa dialect are being lost as speakers replace them with forms from the more prestigious code of Standard Fijian.

2.1   *Factors conducive to dialect leveling in Boumaa Fijian*

Major factors linked with dialect mixing and loss of Boumaa dialect features are:

(1)   **Intermarriage.** The Fijian marriage system, like many other aspects of Fijian social organization, is patrilineal. Marriage is usually exogamous and the social norm is for the woman, once married, to shift and assimilate into the village of her husband. Such an institutionalized norm has far-reaching implications for the sociolinguistic situation at Waitabu, for it defines the female population as the group which instigates much of the linguistic diffusion and change. Women, when marrying into Waitabu, bring with them the speech habits of their birth village. These linguistic habits are often transmitted to their children, i.e. by speaking either a different dialect or Standard Fijian to their children, the parental generation ceases to transmit pure Boumaa Fijian. (Note that this is not a new factor; intermarriage was an institutionalized norm prior to white contact.)

(2)   **Compulsory education.** Education provides a destructive force for the Boumaa dialect on various levels:

    (a) schools provide another context for communication in Standard Fijian;

    (b) by an all Standard Fijian curriculum, the Waitabu students are denied the opportunity of learning their Boumaa dialect at school;

    (c) education promotes Standard Fijian, and, in doing so, casts the Boumaa dialect as a less prestigious code.

(3)   The **Church** is a major catalyst in the dialect leveling phenomenon, through promoting Standard Fijian forms, and not the local Boumaa dialect, in the Bible, prayer books and church services.

(4)   **Media.** None of the media forces employs Boumaa Fijian. For example, the radio programmes listened to in Waitabu are in Standard Fijian. Videos are in English. (These have the additional effect of creating desires, images, and expectations that conflict with traditional culture.) Newspapers are in Standard Fijian and English, and books are mainly in English, except for the Bible, which is written in a special style of Standard Fijian (see Schmidt 1987). Such media promotion of Standard Fijian and English creates the impression of Boumaa Fijian as a less prestigious code.

(5)   **Increased communication** with other dialect regions has led to the usage and acceptance of Standard Fijian as a lingua franca. Standard Fijian is now commonly employed as code of communication in interaction with people outside the Boumaa area.

(6)   **Centralization in Suva.** There is a high urbanization trend throughout Fiji (Lodhia 1977, 1982), and many young people leave their village for education and/or employment in Suva. Due to high unemployment and pressure of kin ties, they may return to their village, bringing with them Standard Fijian and aspirations of westernization.

Focusing now on language change, we will first observe differences between Standard Fijian and Boumaa Fijian dialects, followed by a summary of changes occurring in Boumaa Fijian.

As dialect varieties of the same language, Boumaa Fijian and Standard Fijian are mutually complementary. Most of the differences between the two are formal rather than categorical. The main distinguishing features of the Boumaa dialect include the phonological feature of glottal stop ['], which corresponds to the voiceless velar stop [k] in Standard Fijian. (For Boumaa Fijian speakers, this is the most salient distinguishing Boumaa feature.) Morphologically, the non-monosyllabic transitive affix form of Boumaa Fijian is -*Ca'ina* (where *C* is a consonant), corresponding to -*Caka* in Standard Fijian. There is some variation in the forms of the following grammatical items: pronouns; classifiers, demonstratives, nominal article; discourse marker; and negative marker. Lexically, traditional Boumaa Fijian probably had about 80 percent of its vocabulary either identical or closely cognate (substituting *k* for glottal stop) with Standard Fijian.

In the speech of contemporary Waitabu villagers, there is evidence of the loss or weakening of various Boumaa dialect features. In order to systematically gauge this linguistic attrition, a sample of twenty individuals from a cross-section of the community was selected, ages ranging from 10 to 65 years. Each speaker was presented with a uniform set of 25 Standard Fijian sentences for translation into Boumaa Fijian. These sentences contained a total of 67 opportunities to switch to the Boumaa dialect. (Quantified features consisted of 53 lexical and 14 grammatical items: 5 pronouns; 2 negative morphemes; 5 demonstratives; and 2 non-monosyllabic transitive affixes.)

Individual scores were correlated with age, and speakers ranked on a continuum accordingly. The results are summarized in Figure 8.1.

% score

75	93	70	78	79	76	43	78	60	52	63	48	36	34	52	43	55	28	33	15
65	62	60	59	50	49	45	41	30	27	24	22	22	18	17	16	15	14	12	10

age

8.1   Age and test score correlations in Boumaa Fijian

As the continuum indicates, there is a general tendency for scores gradually to decline with age, indicating a decline in traditional Boumaa features. For example, the highest score was 93 percent by an older speaker of 62 years. The lowest score was 15 percent by the youngest speaker of 10 years.

Having demonstrated that Boumaa dialect features tend to weaken among younger speakers, it is necessary to investigate the relative resilience of Boumaa dialect features to change. The standardized tests described above revealed that there was considerable variation in the tendency of Boumaa linguistic features to weaken. Certain features displayed a strong resilience to loss (e.g. the salient phonological feature of glottal stop, the transitive affix form *-Ca'ina*, and a small percentage of lexical items such as *loga* "mat," *dai* "joke/lie"). These features were used by all of 20 speakers in 100 percent of opportunities. Even the youngest, least fluent Boumaa speakers retain these "strong" features in their everyday speech.

Many of the other Boumaa dialect features showed a gradual weakening among younger speakers (e.g. peripheral and core lexical items, pronouns, nominal article *a*, possessive marker *wei*, and demonstratives).

In contrast, other Boumaa forms appear to have been lost completely. These features include negative marker *cau*, certain possessive pronouns, and various lexical items, e.g. *purelulu* "Wednesday." (For further details of language change in Boumaa Fijian, see Schmidt 1987.)

In short, due to a complex network of sociocultural factors (including education, mass media, societal trends such as westernization, and features of the social organization such as intermarriage), the Boumaa dialect is weakening. Younger speakers are dropping various distinctive features of Boumaa Fijian and replacing them with more prestigious Standard Fijian forms. It is not, however, a case of dialect death. Boumaa Fijian speech (which manifests identification with the Boumaa region) is marked as distinct from Standard Fijian by the retention of a small set of Boumaa features. These include: the salient phonological feature of glottal stop; a small percentage of lexical items, e.g. *loga* "mat," *dai* "joke/lie," and the transitive affix form *-Ca'ina*.

3   Dyirbal

The Dyirbal language is nearing extinction. Originally, this language of at least ten dialects was spoken over more than 8,000 square kilometres in the North Queensland rainforest area. Today, Dyirbal is virtually limited to isolated pockets of the Jambun Aboriginal community. Even within this closed group, Dyirbal is currently being replaced by a variety of English. As a result of the intense contact with English, radical changes are occurring in the grammar of Traditional Dyirbal (TD), this change in progress being manifested in Young Dyirbal (YD).

3.1   *Factors conducive to Dyirbal decline*

Major factors linked with the replacement of Dyirbal by English are:

(1)   **Introduction of radio and colour television.** Many of the houses at Jambun have stereo sets, colour TV and radio. Watching TV is

the main pastime for the family at night and for those not working during the day.

(2)   **Absence of Dyirbal literature.** All-English literature not only confirms English as a prestigious language, but also glossy magazines and books create desires, images and expectations that conflict with the traditional culture.

(3)   **Increased contact with white people** upon fragmentation of the tribe resulted in English as code for communication in the domain of interaction with Europeans.

(4)   **Compulsory education in English schools.** By an all-English curriculum oriented only towards white society and its values, the school provides a negative force for Dyirbal. Rather than education enhancing/enriching Aboriginal cultural identity, it replaces Dyirbal with English and creates an impression that Dyirbal is unimportant.

In line with the diminishing social function of Dyirbal, widespread changes have taken place in the structure of YD. These changes were systematically gauged by a similar method described for Boumaa Fijian (see Section 2 above). A standard set of stimulus sentences was presented to twelve semi-speakers for translation, and speakers were ranked on a continuum according to their retention of TD features. Changes were then traced along a continuum.

Linguistic change is apparent on every linguistic level, affecting phonology, morphology, syntax, semantics, lexicon, and sociolinguistic styles. On the phonological level, changes are comparatively minor, with only slight evidence of English interference. There are signs of phonetic insecurity as the rhotic contrast weakens in non-minimal pairs; YD speakers waver in their realization of the TD phonemes /rr/ and /r/. Also, intrusion of English fricative /f/ is apparent in certain YD pidgin-type pronouns, e.g. *wifela* "we plural," *yufela* "you plural."

Changes on the morphological level are much greater. Innovations in the YD case system include:

(1)   Less fluent YD speakers abandon TD morphological ergativity and regroup core elements on an S–V–O (nominative–accusative type) pattern shown by word order as in English.

(2)   There is allomorphic reduction of ergative-instrumental, locative-aversive, and genitive affixes.

(3)   The TD distinction between alienable and inalienable possession is neutralized. YD speakers extend the alienable possession affix -*gu*, making it a general genitive affix.

(4)   Peripheral case distinctions are collapsed by less proficient YD speakers. They often generalize a single case affix to cover various peripheral case functions.

(5)   Sometimes, less proficient individuals abandon suffixation altogether as a means of marking peripheral case. Alternative role marking devices are English prepositions, or lack of marking.

There is a similar tendency to drop verbal inflectional affixes. The functions of these dying verb inflections are sometimes transferred to alternative linguistic devices, e.g. less-fluent speakers lose future tense *-ny* and negative imperative *-m* affixes, but the notion of future and negative imperative is conveyed by other words in the sentence, but in other cases not, e.g. *bila* "lest," *muŋa* participal. (This exemplifies a distinctive feature of the language death process, i.e. reduction in the structure of a decaying language is not always compensated for by structural expansion and elaboration elsewhere in the system.)

YD speakers show a tendency to eliminate areas of unnecessary (i.e. non-functional) complication in the TD language system. Verb conjugation membership is rearranged so that conjugation corresponds to transitivity value to a greater degree. The irregular verb *yanu* "go" undergoes analogic remodeling to become like regular verbs. In these two areas, YD seems to be shifting in the direction of greater regularity.

Widespread changes occur on the syntactic level:

(1)   There is a breakdown in agreement rules operating in the noun phrase and verb complex.

(2)   The exceptionally free TD word order is rigidified in YD on an S–V–O pattern as in English.

(3)   The TD clause linkage device, S–O pivot, is frequently abandoned in clause subordination and coordination. It survives predominantly in purposive clause conjunctions in the speech of all YD speakers.

(4)   There is a weakening of case-marking on the verb of a relative clause.

(5)   The overall frequency of clause subordination also diminishes in YD.

Lexically, there is a reduction in vocabulary, correlating roughly with YD grammatical proficiency. Some items appear more resistant to dropping than others, e.g. islands of lexemes referring to body parts, human classification, and well-known animates form zones of resistance.

Semantic change is evident in the noun classification system. Most YD speakers radically simplify the complex TD noun class system by re-allocating noun class membership along a system based simply on the principles of animacy and sex.

On the level of sociolinguistic style, *Jalŋuy* "mother-in-law" speech style (used traditionally in the presence of taboo relatives such as parent-in-law of opposite sex or cross-cousin of opposite sex) has ceased to be used due to severe disruptions in the sociocultural sphere. Similarly, a variety of distinct Dyirbal song styles are lost by all but a handful of Traditional Dyirbal speakers.

In short, a complex network of social and psychological factors is contributing to linguistic attrition in Dyirbal and Boumaa Fijian. While the two communities are very different in many aspects of sociocultural organization, both display a common "core" set of features which are conducive to the demise of the local indigenous language variety: education and media promotion of the encroaching code; absence of vernacular literature; and increasing communication links outside of the community. These factors promote the encroaching language variety by instilling a negative impression of the utility and value of the indigenous code; increasing the numbers of contexts for communication in the encroaching code; and importantly, by creating desires, images and expectations that form social identities incongruous with the use of the indigenous language variety.

In terms of language change, the Boumaa Fijian and Dyirbal situations contrast radically. In Boumaa Fijian, the change involved in dialect leveling is predominantly formal as speakers switch to Standard Fijian lexical and grammatical items. Dyirbal, on the other hand, has a much greater range of language change (e.g. allomorphic reduction, collapsing of grammatical categories, and semantic change in noun classification). Despite the obvious contrasts in the Boumaa Fijian and Dyirbal language loss, both communities illustrate a sociolinguistic principle which is common to many cases of language attrition, namely the economy of distinctions.

4   The result of language loss – economy of distinctions

As an integral factor in social interaction, language performs two basic functions: (1) a communication device for transmitting information; (2) a vehicle of identity.

In a dying language variety, the communicative function may diminish as speakers become increasingly reliant on the replacing language/

dialect, its forms and categories, as a means of communication. The identity function, however, is often more resilient, remaining long after the communicative function has decreased.

In Boumaa Fijian and Dyirbal, the importance of language as a vehicle of identity is evident. This is well expressed in the principle of economy of distinctions: in a contact situation where an indigenous language variety is being infiltrated by a more prestigious language variety, speakers of the indigenous code will maintain a reduced number of distinguishing features if they wish to mark their language as distinct from the replacing language.

In other words, speakers of both Boumaa Fijian and Dyirbal do not surrender all features of their dying tongue. Rather, speakers maintain a small set of distinguishing features in order to mark that code as distinct from the replacing language variety.

For example, in Boumaa Fijian, standardized tests indicate that many distinguishing grammatical and lexical features have weakened or been lost (see Section 2). It is not the case, however, that as a consequence of the dialect leveling process, speakers in Waitabu village automatically adopt the dominant encroaching code, Standard Fijian, in their everyday interaction. Rather, they maintain just a few distinguishing Boumaa dialect features (see Section 2) in order to mark their speech as distinct from the replacing language variety. In other words, speakers simply economize on the number of distinguishing features which mark their Boumaa speech as distinct by reducing the range of Boumaa dialect features to a minimal number.

Similarly, in the terminal stages of the Dyirbal language, speakers do not adopt Standard Australian English. Instead, Jambun English, a non-standard variety of English, is used as a common code of communication within the community. Jambun English bears various phonological, grammatical and lexical features of TD, thus distinguishing it from Standard Australian English. On the phonological level, there is replacement of fricatives by stops, reduction of consonant clusters, and deletion of word-initial vowels. TD grammatical influence includes: omission of plural markers -s, absence of number agreement on the verb, deletion of copula and auxiliaries, and absence of prepositions and articles. Lexically, Jambun English is characterized by high intrusion of Dyirbal forms.

These differences, though they be minimal, serve to mark the speech of the Jambun Aborigines as distinct from the encroaching white English language. For Jambun people, Jambun English is thus an important vehicle of identity, symbolizing membership in a closed Aboriginal community.

The important point is that speakers of both Boumaa Fijian and Dyirbal maintain a small set of distinguishing features of their dying code, and use these as shibboleths to mark their identity.

5   Speaker perception: modicum of features as symbols of language

The speaker's perception of language loss often differs markedly from that of the linguist analyzing the same phenomenon. While linguistic analysis may reveal that widespread changes are occurring on many levels of a language system, speakers frequently perceive that their language is "healthy," non-threatened as long as certain formal markers of the language (be they lexical, morphological, or phonological) are used.

In other words, to the speaker, various salient linguistic markers (forms) act as symbols of the language. While **forms** function as symbols of the language, the grammatical and semantic **categories** which these forms denote, do not. Thus, in observing language loss, speakers tend not to focus on collapse of grammatical categories or semantic change, but on the formal salient symbols of the language variety. Hence, use of various salient linguistic markers which symbolize the language variety are often considered as synonymous with "speaking the language." Even a non-fluent semi-speaker, who has lost many distinguishing features of traditional language variety X and who has minimal proficiency in the code, will be regarded as a "speaker of X" by virtue of the fact that he employs a few salient symbols of the language.

This is well exemplified in Boumaa Fijian and Dyirbal data. Younger members of Waitabu village continue to recognize their speech as *vosa va'a-Bouma* "Boumaa Fijian" depsite the loss of most distinguishing Boumaa dialect features. To these speakers, the phonological feature of glottal stop, transitive affix *-Ca'ina* and a few lexical items function as symbols of Boumaa Fijian.

Similarly, in the Dyirbal language, even the least-proficient individuals tend to regard themselves as "Dyirbal speakers." Individuals in the Jambun community may be ranked on a continuum according to their retention of traditional Dyirbal features. For ease of explanation, we will isolate three continuum stages, graphically displayed opposite in Figure 8.2.

> **Stage 1:** at the TD polar extreme are those fully proficient speakers who command the full complex grammar and lexicon of the traditional code (i.e. as described by Dixon 1972).
> **Stage 2:** mid-way along the continuum are ranked less-fluent

speakers who have an imperfect command of Dyirbal grammar and lexicon. A typical speaker of this stage retains some 200–300 lexical items and various grammatical forms, but is reliant on English grammar (e.g. S–V–O word order) in composing utterances.

Stage 3: towards the right polar extreme, "light-weight" speakers (fifteen years and under) recall only some 20–30 Dyirbal lexical items. TD grammar, morphology and other lexical items are lost.

TD	1	2	3	**English**

←——————|————————————————|————————————————|——————→

• TD grammar & lexicon	• some 200 Dyirbal words	• 20–30 Dyirbal words
	• a few Dyirbal grammatical items	• English grammar
	• basic English grammar e.g. S–V–O order	

————————————————————————————————————→

non-linguist's perception of "Dyirbal speaker"

8.2   Attrition stages in Traditional Dyirbal

Despite the range of formal and categorical change occurring along the continuum, individuals at all three stages continue to regard themselves as "Dyirbal speakers." Even least-fluent individuals at Stage 3 take pride in *talkin' guwal* "language," though they retain only some thirty lexical items plugged into an English S–V–O word order.

This not to say that speakers cannot pinpoint change in language attrition. Quite the contrary: in the Dyirbal and Boumaa Fijian investigations, speakers often remarked that younger people's speech was different, describing it as "not so heavy" or "mixed up." In some cases, certain linguistically sensitive traditional speakers could pinpoint actual linguistic differences, e.g. dropping of ergative affix *-gu* in YD speech.

Nevertheless, despite such recognition of linguistic change, the tendency is to regard even least-fluent individuals as Dyirbal or Boumaa Fijian speakers by virtue of the fact that they retain a "lowest common denominator" of distinguishing features, which marks the language variety as distinct from the encroaching code.

6   Conclusion

Despite obvious differences in Boumaa Fijian and Dyirbal language attrition (e.g. Dyirbal has a much greater range of language change than does Boumaa Fijian, such as allomorphic reduction, and collapsing of grammatical and semantic categories), both communities illustrate a sociolinguistic principle which is common to many cases of language loss, namely the "economy of distinctions."

The semi-speaker's perception of language vitality contrasts with that of the linguist. Speakers frequently perceive their language to be healthy and non-threatened as long as a small set of formal linguistic markers, functioning as symbols of the language, continue to be used. Thus, despite the range of changes occurring in the language systems, individuals regard themselves as Dyirbal or Boumaa Fijian speakers by virtue of the fact that they retain a "lowest common denominator" set of distinguishing features, which marks the language variety as distinct from the encroaching code.

References

Dixon, R. M. W. 1972. *The Dyirbal language of North Queensland*. Cambridge: Cambridge University Press.
Lodhia, R. W. 1977. *Report on the census of the population 1976*. Parliamentary Paper No. 13 of 1977, Suva, Fiji.
    1982. *Current economic statistics, April 1982*. Suva: Bureau of Statistics.
Schmidt, A. 1987. *Language in a Fijian village: an ethnolinguistic study*, PhD thesis, Australian National University.

9   Pennsylvania German: convergence and change as strategies of discourse

MARION LOIS HUFFINES

1   Introduction

In most immigrant communities across the United States, English eventually fulfills communicative functions once allocated to immigrants' native languages. The immigrant language falls into disuse, and subsequent generations attain only faulty mastery of its rules if they learn it at all. Of interest in this study is the linguistic integrity of the language as it falls into disuse. If speakers no longer use their native language for daily discourse, does the reduction of function result in a corresponding reduction of linguistic form? Linguistic change due to disuse is only one aspect of first language attrition. Attrition may also occur even while the language continues to fulfill daily discourse functions. In intimate contact with a dominant language, minority languages often exhibit changes which suggest attrition in spite of their maintenance. Linguistic change due to disuse and linguistic convergence toward a dominant language due to contact represent two kinds of attrition, and both may be realized as individual or communal language behaviors.

The purpose of this study is to describe instances of language change and convergence as processes of attrition. First language attrition occurs in individuals whose lives have changed in such a way that they have little or no opportunity to use their native language, perhaps for most of their adult years. The language of such individuals exhibits evidence of faulty application of their native language rules. The speech of whole bilingual communities in which a minority language is spoken for daily discourse may also exhibit evidence of native language displacement. Such evidence reflects the intimate contact with a more dominant language surrounding the community and is realized by the presence of non-native linguistic features which indicate convergence toward the other language model. Individual native language loss and societal native language loss are illustrated by an investigation of linguistic features in Pennsylvania German as it is spoken in sectarian and non-sectarian communities.

2   Background

Of all immigrant groups in the United States, the Pennsylvania Germans are often cited as unusual because they have maintained their culture and language across three centuries. Although studies have long predicted its imminent demise, Pennsylvania German continues to be spoken natively in Amish and Old Order Mennonite communities and can still be heard among those of older generations in non-sectarian enclaves, both rural and urban, in central and eastern Pennsylvania. For the Amish and Mennonites, English and Pennsylvania German fulfill non-overlapping functions: generally, Pennsylvania German is spoken at home and in the sectarian community, English is spoken in school and with all outsiders. This diglossic situation usually obtains, although one can cite individual and communal exceptions. Among non-sectarian Pennsylvania Germans, the switch to English is pervasive. In virtually all non-sectarian Pennsylvania German communities, if Pennsylvania German is spoken, it is spoken only by the elderly. Younger speakers are non-native and non-fluent.

In the following discussion the Pennsylvania German of sectarian groups is compared with the Pennsylvania German of non-sectarian native speakers. The extent of linguistic change and convergence in any specific Pennsylvania German variety can be ascertained only by comparing it with other varieties of Pennsylvania German. Comparisons with modern Standard German or with today's Pfälzisch, from which Pennsylvania German separated two hundred and fifty years ago, are inappropriate. Arguments for or against linguistic change and convergence must be based on norms derived from the Pennsylvania German community itself.

3   Procedures

The observations below are based on data from interviews with 32 native speakers of Pennsylvania German, 13 non-sectarian, 10 Mennonites and 9 Amish. All informants are bilingual. The three main groups are described as followed:

> **Group N**: Non-sectarian speakers of Pennsylvania German. The non-sectarian native speakers of Pennsylvania German range in age from 35 to 75; all but four are 60 years old or older. They live in the farm valleys of southern Northumberland, northern Dauphin, and western Schuylkill counties, where they were born and have spent their adult lives. All but the two youngest (35 and 47 years old), who have monolingual English-

speaking spouses, speak Pennsylvania German with their spouses and peers; all speak English to their children. The two youngest informants in Group N will be referred to jointly as YN and individually as YN1 and YN2 in the lists below.

The sectarian native speakers of Pennsylvania German range from 24 to 65 years of age. All but one were born and raised in Lancaster County but currently reside in Union County, Pennsylvania. All speak Pennsylvania German for daily discourse within the family and community:

> **Group M**: The Mennonites. The Mennonite group consists of members of an Old Order Mennonite community, also called "Team Mennonites." The group is characterized by horse and buggy transportation, distinctive dress, and limited education to the eighth grade.

> **Group A**: The Amish. The Amish group consists of eight members of a conservative wing of the New Order Amish and one member of an Old Order Amish community. As do the Old Order Mennonites, members of the New Order Amish group have electricity in their homes, and the group is also characterized by horse and buggy transportation, distinctive dress, and limited education to the eighth grade. The Old Order Amish informant has no electricity in his home.

The interview consisted of three parts: free conversation, translation of English sentences into Pennsylvania German, and description of pictures. The topics of conversation centered on activities which commonly take place on the farm and at school: daily chores, butchering, weather events, home remedies. The sentences used in the translation task and the pictures used to elicit comparable descriptions without overt reference to English likewise reflect the activities and vocabulary items closely associated with rural family life. The interviewer spoke English, the informants responded in Pennsylvania German, a type of discourse behavior which is common in communities where one language is receding (Dorian 1981). Data based on the translation task are reported separately from those based on the picture descriptions and free conversation.

While speakers often comment on the frequency of lexical borrowings to the point of despairing over the integrity of the language, they fail to notice other changes and convergent behaviors, especially in the area of syntax. Because Pennsylvania German and English derive historically from a common Germanic source, evidence of convergence toward English due to contact with English must be sought in structures which contrast sharply. Three areas of syntactic variation in Pennsylvania German are discussed below, areas where Pennsylvania German structures contrast with English structures in form and/or function: (1) case usage, specifically the status of dative pronouns; (2) verbal aspect, specifically the use of the auxiliary *du*; and (3) word order, specifically the position of the past participle in independent clauses.

4   Results

4.1   *Case usage*

The Pennsylvania German pronoun system consists of three cases: the nominative, accusative, and dative. Distinctive dative pronouns, stressed and unstressed forms, exist for the first, second, and third persons singular and for the third person plural. All other forms are identical to the accusative. See Table 9.1. The nominative/accusative distinction does not exist for nouns; both nominative and accusative functions are expressed by the common case. Although all prescriptive grammars carefully distinguish dative forms and functions, variability in the use of the dative is reported by Anderson and Martin (1976) for the Pennsylvania German spoken by the Old Order Mennonites in Pennsylvania and Ontario, by Enninger (1980) for the Pennsylvania German spoken by the Old Order Amish in Delaware, and by Costello (1985). All three indicate a trend toward the use of the common case for nouns and the accusative case for pronouns to fulfill dative functions.

In the Pennsylvania German spoken in the communities under consideration, the sectarian and non-sectarian informants diverge sharply in their use of the dative, a divergence which obtains across interview tasks. Table 9.2 opposite reports the case of personal pronouns in dative functions in the translation task. Although speakers in Group N show variation, they also show firm control of dative case usage. Much of the

Table 9.1 *Pennsylvania German pronouns*

	nom.	dat. str.	dat. unstr.	acc.
1 sg	Iç	mir	mər	mIç
2 sg	du	dir	dər	dIç
3 sg masc/neut	ar/əs	im	əm	in
3 sg fem	si	irə	rə	si
1 pl	mir/mər	Uns		Uns
2 pl	dir/dər	aiç		aiç
3 pl	si	in	nə	si

Table 9.2 *Case of personal pronouns in dative functions (translation task)*

Group	dat.	acc.
N	83	22
M	1	86
A	2	90

Table 9.3 *Dative personal pronouns (free conversation and picture descriptions)*

Group	1 sg	2 sg	3m sg	3f sg	3 pl	Total
N	14	5	9	8	3	39
M	0	1	0	0	0	1
A	0	0	0	0	0	0

variation in Group N can be attributed to the two youngest speakers of that group, who do not speak Pennsylvania German in their homes as the others in the group regularly do. Among the sectarians, the dative is virtually non-existent. Examples from the translation task appear in List 1.

List 1: Examples of pronouns in dative functions (translation task)

> N: *iç hap inə gEšdər ghɔlfə*
> M: *iç hap si gEšdər ghɔlfə*
> A: *iç hap si ghɔlfə gEšdər*
> YN: *iç hap si ghɔlfə gEšdər*
> "I helped them yesterday."

> N: *əs ghErt nEt tsu dir*
> M: *əs ghErt nEt tsu dIç*
> A: *əs hErt nEt tsu dIç*
> YN1: *sEl bilaŋt nEt tsu dir*
> YN2: *sEl bilaŋt nEt tsu dir / tsu diç / sEl bilaŋt nEt tsu dIç*
> "It doesn't belong to you." (/ = sentence pause)

> N: *sai dadi gEpt mir ɔft gEld*
> M: *sai dæd gEpt mIç ɔft gEld*
> A: *sai dæd gEpt mIç als gEld*
> YN: *sai dadi gEpt mər als gEld*
> "His daddy often gives me money."

The occurrence of dative pronouns in free conversation and picture descriptions supports the results of the translation data. See Table 9.3 (previous page). List 2 shows one example of comparable structures from the picture description task:

List 2: Examples of pronouns in dative functions (picture description)

N: *si šmaist tsu **im***   *ar šmaist tsu **irə***
"She throws to him. He throws to her."

M: *s medli šmaist tsu **dər** bu*
"The little girl throws to the boy."

A: *s medli šmaist **dər** balə tsu **dər** bu*
"The little girl throws the ball to the boy."

YN1: *si šmaist dər bal tsu **dər** / tsu sEl anərə yuŋə*
"She throws the ball to the / to that other boy."
ar wll ən faŋə / ar hat nɔx nEt
"He wants to catch it / he has not yet."

YN2: *s medl šmaist tsu **dər** bu*
"The little girl throws to the boy."

List 3 gives examples of dative functions from the free conversation data. Group N uses the dative case to express those functions; Groups M and A use the accusative case. The YN informants alternate between dative and accusative forms.

List 3: Examples of pronouns in dative functions (free conversation)

N: *əs get **mər** wUndərbar hart*
"It is awfully hard for me."

N: *iç kan **dir** nEt sayə*
"I can't tell you."

M: *iç wll **mIç** nɔx ən frak maxə*
"I still want to make myself a dress."

M: *wEn mər **dIç** Epəs lEts gsat hEn*
"If we said something wrong to you."

A: *as nEkšt war tsu **mIç***
"Who was next to me."

A: *iç kan əs **dIç** nEt sayə*
"I can't tell you that."

YN2: *si hEn **mər** ən gle kæf gšikt e mɔl*
"They gave me a little calf one time."

YN2: *mir hEn **in** als ən rʌfi tsait gEvə*
"We used to give him a rough time."

Group N maintains a vigorous dative case which fulfills dative functions. Variation exists within Group N, where the two youngest members resort to accusative forms, but even their speech has evidence of operative dative rules. They maintain the first person dative pronoun and alternate between accusative and dative forms for other pronouns. These speakers also resort to repairs and elaborate paraphrasings in order to maintain discourse in Pennsylvania German.

In the Pennsylvania German of Groups M and A, the merger of the dative and accusative cases is complete (see also Huffines 1989). These speakers have a one case system for nouns and a two case system for pronouns. One must note that this case merger need not necessarily be caused by the close contact with English; northern European German dialects and the dialect of Berlin have also merged the dative and accusative cases and done so without intimate contact with English. However, in contrast to non-sectarian Pennsylvania German, the sectarian Pennsylvania German case system now parallels the English case system.

4.2   *The auxiliary* du

The Pennsylvania German verb *du* "to do" serves a limited function in the Pennsylvania German verb aspect system as an auxiliary. It is the obligatory auxiliary in the formation of the present subjunctive for most Pennsylvania German verbs, a usage which is not under consideration in this discussion. The use of the auxiliary *du* with the infinitive of the main verb expresses present tense iteration (Huffines 1986); it occurs most frequently in discussions describing repeated activities, such as those which regularly take place during annual family butcherings: *no dUd dər bUtšər əs mIksə* "then the butcher mixes it"; *del lait dunə šperlbs šnaidə* "some people cut up spareribs." Data from this sample do not support the description of the auxiliary *du* by Buffington and Barba (1965) as an emphatic form used most frequently to ask questions and to make negative statements. See Table 9.4. YN speakers account for the use of the auxiliary *du* in two questions and two negatives. Sectarian

Table 9.4 *Use of the auxiliary* du *(translation task)*

Group	Total	Quest.	Neg.	Emphasis
N	30	10	7	1
M	23	2	6	1
A	24	11	4	1

Table 9.5 *Use of the auxilliary* du – *scored** (*free conversation*)

Group	# occ. aux /du/	Av. # words per speaker	Score
N	24	1303	18
M	32	1520	21
A	40	1255	31

*The number of occurrences of the auxiliary *du* divided by the average number of words per speaker for each group, multiplied by 10^3.

informants, especially the Amish, tend to use the auxiliary *du* more frequently than do non-sectarian informants in free conversation although the use of auxiliary *du* forms is not particularly frequent for any group. See Table 9.5. In free conversation no more than three instances of *du* occur in negative statements for each group. No instance of *du* occurs to formulate questions.

Three significant differences in the use of the auxiliary *du* emerge from the speech of the sectarian informants when it is compared with that of the non-sectarians (see List 4):

List 4: Use of the auxiliary *du* by Groups M and A

(1)   Sectarian informants frequently use the auxiliary *du* in collocation with adverbs and temporal clauses which indicate repeated time:
Iç du alsəmɔl yogUrt maxə
"Sometimes I make yogurt."
wan mir bUtšərə dun Iç fleš kænə
"When we butcher, I can meat."
mər dUd s aləgəbɔt štarə
"One stirs it once in a while."

(2)   Sectarian informants employ the auxiliary *du* in pro-form functions, i.e. the auxiliary stands alone in place of the main verb:
si dun als nɔx
"They still do."
Iç wes as sʌm lait dun
"I know that some people do."
nau dun mir a
"Now we do too."

(3)   Sectarian informants extend the use of the auxiliary *du* to verbs which cannot be iterative:
Er dUd aləs wIsə wi sEl
"He knows everything like that."

> *əs dUd mIç glaiçə*
> "It likes me."
> *blumə wu gut šmakə dun*
> "flowers which smell good"

This evidence indicates that in the Pennsylvania German of the sectarian community constructions with *du* no longer have a semantic force strong enough to express present iteration; that function is being carried out by adverbs and other temporal phrases. This observation is supported by the use of *du* in pro-form function and by the extension of the construction to verbs which cannot be iterative.

The use of *du* exhibits convergent behavior which is more complex than was seen in the use of the dative: Pennsylvania German *du* does not parallel functions or assume the role of English *do*. All groups provide uniform and unambiguous evidence of that fact. Pennsylvania German *du* is not used with any special frequency in the formation of questions or negatives, and it is not used emphatically. In sectarian communities a subtle semantic shift is occurring. The loss of iterative meaning results in the increased availability of *du* to perform functions more similar to the English model. The use of *du* as a pro-form is such a function.

4.3   Word order

Pennsylvania German and English contrast sharply in rules governing word order. A frequently cited characteristic of all varieties of American German is the trend toward word order patterns which parallel those in English. The question arises to what extent these trends actually reflect contact with English and to what extent the word order variation was already present in German dialects. Published Pennsylvania German writings are of little help. Early writers of Pennsylvania German had often been trained in standard varieties of German, and the relationship of written Pennsylvania German to spoken Pennsylvania German is unclear.

In order to determine whether convergence obtains, this study investigates one distinctive word order pattern of Pennsylvania German which contrasts with English placement rules: the position of the past participle in independent clauses.

In independent clauses, the prescribed position for the past participle is at the end of the clause. Although Frey (1981) and Haag (1982) state categorically that in independent clauses the past participle comes at the end, Buffington & Barba (1965) suggest that variation exists in the application of this rule: "[I]t is not uncommon to place adverbial modifiers

Table 9.6 *Position of the past participle in independent clauses*
(translation data)

Group	Total # participles	# non-final	% non-final
N	110	39	35
M	91	59	65
A	96	62	65
YN	25	14	56

Table 9.7 *Position of the past participle in independent clauses*
(free conversation)

Group	Total # participles	# non-final	% non-final
N	678	94	14
M	496	117	24
A	357	111	31
YN	39	11	28

after the past participle'' (63). The data from the communities under
investigation suggest that variation does, indeed, characterize Pennsylvania German. See Tables 9.6 and 9.7. In the translation task Groups M
and A place past participles in non-final position almost twice as frequently as Group N. All groups place past participles in non-final position more frequently in the translation task than in free conversation, and
this placement may be a function of a strategy to translate a sentence
linearly, as it is presented in English. In both interview tasks Group N
places past participles in non-final position less frequently than do the
sectarian groups. The YN informants show substantially more non-final
participles in independent clauses than do the other speakers in Group
N. Their percentages approach those of the sectarians in the translation
task and surpass the Mennonites in free conversation. For all groups, if the
past participle is not in final position, typically one prepositional phrase
or one adverb follows it. See examples from the translation task in List 5.

List 5: Word order in independent clauses (translation task)

    N,YN1: *əs hat gEšdər gərEyərt*
  YN2,M,A: *əs hat gərEərt gEšdər*
               "It rained yesterday."

> N: *si hEn s im no špetər gšIkt*
> M,A: *si hEn s tsu ən gšIkt špetər*
> YN1: *si hEn əs nɔx gšIkt tsu əm špetər*
> YN2: *si hEn əs špetər šIkt*
> "They sent it to him later."

Observations based on translation data alone would consistently overrate the trend which suggests convergence toward English.

5   Conclusion

The speech of the non-sectarian native speakers of Pennsylvania German (Group N) shows evidence of a more conservative norm, a norm which more closely reflects prescribed usage: the dative case fulfills dative functions; the auxiliary use of *du* is limited and expresses present iteration; Group N clearly prefers past participles in final position. Group N also exhibits variation which indicates the presence of other language patterns, especially in the speech of younger speakers: the use of the common case to fulfill dative functions; one instance of the auxiliary *du* used emphatically, and the use of the final position in independent clauses for adverbial material. The speech of the YN speakers is characterized by more variation and faulty application of Pennsylvania German rules than is found in the speech of other Group N speakers. Constructions based on an apparent English model occur, but Pennsylvania German linguistic rules are clearly still operative even if their application is faulty.

The variation within the non-sectarian community and its frequent occurrence in the speech of younger speakers suggest the incipient loss of a community norm. Individuals accommodate their linguistic environment as best they can – by using Pennsylvania German rules when speaking Pennsylvania German and by switching to English when those rules fail them. The essential accommodation to the English speaking environment by Group N is the switching behavior. As Pennsylvania German falls into disuse, the resultant variation and the lack of a clear norm within the community are characteristic features of impending language death. Group N is the last of the native speakers of Pennsylvania German in their community, but they still exhibit firm control of Pennsylvania German rules. The language is dying, but it is dying relatively intact, and it shows little evidence of convergence to English.

The Mennonites and the Amish (Groups M and A) contrast in their language behavior with Group N: the dative and the common case have merged; the auxiliary *du* has shifted semantically and is beginning to assume English-like functions; the past participle in independent clauses occurs significantly more frequently in non-final position than the more conservative Group N norm suggests as typical. Each of the resulting language patterns parallels an English model.

Particularly striking in the language behavior of the sectarian communities is its uniformity. Accommodation to English is communal, and the community maintains a norm. Individuals do not accommodate their linguistic environment, the community accommodates the environment, not by switching to English but by making their Pennsylvania German more like English. The sociolinguistic norms for language behavior in sectarian communities prescribe usage not form, and convergence is the means by which Pennsylvania German is maintained. The displacement of native language forms, functions, and constructions by non-native language formulations also represents instances of language attrition. In the case of sectarian Pennsylvania German, language attrition does not proceed into language death but is a strategy of language maintenance.

The lifestyle associated with the sectarians would not have led one to predict the greater convergence in their variety of Pennsylvania German. Sectarians live as a people separate "from the world" and generally associate with outsiders only in transactional settings. Non-sectarians, on the other hand, live in mainstream American society, associating with monolingual English speakers socially and otherwise. The explanation for the observed linguistic pattern seems to lie in the different switching behaviors of each group. Non-sectarians speak Pennsylvania German with their linguistic peers when appropriate. If their Pennsylvania German fails them and cannot efficiently fulfill the communicative function at hand, the non-sectarians switch languages. Switching to English is inappropriate within sectarian communities. No productive relationship exists between Pennsylvania German and varieties of modern European German, and most sectarians have only a limited passive knowledge of Standard German in liturgical contexts. If Pennsylvania German is to continue to meet the changing needs of their community, the sectarians must elaborate and develop it by using linguistic resources from English. The lack of switching to English exposes sectarian Pennsylvania German to influence from English. This dependence on English in a context which does not allow switching accounts for the greater convergence in the Pennsylvania German spoken by the sectarians. For non-sectarians the frequent switching almost paradoxically protects their Pennsylvania German from innovations based on English while at the same time it increasingly contributes to the disuse and death of Pennsylvania German.

References

Anderson, K. O., and W. Martin. 1976. "Language loyalty among the Pennsylvania Germans: a status report on Old Order Mennonites in Pennsylvania and Ontario," in E. A. Albrecht and J. A. Burzle (eds.), *Germanica-Americana 1976*. Lawrence, Kansas: University of Kansas.

Buffington, A. F., and P. A. Barba. 1954, revised 1965. *A Pennsylvania German grammar*. Allentown, PA: Schlechter.

Costello, J. R. 1985. "Pennsylvania German and English: languages in contact," in H. Kloss (ed.), *Deutsch als Muttersprache in den Vereinigten Staaten Teil II*. Wiesbaden: Franz Steiner.

Dorian, N. C. 1981. *Language death: the life cycle of a Scottish Gaelic dialect*. Philadelphia: University of Pennsylvania Press.

Enninger, W. 1980. "Syntactic convergence in a stable triglossia plus trilingualism situation in Kent County, Delaware, USA," in H. P. Nelde (ed.), *Sprachkontakt und Sprachkonflikt*, Zeitschrift für Dialektologie und Linguistik, Beiheft 32. Wiesbaden: Franz Steiner.

Frey, J. W. 1942, reprinted 1981. *A simple grammar of Pennsylvania German*, reissued with a new preface by C. R. Beam, Lancaster, PA: Brookshire Publications.

Haag, E. C. 1982. *A Pennsylvania German reader and grammar*. University Park, PA: The Pennsylvania State University Press.

Huffines, M. L. 1986. "The function of aspect in Pennsylvania German and the impact of English," *Yearbook of German-American Studies* 21: 137–154.

Huffines, M. L. 1989. "Case usage among the Pennsylvania German sectarians and nonsectarians," in N.C. Dorian (ed.), *Investigating obsolescence: Studies in language contraction and death*. Cambridge: Cambridge University Press.

10   Lexical retrieval difficulties in adult language attrition

ELITE OLSHTAIN AND MARGARET BARZILAY

1   Introduction

Primary language attrition in adults is likely to occur when the subjects have been uprooted from their natural mother tongue context and transferred to a new language environment. From the point of view of the speakers, a second language is now the dominant language in the new context while their first language has become a restricted mode of communication. The degree of such restriction, the prestige of the first language in the new environment, the level of social distance between the immigrant community and the host community, and the individual degree of acculturation into the new speech community may all have an impact on the degree of erosion which takes place in the subjects' level of competence in their first language.

This chapter will attempt to describe some features of attrition in a context least conducive to primary language erosion and yet exhibiting interesting changes in linguistic competence. The subjects in our study are American speaking immigrants to Israel who continue to maintain English as their dominant language even ten and twenty years after immigration. Although some of the subjects have attained near native proficiency in Hebrew, most have only acquired the language to an extent that fulfills their immediate needs. All subjects continue to use English for reading, entertainment and professional functions.

An important feature of the new environment is the fact that English, the primary language of the attriters, happens to be considered a language of high prestige and utilitarian value in the new community. Consequently, the knowledge of English is regarded as an asset worth keeping. Thus, we are concerned with attrition of L1 (English) in an L2 (Hebrew) environment according to Van Els' (1986) definition, but in a unique language setting where least attrition is to be expected.

Under the special circumstances described above, we noticed in interpersonal interactions and during informal observation that word retrieval processes seemed to be slightly impaired in the primary language of

American immigrants living in Israel for longer periods of time. We were motivated, therefore, to find out more about the type of changes which take place in the English of such subjects. In this chapter we will focus on the facility of lexical retrieval of specific English words as our criterion variable (Lambert 1982; Lambert & Moore 1986), and on extended stay (over eight years) in a Hebrew speaking environment as our predictor variable.

2   Lexical retrieval and language attrition

Vocabulary accessibility in one's L1 and its susceptibility to attrition is quite different from attrition in L2 vocabulary. Cohen (1986) lists the various features that can be forgotten with respect to a word in the language suffering from attrition: form, position, function and meaning (146). We have noticed vocabulary attrition among adult native speakers mostly in the limited area of specificity in meaning. Thus, in accordance with Obler (1982), the most susceptible items to suffer from language attrition are infrequent, specific, nouns. In the data that we collected six such specific nouns stand out as a test case for retrieval difficulties, and they will each be analyzed in detail. It will be our contention that what Sharwood Smith (1983) calls "reduction in accessibility" of lexical items which are attrition prone is one of the outstanding features of attrition among adult attriters who continue to maintain their primary language as their own dominant language while living in an L2 dominant linguistic environment.

The main assumption underlying the notion "reduction in accessibility" is that the subjects participating in this study were at some point in the past fully capable of using the specific lexical items focused on here, both in production and reception. In this respect, our study bears some similarity to studies which have focused on semantic priming and object naming with aging subjects and with cases suffering from various types of dementia (Bayles & Kaszniak 1987). Thus, patients with mild dementia exhibit some slight disorder of their semantic memory and take more time to respond on semantic naming tasks. Studies of such difficulties of lexical accessibility may shed light on retrieval processes in general, and the study presented here attempts to add an additional perspective to these processes, based on the qualitative analysis of the data collected from our attriter subjects.

Our main objective was to try and describe features of language attrition as exhibited by the subjects' systematic and consciously directed search of their semantic memory for lexical items which prior to the onset of attrition were easily accessible. While in natural interactions attriters may find ways to avoid such a conscious retrieval process, either by paraphrasing in English the meaning of the inaccessible word or by mixing codes and using words from L2, the task designed for this study urged them to use a direct retrieval process. Our analysis of this process follows.

3   The study

3.1   Subjects

Fifteen Americans living in Israel for an extended period of time (henceforth referred to as American Israelis) and six Americans living in the USA who have never lived in Israel (henceforth referred to as Americans) participated in this study. The six Americans ranged in age from twenty-eight to fifty-six. They had no knowledge of Hebrew and had continually lived in an American English speaking environment. The fifteen American Israelis ranged in age from twenty-three to fifty-five. They had all been native speakers of American English with full competence in their first language, before immigrating to Israel. At the time when the study was conducted, they had been living in the second language environment for a minimum of eight years to a maximum of twenty-five years. They came from different geographical areas within the United States and thirteen out of the fifteen were women. The American Israelis all speak Hebrew at various levels of proficiency but most of them have difficulty reading Hebrew.

3.2   Data collection

The data for this study were collected by having subjects tell two frog stories based on two booklets, *Frog, where are you?* and *A boy, a dog and a frog*, both by Mercer Mayer (New York, The Dial Press, 1969). The first of these two books provided the bulk of the data analyzed here while then second served more as additional back-up for the examples identified in the first story.

The frog booklets are very useful instruments for data collection of the type we were interested in, since the story line is conveyed through a series of detailed pictures without any written text. The subjects were asked to leaf through the whole booklet for a while and then tell the story. Such an elicitation technique provides a rather free and open framework enabling each subject to be as detailed or general as they like and to

produce language without any necessary interference from the researcher. Each subject was interviewed individually and all sessions were
tape recorded and then transcribed. The transcriptions of the data collected from the American Israelis were analyzed for language attrition
features. Identical data, using the frog stories, were collected from the six
Americans and provided the "native speaker" sample.

Eliciting data with the frog stories should result in a natural flow of
speech, which focuses on the content represented in the pictures. Thus, it
is difficult for the subjects to ignore key elements in the pictures, especially if they are repeated throughout the story. Very few subjects tried to
practice "avoidance" strategy. In fact, an object naming task is embedded in the global task of story telling and this object naming task
enabled us to focus on a group of nouns which are needed for the story,
carry a specific meaning and are not necessarily frequent in the speech of
our subjects: *jar, cliff, pond, gopher,* and *deer.*

3.3   Findings

On the whole, the American Israelis had no difficulty telling the
frog stories and they acted as fully competent speakers of the language.
However, they did have difficulty with the specific words chosen for
analysis. Being faced with the task of fluent story telling, they could not
ignore these key words in the story and had in fact a number of options
available: (a) the use of circumlocution or paraphrase; (b) the replacement
of the word with a word with similar meaning which is more accessible in
their semantic memory and which is triggered by the word in the picture
(Saffron, Schwartz, & Marin 1976); or (c) the activation of a conscious and
systematic retrieval process of the specific word. Our subjects employed
all three options but word replacement and a systematic word retrieval
process were definitely their preferred strategies. This is evidenced by the
variety of substitutions they provided for the nouns in question (see
Tables 10.1–10.5) and by the fact that they often commented that they
forgot their English or that they forgot the particular item and insisted on
finding the proper word by further probing their semantic memory.

The subjects who provided the native data stock and whom we have
identified as the Americans had, obviously, no difficulty with any of the
five words analyzed here. From the data presented in Tables 10.1–10.5, it
is clear that the native speakers had some variability in their responses but
considerably less that the attriters. All the Americans used the word *jar*
whenever a picture of this object appeared in the booklet and had no
hesitations about it. They used either *gopher* or *groundhog,* which share

Table 10.1 *Responses given on the first encounter of the picture of a "pond"*

Word	American Israelis N = 15	Americans N = 6
pond	3	5
swamp	1	1
water	4	–
body of water	1	–
pond of water	2	–
puddle of water	1	–
riverbed	1	–
ocean	1	–
puddle	1	–
	15	6

Table 10.2 *Responses given on the first encounter of the picture of a "deer"*

Word	American Israelis N = 15	Americans N = 6
deer	8	4
stag	1	2
antelope	4	–
elk	1	–
little animal	1	–
	15	6

Table 10.3 *Responses given on the first encounter of the picture of a "gopher"*

Word	American Israelis N = 15	Americans N = 5
gopher	1	2
groundhog	1	3
skunk	2	–
chipmunk	1	–
mole	4	–
hedgehog	1	–
muskrat	1	–
rabbit	1	–
squirrel	3	–
	15	5

Table 10.4 *Responses given on the first encounter of the picture of a "cliff"*

Word	American Israelis N = 15	Americans N = 5
cliff	12	4
precipice	1	1
mountain	1	–
little hill	1	–
	15	5

Table 10.5 *Responses given on the first encounter of the picture of a "jar"*

Word	American Israelis N = 15	Americans N = 6
jar	10	6
bottle	3	–
bowl	1	–
jug	1	–
	15	6

the same semantic features, for the animal depicted in the pictures. Four out of six used the word *deer*, while the remaining two used the word *stag*, which includes the additional semantic feature of "male." Five out of the six used the word *pond*, while one used the word *swamp*, which resulted from a certain ambiguity in the drawing. Four out of the five subjects used the word *cliff*, one used *precipice*. In spite of this limited variability, the native speakers' data exhibit a certain uniformity and seem to indicate that specific semantic features of such words are easily available in their semantic memory. When deviation occurs, it is in the area of added specificity or in the inclusion of additional semantic features. This stands in sharp contrast to the difficulties encountered by the American Israelis in supplying suitable nouns for the five cases selected for analysis. The actual choices made by both groups, on their first encounter of these words, are given in the Tables 10.1–10.5.

For the American Israelis, the most difficult items for retrieval proved to be the words *pond* and *gopher*. Only four out of the fifteen subjects used the word *pond* or *swamp*, while five out of the fifteen used either *water* or *body of water*, retaining only the most general (inherently neutral specificity) semantic features. In other cases subjects used such words as *puddle* or *ocean*, while some spoke of *pond of water* as if the feature "water" was not already included in the word *pond*. This phenomenon was even more pronounced with the word *gopher*. Only two of the fifteen subjects used the word *gopher* or *groundhog*, while most of the subjects chose specifications which included the addition of incorrect semantic features, such as *chipmunk*, *rabbit*, and others.

The word *deer* was used only by eight out of the fifteen subjects, while one subject chose the word *stag*. In their place, subjects substituted such words as *antelope* and *elk*, or simply used the most general term, *little animal*. For the word *cliff*, appropriate responses were made by twelve out of the fifteen subjects, although one subject used *cliff* and *mountain* interchangeably. Where difficulty of retrieval was evident, subjects used *little hill* or *mountain*, again retaining only a very general feature of the word.

The word *jar* presented relatively less difficulty of retrieval for most American Israelis. Ten out of the fifteen responded initially with the use of the appropriate term, while the others used *bottle*, *bowl*, or *jug*. Eventually all the subjects managed to retrieve the word *jar*, which would not be considered an infrequent or unique item in the household. It is possible that the subjects who had difficulty with the initial retrieval of this word usually use the Hebrew word *cincenet* rather than *jar*. Such code mixing of household items might be quite common in an English speaking family in Israel where many daily expressions are replaced by Hebrew words (Blum-Kulka & Olshtain 1987).

4   Discussion: Features of the retrieval process

From the data analyzed in this chapter it becomes apparent that all the American Israelis participating in this study exhibit some reduction of lexical accessibility in English when they are placed in a situation where certain lexical specification is necessary (the picture booklets). They also happen to be fully aware of the fact that there is an appropriate word which they used to know but which suddenly requires an intensified search of their semantic memory. They often express their frustration by saying "I forgot the word" or "I forgot my English." In a general sense we might summarize the following features as representative of overall first language attrition within the lexical domain:

(1)   A more restricted stock of items is available to the attriter and therefore some items are less accessible for retrieval in active

production of language although they are most probably available for interpretation.

(2)   Less specificity is maintained in an attriter's language. Basic meanings are retained but sensitivity to specific selectional restrictions is reduced.

These features of attrition are often overcome by the attriters by working their way along (what we would like to call) the "lexical retrieval path." We are proposing, therefore, a description of this retrieval process, which can be viewed as a series of options which the attriter might go through while activating the "retrieval path." The potential retrieval process, which will usually be activated for highly specific items, presents the speaker with a hierarchical sequence of points at each of which at least two options are possible (Figure 10.1), the first leading to the correct or anticipated selection and the other to a less appropriate word from the

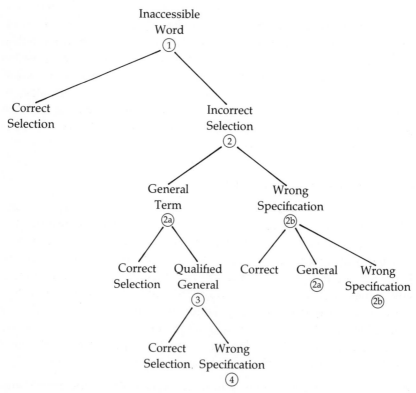

10.1   Lexical retrieval options in language attrition

same semantic field. The first decision making point (1) is when the speaker is faced with the need for an inaccessible word and s/he makes a conscious effort to remember that word. The possibilities are that either the correct selection will be made already at this early node (all the correct responses in the tables presenting the data for the five analyzed words) or that an incorrect item will be selected. If the correct selection is made, the process stops here, at the first point of departure, and to the hearer it may not even be obvious that there was some difficulty of retrieval in the speaker's language. If however the speaker makes an incorrect selection (2), this incorrect selection can be expected to be either a reference to the most general semantic specification of the inaccessible word (2a) or another lexeme which, although it belongs to the same overall semantic domain, carries a different set of specifications than the anticipated item (2b). Thus, when faced with the need to retrieve the word *pond*, some of our subjects offered a very general lexeme within the domain such as *body of water*, while others suggested specific types of "bodies of water," such as *lake* or *ocean*, which had different specifications from the required lexeme *pond* (see Table 10.1).

According to the two options described above, the speaker might either abandon the search or continue along the path to additional option nodes. If his/her selection was a general term such as *water* for *pond*, the two new possibilities available are either the correct or anticipated selection, or a qualification of the previously selected general term (3). Some subjects therefore followed the word *water* with the qualification *a small body of water* (3), which is still not the expected word but it is much closer in meaning. If at the next point along the path the speaker manages to retrieve the correct form the search will end successfully but there is also a possibility that following the qualified general term the next step will be another incorrect specification (4), such as *lake* for instance, in the example above, in which case the search was not fully successful but came close.

Let us now return to node (2b), where the wrong specification of a member of the semantic class was made. From this point on there are three options open: the correct item, the use of the general item or an alternatively wrong specification such as *ocean* or *river*. If the general term is chosen by the speaker the search might continue through a qualification, as before, on the left hand branching. The subjects may opt for another attempt leading to an unsuccessful completion of the task (such as choosing *muskrat* or *gopher*). In such cases subjects may be fully aware of their inappropriate choices yet decide to terminate the search.

It is obvious then, that the retrieval process is sometimes short and painless, when the attriter manages to come upon the proper word early on, but it can also be very long and painful if the speaker insists on continuing the search until s/he finds the right word. The retrieval path suggested here is the result of an attempt to describe what attriters might do in order to overcome the reduction in word accessibility when they force themselves into a conscious effort to search for the accurate term in their memory. The retrieval path presents the options available to the speaker when this natural, self-prompted effort takes place. It is very possible that in "think aloud protocols" of the retrieval process we might get a similar procedural path; in our case, however, the retrieval path represents the natural self-induced sequence evidenced in the data we collected.

In general, the lexical retrieval process as carried out by adult attriters in the particular context which we are concerned with can be viewed as a continuous series of efforts made by the speaker to find the anticipated word. The strategies for this search are however quite different from the associative devices described by Cohen (1986), where L2 attriters seem to be mostly concerned with the phonetic shape of the word. In our case the speaker focuses on meaning and on the semantic features of the word and thus s/he may either cling to what Cruse (1977) identifies as Inherently Neutral Specificity (INS) and use, in our example, just the word *water* (for the word *pond*) or attempt overspecification such as *lake* and do so inappropriately, or use underspecification and come up with the general term *a body of water*. In our study subjects exhibited such strategies of over- and underspecification when making the wrong choices while following the retrieval path. In all examples they stayed within the semantic category and failed only with respect to more specific selectional rules. In the following examples we can see how subjects maintained some of the main features and altered others:

(1)   For the word *pond*, which is specifically a small, enclosed and shallow body of water, the replacements were more frequent and general words which share the semantic feature of "body of water", such as *lake, river, ocean*. Specificity here was lost in the sense that the replacements did not provide the features of shallowness, and in the case of *river* specifications of "static" and "enclosed" were replaced by the feature "flowing water."

(2)   The word *cliff* retained the meaning of "a high place" but lost its specific shape and texture when it was replaced by *precipice, hill, mountain*.

(3)   The word *jar* retained the meaning of "a round container" but lost its unique shape when it was replaced with items such as *bottle, glass bowl, container, jug.*

When faced with the need to retrieve the item quickly, under the strain of face to face communication, attriters will use more general terms which share some of the features of meaning of the intended word, or they will make use of paraphrase or circumlocution. Thus, they might avoid the painful retrieval process. Our subjects often used paraphrases or circumlocution when on the one hand they felt the full search might be too difficult and on the other hand they could make themselves perfectly well understood via paraphrase. The following are examples from one of the subjects:

(a)   *ground of the living room* was used instead of *floor*
(b)   *The dog goes into this little river, body of water, whatever it is, but it's very shallow, and they're safe.*

The second example follows the retrieval path where an incorrect selection at node (2) leads to the wrong specification (2b) *little river* and then moves to the general term (2a) *body of water* following some qualifications (3) *very shallow,* and finally the process is discontinued at this point.

In some cases the retrieval path is initiated and followed through within the same sentence, with the subject finally coming up with the correct lexical item. The following example exhibits such a case from another subject in our study:

(c)   *They're looking at a frog who's sitting in a round glass, bowl . . . and the frog is tip-toeing out of the jar.*

5   Conclusion

This chapter presented a study of a rather unique type of primary language attrition – reduction in specific lexical accessibility as evidenced by adult speakers of English living in a Hebrew dominant environment. The special context of English speakers in Israel is such that primary language maintenance is highly valued and all the American Israelis in our study exhibited frustration when they realized that they had developed retrieval difficulties in their dominant language. This is perhaps a unique context in which language attrition has the least chance to develop and yet we found an obvious feature of reduction in vocabulary retrieval.

References

Bayles, K., and A. Kaszniak. 1987. *Communication and cognition in normal aging and dementia*. Boston: Little, Brown and Company – College Hill.

Blum-Kulka, S., and E. Olshtain. 1987. ''Code-switching and code-mixing within the family: Hebrew–English bilinguals living in Israel.'' Paper presented at the conference on Variation in Second Language Acquisition, held at the University of Michigan, Ann Arbor.

Cohen, A. 1986. ''Forgetting foreign-language vocabulary,'' in Weltens, de Bot, and Van Els (eds.).

Cruse, D. A. 1977. ''The pragmatics of lexical specificity,'' *Journal of Linguistics* 13.

Lambert, R. 1982. ''Setting the agenda,'' in Lambert and Freed (eds.).

Lambert, R., and B. Freed. (eds.). 1982. *The loss of language skills*. Rowley, MA: Newbury House Publishers.

Lambert, R., and S. Moore. 1986. ''Problem areas in the study of language attrition,'' in Weltens, de Bot, and Van Els (eds.).

Obler, K. L. 1982. ''Neurolinguistic aspects of language loss as they pertain to second language attrition,'' in Lambert and Freed (eds.).

Saffran, E. M., M. F. Schwartz, and O. S. M. Marin, 1976. ''Semantic mechanisms in paralexia,'' *Brain and Language* 3: 255–265.

Sharwood Smith, M. 1983. ''On first language loss in the second language acquirer: problems of transfer,'' in Gass and Selinker (eds.), *Language transfer in language learning*, Rowley, MA: Newbury House Publishers.

Van Els, T. 1986. ''An overview of European research on language attrition,'' in Weltens, de Bot, and Van Els (eds.).

Weltens, B., K. de Bot, and T. Van Els (eds.). 1986. *Language attrition in progress*. Dordrecht: Foris.

11 Spanish language attrition in a contact situation with English

CARMEN SILVA-CORVALÁN

1 Introduction

This chapter examines processes of simplification and loss of tense–mood–aspect morphology in the Spanish spoken by adult Spanish–English bilinguals living in the eastern section of Los Angeles, California. It is part of a larger project which investigates the speech of fifty Mexican–American bilinguals who represent three different immigrant groups according to length of stay in the US. A subset sample of fourteen speakers is included in the study of verbal morphology: six speakers from group 1, and four each from groups 2 and 3.

Group 1 includes only speakers born in Mexico who immigrated to the US after the age of eleven. Group 2 encompasses speakers either born in Los Angeles or who have immigrated from Mexico before the age of six. Group 3 also comprises speakers born in Los Angeles; in addition, at least one parent must respond to the definition of those in group 2.

The complexity of this community accounts for the existence of what I call a **bilingual continuum**, similar to a creole continuum in that one may identify a series of lects ranging from full-fledged to emblematic Spanish and, vice versa, from full-fledged to emblematic English depending on whether the bilingual is more or less dominant in Spanish or English. Even further, these individual lects do not correspond to fixed dichotomies of the type "compound–coordinate", or "balanced–unbalanced". Rather, at the individual level they represent a wide range of **dynamic** levels of proficiency in the subordinate language, i.e. it is in principle possible for an individual to move or be moving toward one or the other end of the continuum at any given synchronic stage of his life.

The data for this study were obtained through recordings of conversations between the author[1] and the Mexican–American speakers. Analyzed here are, in group 1 (also referred to as first generation immigrants): Eli (f20), Lou (f23), Sil (f24), Ali (f62), Eva (f,44, married to Phil), and Phil (m54). Group 2: Lau (f22, Eva and Phil's daughter), Rra (m20, Eva and Phil's nephew), Alb (m60, married to Ali), and Vir (f18).

Group 3: Son (f19) and Rro (m46), daughter and father (Son qualifies for this group because her mother qualifies as a member of group 2); the other two are Aal (f31), Ali and Alb's daughter, and Dan (m45).

2   Theoretical Considerations

Given attested simplification in other areas of the grammar across the continuum (cf. Silva-Corvalán 1986), as well as in other contact languages in similar sociolinguistic situations (Dorian 1981; Gal 1984; Mougeon, Beniak, & Valois 1985; etc.), I hypothesized that intensive and prolonged contact with a superordinate language, and consequent reduction of domains of use, would have consequences on the Spanish verb system of bilinguals such that it would evidence processes of simplification resulting in loss of tense forms[2] and restructuring of the system, with possible transfer from and consequent convergence with English.

Such theoretical notions as simplification, transfer, and convergence need to be defined in the context of this study, especially since researchers in fields related to that of language contact are not infrequently in disagreement about the meaning of these terms, as well as about what constitutes unarguable evidence in support of the existence of these phenomena in the relevant sociolinguistic situations (cf., among others, several contributions in Andersen 1983; Kellerman 1979; Meisel 1977, 1983; Mougeon, Beniak, & Valois 1985; Mühlhäusler 1981; Traugott 1976; Trudgill 1983).

I consider **simplification** a complex process which implies also rule generalization in the sense that a given form is being expanded to a larger number of contexts. **Simplification**, then, involves the higher frequency of use of a form X in context Y (i.e. generalization) at the expense of a form Z, usually in competition with and semantically closely related to X, where both X and Z existed in the language prior to the initiation of simplification. Thus, X is an **expanding form**, while Z is a **shrinking/contracting form**. The final outcome of simplification is **loss** of forms, i.e. a simplified system with fewer forms, and possibly, though not necessarily, loss of meanings. In the context of my research, I further speak of loss of a form when this form is not attested in the data, without necessarily claiming that it has undergone a **process** of simplification.

Transfer is defined as a process which may involve either one or more of the following (cf. Weinreich 1974: 30): (a) the replacement of a form in language S with a form from language F, or the incorporation from language F into language S of a form (with or without its associated meaning) previously absent in S (this is usually referred to in the literature as "borrowing"); (b) the incorporation of the meaning of a form R from language F, which may be part of the meaning of a form P in S, into another form, structurally similar to R, in the system of S (cf. Weinreich's extension or reduction of function); (c) the higher frequency of use of a form in language S, determined on the basis of a comparison with more conservative internal community norms (cf. Klein-Andreu 1986; Mougeon *et al* 1985; Silva-Corvalán 1986), in contexts where a partially corresponding form in the system of F is used either categorically or preferentially; and (d) the loss of a form in language S which does not exist in the system of F (cf.Weinreich's "neglect" or "elimination" of obligatory categories). Transfer leads to, but is not the single case of, **convergence**, defined as the achievement of structural similarity in a given aspect of the grammar of two or more languages, assumed to be different at the onset of contact. Indeed, convergence may result as well from internally motivated changes in one of the languages, most likely accelerated by contact, rather than as a consequence of direct interlingual influence (Silva-Corvalán 1986).

A change in a language L is considered to have **accelerated** in the speech of a group X when both the number of context types (as opposed to tokens of the same context), and the frequency of use of the innovation in a token count in the various contexts are higher as compared with an older age group Y in the same speech community as X, and this increase is in turn higher than any possible increase identified in the speech of a group P, as compared with an older-age group Q in the same speech community as P. This definition follows from the assumption that change-related variation observed in apparent time (i.e. across generations) may reflect stages of diffusion in real time (cf. Labov 1972).

Hypothesizing the possibility of transfer from English implies making predictions about the permeability of the Spanish verb system to change and to influence from another language. At the same time, however, there exist other factors which have been shown to play a role in situations of contact and change, which must be taken into account and which may or may not predict similar results. Indeed, although these distinct factors are related to phenomena of a different nature – on the one hand, cognitive (e.g. higher cognitive complexity of certain types of discourse (see, Levelt 1979; Silva-Corvalán 1987) and social (e.g. absence of normative pressures, specific communicative needs), and on the other, intra- and interlinguistic – it is usually the case that more than one, or even all, may be motivating and constraining a specific process of change.

Thus, consideration of socially motivated circumstances[3] makes it reasonable to expect that simplification and loss would affect first those forms used in contexts of higher hypotheticality or weaker assertiveness, i.e. conditional and subjunctive forms. However, hypothetical texts are cognitively more complex to produce,[4] a fact which makes a cognitive explanation for the occurrence of the phenomenon quite plausible. Even further, at least simplification of conditional morphology could also have intralinguistic motivation since it is attested both in first generation immigrants' speech and in non-immigrant varieties in Mexico. Finally, given that English lacks subjunctive tenses and the conditional is not marked by bound morphology, it seems justifiable to invoke the impact of interlinguistic factors as well.

Conversely, cognitive and interlinguistic factors appear to predict contradictory results in the case of the preterite–imperfect opposition. Indeed, the cognitively motivated principle of **semantic transparency**, defined by Slobin (1977: 186) as a tendency "to maintain a one-to-one mapping between underlying semantic structures and surface forms, with the goal of making messages easily retrievable for listeners", held to be responsible for a number of linguistic phenomena characteristic of language acquisition, attrition, loss, development, and change, predicts the retention of the preterite–imperfect opposition. By contrast, direct transfer from English leads us to expect the neutralization of an opposition not marked by bound morphology in this language.

The complexity of the question of permeability to change and the factors which both motivate and constrain it is undeniable. Given a situation of this sort, it seems to me appropriate to propose that those forms whose loss or simplification may be motivated by a higher number of factors (of the four discussed above) will be more permeable and thus affected first. If these factors predict contradictory results, it is likely that cognitive considerations will take precedence. Indeed, one may assume as correct the generally accepted hypothesis that in intensive language contact situations, bilinguals tend to develop a simplified variety of the less used language, as well as to approximate the systems of the languages involved, both unconscious strategies aimed at achieving a cognitively lighter linguistic load.

In this respect, what Seuren & Wekker (1986: 66) refer to as the strategy of **universality** may play an important role. According to this strategy, those grammatical processes and rule systems which are least language specific will be preferred, while language-particular morphological systems and so-called "secondary constructions," for instance, will be avoided. In my interpretation of this strategy, universality must involve the consideration of Universal Grammar, where universal grammar is defined as what crosslinguistic studies have shown to be grammatically possible in natural languages. For our specific purposes, then, we are interested in what tense systems have been shown to be possible, and preferred – inasmuch as they exist in a greater number of languages.

3   The Verb System: Analysis

At this point, it becomes necessary to present the verb system examined. Note that in addition to the tenses traditionally postulated for most varieties of Hispanoamerican Spanish, I have included the so-called periphrastic future, on the basis that (a) ''morphological boundness is not in itself a necessary criterion'' (Comrie 1985:11) to decide whether a given category is grammaticalized; and (b) it is by far the most frequent form used to locate situations in the future. I also examine two uses of the simple future and conditional forms, but this should not be interpreted to mean that these uses are considered part of the system of forms.[5]

The perfect present participle, the past perfect and the future perfect are in parentheses in Table 11.1 (overleaf) to indicate that they are never used by any of the speakers in the sample. In fact, the past perfect is not used in any variety of spoken Spanish and is quite rare in written Spanish, and the perfect participle appears to be restricted to the written mode; their absence in spoken Mexican American Spanish is not surprising, therefore. The future perfect is still in use in spoken and written Spanish to refer to past hypothetical **situations**[6] (as shown in example 1 below), as well as to future situations viewed as completed after a reference point also located in the future.

(1)   A: *Los Castro se han ido ya.*
        B: **Habrán vendido** *su casa entonces.*
        A: ''The Castros have already left.''
        B: ''(They) must have sold their house then.''

Furthermore, the morphological future (-*rá*) is used to refer to future time only in a restricted number of registers in Hispanoamerican Spanish. Likewise, the conditional is extremely rare in its tense function, i.e. when it is used to refer to future in the past, as in reported speech (2b):

(2)   a. *Lo* **miraré** *mañana.*
           ''I'll look at it tomorrow.''
        b. *Dijo que lo* **miraría** *mañana.*
           ''He said he'd look at it tomorrow.''

In examples of the type of (2a–b), the form used is almost exclusively the periphrastic construction with *ir a* ''go to'' + infinitive. In the

Table 11.1 *Verb forms examined across the continuum*

Non-finite forms: inf. *mirar* "look at" pres. part. *mirando* past part. *mirado*	
	perf. inf. *haber mirado* (perf. pres. part. *habiendo mirado*)
Finite forms: *Indicative* pres. (*él*) *mira* "(he) looks at"	
pret. *miró* imperf. *miraba* future *va a mirar* *mirará*	pres. perf. *ha mirado* (past perf. *hubo mirado*) pluperf. *había mirado* (future perf. *habrá mirado*)

[functions: fut. "tense"; pres. hypothetical reference]
condit. *miraría*   condit. perf. *habría mirado*
          [functions: fut. hypothetical reference; past hypoth. ref.]

Subjunctive pres. *mire* imperf. *mirara*	pres. perf. *haya mirado* pluperf. *hubiera mirado*
Imperative pres. (*tú*) *mira* "(you) look" (*usted*) *mire* "(you-polite) look"	

Mexican American Spanish data, the morphological conditional is never used in its tense function, and the morphological future occurs with a very low frequency in the speech of first generation immigrants, especially so in its tense function. Given the acceleration of change in contact languages, the early loss of these forms in the other two groups is predictable.

To identify patterns of simplification and loss I have compared the linguistic behaviour of second and third generation speakers, groups 2 and 3, with that of those in group 1, i.e. with the speech of members of the same bilingual community. This was done taking a number of different contexts into account, as explained below:

(i) Firstly, obligatory syntactic contexts, i.e. those requiring one or another verb form, were considered, e.g. contexts which impose consecutio temporum constraints in a number of subordinate clauses. Thus, the pluperfect subjunctive provided by the researcher in the protasis of ex. 3A constrains the choice of verb form in the apodosis to pluperfect subjunctive or indicative or to conditional perfect. The choice of other verb forms (as in 3B) was considered to indicate simplification or loss of these perfect forms. Likewise, failure to use subjunctive in certain subordinate clauses (ex. 4) which require it in group 1 was ascribed to simplification or loss.

(3)   A: *¿Y qué me dices de tu educación si tus padres se **hubieran quedado** en México?*
        B: *No **estudiaba** (imperf.) mucho, yo creo.*
        (H, m21, 2, ELA11A275)[7]
        A: "So what can you tell me about your education if your parents had stayed in Mexico?"
        B: "I **didn't study** much, I think."

(4)   *Lo voy a guardar antes que **llega** (pres. indic.).*
        "I'm going to put it away before he **comes** home."
        (Son, f19, 3, ELA66B490)

   (ii) Secondly, obligatory contexts created either by intrasentential linguistic material (e.g. an adverbial expression) or by the verb form used in the preceding sentence were taken into account to determine whether the form under examination was correct. Accordingly, the use of imperfect in (5), and of preterite in (6b–7b) were regarded as signs of simplification of the preterite–imperfect opposition.This is because the complement *un accidente* "an accident" in (5) forces an interpretation of the **situation** as singular and perfective so that the preterite is required. Examples (6a–7a), on the other hand, have created an imperfective frame which (6b–7b), being part of the same temporal–aspectual sequence, should, but fail to, maintain.

(5)   *Iba a ser profesional, pero creo que **tenía** (imperf.) un accidente.*
        (Rra, m20, 2, ELA5OA320)
        "He was going to become professional, but I think he **had** an accident."

(6)   a. *Después mi hermano **era** (imperf.) el que **iba** (imperf.) a misa*
        b. *y **entregó** (pret.) el sobre.*
        (Son, f19, 3, ELA66B540).
        a. "Afterwards my brother **was** the one who **went** to church
        b. and **handed in** the envelope."

(7)   a. *Porque este mejicano no **sabía** (imperf.) el inglés,*
        b. *no más **habló** (pret.) español,*
        c. *pero **era** (imperf.) muy bravo y muy macho.*
        (Dan, m45, 3, ELA43B455)

> a. "Because this Mexican **didn't know** English,
> b. he only **spoke** Spanish,
> c. but he **was** very tough and very macho."

(iii) Thirdly, discourse constraints on the occurrence of a form in a given context provided information needed to evaluate the correctness of the form used. For instance, narrative abstracts and statements which orient or evaluate the narrative events **as a whole** must be coded in the preterite in Spanish (Silva-Corvalán, 1983, 1988). This rule, never broken by first generation immigrants (8–9), is frequently violated by speakers in groups 2 and 3, who use the imperfect form instead, (10–11, both from group 2, are illustrative).

(8)   *Fue* (pret.) *una manifestación muy grande—. Fue* (pret.) *como desde la cuarta hasta como a la sexta o séptima avenida.*
        (Lou, f23, 1, ELA45A635).
        "It **was** a big demonstration—. It **was** from about fourth to sixth or seventh avenue."

(9)   *Dicen que fue* (pret.) *muy trágico. Yo no alcancé a ver lo demás. Pero estuvo* (pret.) *muy feo eso.*
        (Lou, f23, 1, ELA45A550).
        "They say it **was** really tragic. I **didn't have a chance** to see the rest. But that **was** real ugly."

(10)   [Produced at the end of a narrative about the speaker's prom.]
        Y estaba (imperf.) *muy bonito el prom.*
        (Rra, m20, 2, ELA50B395)
        "And the prom **was** real nice."

(11)   [R: ¿*Y la otra vez, qué pasó?*] *Era* (imperf.) *en el seventh grade, con un muchacho del sixth grade.*
        (H, m21, 2, ELA11A240)
        [R: "And the other time, what happened?] It **was** in seventh grade, with a guy from sixth grade."

(iv) Finally, favoring discourse-pragmatic contexts for the occurrence of a form were identified in the speech of first generation immigrants. If the same favoring contexts failed to elicit the expected forms in the speech of those in groups 2 and 3, the forms in question were considered to be undergoing simplification or to be lost, depending on whether they did or did not appear in other contexts. This methodology is illustrated through a comparison of (12) and (13) from a speaker in group 1 and in group 3, respectively. Both passages are selected from conversations dealing with racial discrimination and prejudices.

(12)   C: *Si, si viniera un día y te dijera, ''Mira, me voy a casar con un negro.''*

        S: *Con un negro, ah, bueno, yo pienso que yo si* **aceptaría** *(cond.). porque claro mi hermana no va – no se va a casar con cualquier negro simplemente. Pues tomarlo como cualquier persona que* **sea** *(pres. subj.).— Y yo pienso que tan sólo por – por, cuando* **vengan** *(pres. subj.) los hijos, por ser hijo de mi hermana, pos yo lo* **querría** *(cond.) bastante también, aunque* **sea** *(pres. subj.) negrito, no le hace.*
          (Sil, f25, 1, ELA76B70)

    C: ''Yes, if one day she told you, 'Look here, I'm going to marry a black'.''

        S: ''A black ah, well, I think that I **would accept** it, because of course my sister is not – is not going to marry just any black. So take him like I would any other person. And I think that just because – because – when children **come**, because he's my sister's son, well I **would love** him well, even if he **were** black, it doesn't matter.''

(13)   C: *—¿Qué crees tú que dirías en este caso, qué, cuál reacción, cuál sería tu reacción, verdad, qué – ?*

        D: *Antes que me* **dice** *(pres.) eso, yo* **creo** *(pres.) que va a ir,* **vamos a tener** *(perf. fut.) mucho más oportunidades para yo conocer el hombre, de cualquier color, negro, blanco, café y yo* **puedo** *(pres.) decir algo de esa persona, si es bueno o no es bueno. Y mismo tiempo ella* **va a hacer** *(perf. fut.) que ella* **quiere** *(pres.).*
          (Dan, m45, 3, ELA9OA135)

    C: ''—What do you think you'd say in this case, what, what reaction, what would your reaction be, right, what – ?''

        D: ''Before she **says** that to me, I **think** there's going to, **we're going to have** much more opportunity for me to know the man, of any color, black, white, brown, and I **can** say something about that person, if he's good or if he's not good. And at the same time she's **going to do** what she **wants**.''

Note that (12–13) are samples of **hypothetical texts**, i.e. texts which convey imaginary, conjectural information, rather than facts stemming from perception and memory (Klein, Stutterheim n.d.: 31). In texts of this

Table 11.2 *Stages of loss of "tense–mood–aspect" morphemes*

Group	1 Eli	1 Sil	1 Eva	1 Phi	1 Ali	1 Lou	2 Lau	2 Alb	3 Rro	2 Vir	2 Rra	3 Son	3 Dan	3 Aal
NON-FIN.														
Inf.	+	+	+	+	+	+	+	+	+	+	+	+	+	+
Pres. part.	+	+	+	+	+	+	+	+	+	+	+	+	+	+
Past part.	+	+	+	+	+	+	+	+	+	+	+	+	+	+
INDIC.														
Pres.	+	+	+	+	+	+	+	+	+	+	+	+	+	+
Fut. (*ir a*)	+	+	+	+	+	+	+	+	+	+	+	+	+	+
Pret.	+	+	+	+	+	+	~	~	~	~	~	~	~	~
Imperf.	+	+	+	+	+	+	+	+	x	+	@	@	@	@
IMP.														
Pres.	+	+	+	+	+	+	+	+	+	o	o	o	o	]
SUBJ.														
Pres.	+	+	+	+	+	+	+	+	+	o	x	o	o	]
INDIC.														
Pres. Perf.	+	+	+	+	+	+	+	+	+	+	+	o	–	–
SUBJ.														
Imperf.	+	+	+	+	+	+	x	x	x	o	–	–	–	–
INDIC.														
Condit. (fut. ref.)[8]	+	+	+	+	+	+	+	+	{	–	]	–	–	–
Condit. (past ref.)	+	+	+	+	+	+	+	+	–	–	–	–	–	–
NON FIN.														
Perf. inf.	+	+	+	+	+	+	+	+	–	–	–	–	–	–
SUBJ.														
Pres. perf.	+	+	+	+	+	+	+	+	–	–	–	–	–	–
Pluperf.	+	+	+	+	+	+	x	x	–	–	–	–	–	–
INDIC.														
Pluperf.	+	+	+	+	+	+	x	–	–	–	–	–	–	–
Future (pres. ref.)	+	+	+	+	+	+	–	]	–	–	–	–	–	–
Future (fut. ref.)	+	+	+	+	{	{	–	–	]	–	–	]	–	–
Condit. perf.	+	+	–	–	–	–	–	–	–	–	–	–	–	–

type, one would expect frequent use of weak assertive verb morphology, e.g. conditional and subjunctive. As expected, (12) (from group 1) contains two conditional and three subjunctive forms. By contrast, every finite form in (13) (from group 3) is either present indicative or periphrastic future. Given a situation of this sort, one may postulate that the speaker who produces (13) has failed to produce a conditional and/or a subjunctive form. Furthermore, if no favouring context (in two to three hours of transcribed conversation) prompts the use of these forms, it seems safe to conclude that they are non-existent in this speaker's verbal system.

4   The Continuum

The analysis allowed us to identify a clear-cut qualitative difference between first generation immigrants and the rest of the speakers,[9] as displayed on the previous page in Table 11.2. Those in the former group use the verb system in the manner predicted for a full-fledged variety of spoken Spanish. Speakers in groups 2 and 3 evidence a range of systems which may be ordered according to whether they are more or less different from that of those in group 1. Table 11.2. displays visually the variation characteristic of the continuum.

The symbols in Table 11.2 mean the following: sign '' + '' stands for a tense form which is used according to the norms of general spoken Spanish, regardless of whether it has acquired expanded uses as other forms are simplified and lost; '' − '' indicates that the form is not part of the speaker's verb system; a tilde '' ~ '' is used to indicate that the preterite–imperfect opposition has become neutralized in a closed list of verbs which appear with imperfect morphology in both perfective and imperfective contexts; ''@'' signals that a speaker has used a number of preterites instead of imperfects; ''x'' reflects a high but not categorical occurrence of a form in an obligatory context; ''o'' signals a **shrinking** form, i.e. one which fails to occur in a high percentage of required contexts; ''{'' signals that the form appears to be lexicalized, i.e. it is used with just one or two verbs; '']'' indicates that the form occurs in one or a maximum of three different frozen expressions.

The two extreme ends of the continuum, from most developed to most simplified, are represented by Eli and Sil (group 1), and by Aal (group 3). The most developed system used by group 1 does not differ from the norms of general spoken Spanish.

The absence of future morphology clearly differentiates groups 2 and 3 from the first generation immigrants. Further qualitative differences between them are established by processes of simplification affecting the preterite, the imperfect subjunctive, and the pluperfect indicative and subjunctive. The pluperfect indicative is in fact used, albeit not in all required contexts, by one speaker beyond group 1, Lau.

With only minor exceptions, then, the progression[10] of simplification (S) and loss (L) falls into eight stages, implicationally ordered as shown overleaf in Table 11.3, such that if an individual uses the forms in (i), it may be assumed that the forms listed in (ii)–(viii) will form part of his verb system and will not be affected by processes of simplification. Conversely, loss of present subjunctive and imperative (stage viii) implies as well the absence of the forms listed in (i) through (vii), and the simplification of the preterite–imperfect opposition, as indicated in (ii) and (iv):

Table 11.3 *Stages of simplification and loss*

(i)	L:	morphological conditional (tense function)
		conditional perfect
	S:	morphological future
(ii)	L:	morphological future
	S:	pluperfect indicative
		imperfect subjunctive
		pluperfect subjunctive
		preterite (with closed list of stative verbs)
(iii)	L:	pluperfect indicative
(iv)	L:	pluperfect subjunctive
		present perfect subjunctive
		perfect infinitive
		morphological conditional (hypothetical function)
	S:	imperfect indicative
		present and imperfect subjunctive
		imperative
(v)	L:	imperfect subjunctive
(vi)	S:	present perfect indicative
(vii)	L:	present perfect indicative
(viii)	L:	present subjunctive
		imperative

Note: L = loss; S = simplification.

Table 11.4 *Tense systems across the bilingual continuum*

	US born bilinguals				
	I	II	III	IV	V
Relative tenses					
Inf.	+	+	+	+	+
Pres. part.	+	+	+	+	+
Past part.	+	+	+	+	−
Absolute tenses: indicative					
Pres. (pres.)	+	+	+	+	+
Pret. (past)	+	+	+	+	+
Imperf. (past, imperf.)	+	+	+	+	+
Future-periphr. (future)	+	+	+	+	+
Pres. perf. (past with pres. relev.)	+	+	+	+	−
Absolute-relative tenses					
Condit.-periphr.[11] (fut. in the past)	+	+	+	+	+
Pres. subj. (fut. in the past/pres.)	+	+	+	+	−
Imperf. subj. (fut. in the past)	+	+	+	−	−
Pluperf. subj. (fut. perf. in the past)	+	+	+	−	−
Pluperf. indic. (past of past)	+	+	−	−	−
Condit. perf. (fut. perf. in the past)	+	−	−	−	−
Fut. perf. (fut. of fut.)	−	−	−	−	−

What is remarkable about the manner in which the system changes is its regularity. Patterns of simplification and loss are never random but at all stages conform to a predictable trend to develop a least grammaticalized system within the constraints of universal grammar possibilities and preferences. Disregarding a few frozen expressions, and a small residue of forms undergoing advanced simplification, it is possible to single out five different systems which represent a steady progression toward a less grammaticalized one. These systems are presented on the previous page in Table 11.4 following Comrie's (1985) framework for the analysis of tense.[12]

In Spanish, absolute tenses include present, preterite, imperfect, future, and present perfect indicative (semantically "past with present relevance", Comrie 1985: 77–82). Absolute–relative tenses encompass the conditional (as future in the past), the present and imperfect subjunctive, and indicative and subjunctive compound forms. Relative tenses comprise the non-finite forms.

Fig 11.1 represents system I diagrammatically.

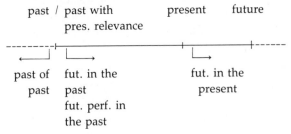

11.1   Representation of tense distinctions in system I.

Observe that systems I and II have five grammatical distinctions in the past and only one in the future, "in accordance with the general tendency of languages to have a better developed past than future system" (Comrie 1985: 85). System III, the most developed one attested among US born bilinguals, has lost two of the past distinctions, pluperfect indicative and conditional perfect, and retains four absolute–relative forms, two for future in the past (periphrastic conditional and imperfect subjunctive); one for future in the past or present (present subjunctive) and one for future perfect in the past (pluperfect subjunctive). Of these, system IV retains the present subjunctive and the periphrastic conditional, and system V preserves only the periphrastic conditional for future in the past. System V consists of only four absolute and one absolute–relative tense plus two pure relative forms. The last distinctions to disappear are past with present relevance and future in the past/present. System V is represented overleaf in Figure 11.2 for an easier visual comparison with system I.

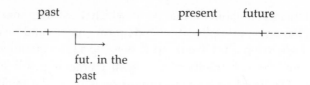

11.2   Representation of tense distinctions in system V.

Given widespread acceptance of the fact that simplified languages (e.g. child language, pidgins, early stages of second language acquisition) rely heavily on the context, it seems safe to assume that the most simplified tense system could consist of basically non-finite forms with perhaps a small number of auxiliary verbs, but this stage is not attested in the data analyzed here.

5   Conclusion

Having established patterns of simplification and loss in the verb system, one can ask at least two questions: (1) What is the universality of the systems and processes identified?; and (2) What accounts for the type and stages of simplification and loss?

With respect to the first question, we note certain parallels with simplification and loss in other contact languages, such as those described by Dorian (1981) for East Sutherland Gaelic, by Gal (1984) for Austrian Hungarian, by Mougeon, Beniak & Valois (1985) for Canadian French, and by Trudgill (1983) for Arvanitika. For instance, the early loss of one of two ''same meaning'' structures (or ''stylistic shrinkage'') has been documented as well in every one of these bilingual communities (cf. loss of conditional perfect, in competition with imperfect subjunctive, in Los Angeles Spanish).

Specifically in regard to tense in Gaelic, Dorian (1981: 141) notes early simplification of future and conditional in the larger part of the less proficient speakers of Gaelic, and, even further, loss of these tenses in the lower levels of the proficiency contiuum. Thus, the system of three morphophonologically marked tenses,[13] past, future, and conditional, is reduced to one, past. Similar observations are made by Trudgill regarding Arvanitika. Trudgill notices that ''of the forms that remain in full use, only the present and past definite are inflected.'' (1983: 117)

It is arresting, furthermore, to note that language loss is to a large extent the mirror image of development in creolization, and in first and second language acquisition. That is to say, in acquiring the verb system of Spanish (see Andersen, n.d.; Jacobsen 1986), and indeed of various other languages (see Klein 1985; Meisel 1985), learners go through stages of development which are the reverse of loss: the earliest tense forms to be acquired are present and past (both perfective and imperfective), while future, conditional and compound tenses are acquired much in the same order in which they are lost across the bilingual continuum. This correspondence may in fact reflect the freezing, at different levels of development of grammatical proficiency, of the bilingual's secondary language. However, the possibility of **loss at the individual level**, though not documented in this study, could not be dismissed a priori.

In regard to creolization, Muysken (1981) claims that the emergence of tense, mood, and aspect (TMA) categories in Creole languages is in each case governed by a theory of markedness. For the category **tense**, which we are interested in comparing with the bilingual continuum, a markedness index based on dissociation versus association of three points (moment of speech, moment of the event, theoretical reference point) justifies the hierarchy from least to most marked in Table 11.5. This markedness hierarchy, proposed to account for order of appearance of tense morphemes in Creole languages, seems to be valid as well as a predictor of order of disappearance in subordinate contact languages, such that the most marked tense disappears first. Within my view of language as a system of human communication, however, a theory of markedness describes, but does not explain, the facts observed. To be explanatory, a markedness hierarchy needs to be justified with reference to factors which lie outside the linguistic system (e.g. interactive, cognitive).

One may further ask why languages develop such grammaticalized systems as those in Table 11.4 to the exclusion of other logical possibilities. The answer, it seems to me, must be sought in relation to the same four general factors proposed to play a role in contact languages, namely cognitive, social, intra- and interlinguistic.

In regards to interlinguistic considerations, examination of the pro-

Table 11.5 *Hierarchy of markedness*

	Markedness index
Simple present	0
Simple past	1
Present perfect	1
Simple future	2
Past perfect	2
Future perfect	3

gression of simplification and loss, summarized in Tables 11.2–11.4 leads us to conclude that the impact from English is only indirect. That is, evidence does not seem to be sufficient to conclude that contact with a typologically different language would have resulted in a system different from system V. Note that direct influence from English does not justify (a) the early simplification and loss of pluperfect indicative;[14] (b) the loss of perfect infinitive (at stage iv); (c) the loss of present perfect (at stage vii) as compared with the later loss of present and imperfect subjunctive; nor, finally, (d) the retention of imperfect indicative down to very low points in the continuum. Thus, as previous studies have shown (Dorian 1978, 1981; Silva-Corvalán 1986, among others), some changes occur rather as a result of reduction of both exposure to and use of a full-fledged variety of a subordinate language in contact with a superordinate one. Nonetheless, it seems to me that transfer may play a role once forms have become lost. At this stage, and under pressure to communicate a given message, bilinguals make use of the forms available to them in the recessive language, and tend to distribute them according to the syntactic and semantic rules of the dominant language.

Earlier studies have given evidence that internal processes of change are accelerated in contact situations. This observation is supported by the early loss of conditional perfect and simple future. On the other hand, although simplification of present perfect and pluperfect indicative, and of subjunctive forms, is attested in a number of Spanish varieties spoken in Argentina, Paraguay and Venezuela, for instance, it is doubtful that internal causation may be adduced for the changes in Mexican–American Spanish. One may identify both intra- and interlinguistic favoring factors such as the cross dialectal facts mentioned, and the lack of subjunctive in English, but these factors alone predict neither the order nor the type of loss evidenced in the data examined.

Simplification and loss appear to be more appropriately accounted for by cognitive and social considerations. Note that the simplest system of grammaticalized tense, system V, appears to be cognitively less complex and interactionally most justified. With respect to cognitive complexity, there seems to be widespread agreement that grammaticalized distinctions marked by bound morphology are dispreferred in situations of linguistic stress (e.g. language acquisition, pidginization, cf. Givón 1979) because of their low semantic transparency, as compared with more or less corresponding lexical and periphrastic constructions. In addition, absolute–relative tenses are cognitively more complex. They are in a sense like secondary constructions since their meaning combines two points of reference: location of a reference point in relation to the present with relative time location of a situation. Furthermore, interactional factors do not favour the retention of absolute–relative tenses in a contact situation where the domains to which the subordinate language is restricted call much more frequently for reference to immediate concrete worlds. By contrast, interactional factors favor the retention of preterite–imperfect morphology, an opposition which plays a crucial communicative role in reference to past situations (Silva-Corvalán 1983), which constitute a favorite topic of conversation.

As we have seen, all four factors contribute to the simplification and loss of forms in the various stages of restructuring of the verb system. Moreover, our hypothesis regarding the higher importance of cognitive factors, reflected in universal grammar, appears to be upheld. Mülhäusler (1981: 120) has stated that in the creolization phase of a pidgin "the increase in overall complexity is as it were preprogrammed in a way similar to the developmental continuum of a child learning a first language or the inter-language of a second language learner." Our study has shown that the same statement is true in the case of language simplification and loss. The various verb systems identified in the data from Mexican–American bilinguals conform to universal principles of, as it were, language development in reverse. Thus, as also observed by Mühl-häusler in regard to the impact of the languages which contribute to the development of a pidgin, a language is permeable to interlinguistic influence only within the constraints imposed by cognitive factors which underline possible and preferred linguistic systems as attested in natural languages.

Finally, turning to the question of convergence with English, it **seems** clear that despite the rather drastic changes that Spanish has gone through, there is only one which approximates it to English, the loss of the subjunctive mood. There is no doubt that the Spanish verb system is permeable to change, but transfer and convergence appear to operate at more "superficial" and idiosyncratic levels, such as preferential use of certain forms in contexts where the more or less corresponding English form would also be preferred, and certainly at the purely lexical level as well.

Notes

This material is based upon work supported by the National Science Foundation under Grant BNS-8214733. Part of the research was carried out while the author was a guest researcher at the Max-Planck-Institüt für Psycholinguistik, Nijmegen

(1986). The hospitality and support of the Max-Planck-Institüt are gratefully acknowledged.

(1)   Two exceptions are Sil and Lou, who were recorded by a friend of theirs who is one of the author's students at the University of Southern California.

(2)   After Comrie (1985), we consider tense to be "the grammaticalization of location in time" (see, in particular, Ch. 1) and include as such those forms discussed under the labels of **preterite, pluperfect, future, non-finite forms,** etc. It must be kept in mind, however, that these forms are usually used to convey mood and aspect distinctions rather than strictly tense.

(3)   For instance the **principle of distance** proposed in Silva-Corvalán (1985: 565). According to this principle, if a language system has several closely related forms in the same syntactic–semantic sphere, the form which is farthest away from the speaker, in the sense that it refers to objects or events which are the farthest from him in his objective (e.g. actual distance) or subjective (e.g. possibility of actualization) world, will tend to be lost. Interactional, and perhaps also memory factors underlie this principle; since speakers tend to speak about themselves and their immediate objective world rather than about distant and hypothetical situations, the infrequently used forms, if any, will disappear first.

(4)   The source of this complexity seems to be the question of linearization of information, which does not stem from perception and memory. In regard to this issue, see Klein & von Stutterheim (n.d.), and Levelt (1979).

(5)   Statements about uses of this verbal system do not necessarily apply to varieties of Iberian Spanish.

(6)   After Comrie (1976), who proposes **situation** as a technical term to refer inclusively and indistinctly to actions, processes, events, states, etc.

(7)   The information given in parentheses corresponds to speaker's name (code or initial), sex and age, group (1, 2, 3), cassette-tape identification and place of example in the tape. Dashes in the examples stand for language material left out because it is not relevant to the discussion.

(8)   No occurrences of the conditional in its tense function (future in the past) are attested in the data. Future reference and past reference stand for modal uses in future and past contexts. Note that the tense versus modal or aspectual function of tenses has been investigated exclusively for future and conditional. In all other cases, the term tense may subsume tense, mood, and aspect meanings.

(9)   This qualitative difference appears to contradict the notion of the bilingual continuum. More second generation speakers need to be examined, however, before a definite conclusion may be reached.

(10)   It must be specified that progressive loss is a group phenomenon because, given the fact that data were collected with only a maximum of eight months between the two recording sessions with each person, there is no empirical evidence to support a claim of loss at the individual level, i.e. forms absent in the speech of any given individual may have never been part of his linguistic repertoire at earlier stages. In addition, it should be made clear that this study examines the **use** of a system, i.e.

languagé **production**. It will be obvious to any observer of the community studied, that speakers' comprehension of the receding language (Spanish in our case) is much more highly developed. As is the case in other sociolinguistic situations of this type, some members of the community are able to participate in conversations held mainly in Spanish, though they themselves use English almost exclusively. This clearly indicates that comprehension is a different skill from production, and that these bilinguals are more proficient in the former skill.

(11)   Though not current practice, I have included the periphrastic conditional (formed with the imperfect of *ir* "to go" + infinitive) in Table 11.4 for the same reasons which justify the inclusion of the periphrastic future (see section 3).

(12)   Comrie incorporates the notions of **relative, absolute,** and **absolute–relative** tenses in his cross linguistic study. Absolute tenses locate a situation in time relative to the present moment; absolute–relative tenses locate a situation in time relative to a reference point which is in turn established (absolutely) to be before or after the present moment; with pure relative tense the reference point is some point in time given by the context, not necessarily the present moment.

(13)   In Gaelic, only the verb for *to be* has a present tense. The present of all other verbs, including the "habitual" meaning, is formed with the present of *to be* plus the corresponding gerund.

(14)   In English these speakers use the pluperfect indicative as expected.

References

Andersen, Roger W., (ed.). 1983. *Pidginization and creolization as language acquisition*, Rowley, MA: Newbury House Publishers.

(n.d.). "Interpreting data: second language acquisition of verbal aspect," MS, University of California at Los Angeles.

Comrie, Bernard. 1976. *Aspect*. Cambridge: Cambridge University Press.

1985. *Tense*. Cambridge; Cambridge University Press.

Corder, S. P., and E. Roulet (eds.). 1976. *The notions of simplification, interlanguages and pidgins and their relation to second language pedagogy* (Actes du 5ème Colloque de Linguistique Appliquée de Neuchâtel), Université de Neuchâtel, Faculté des Lettres.

Dorian, Nancy. 1978. "The fate of morphological complexity in language death," *Language* 54, 590–609.

1980. "Maintenance and loss of same-meaning structures in language death," *Word* 31: 39–45.

1981. *Language death*. Philadelphia: University of Pennsylvania Press.

Fisiak, Jacek (ed.). 1985. *Historical semantics – Historical word formation*. Berlin: Mouton.

Fleischman, Suzanne. 1982. *The future in thought and language: diachronic evidence from Romance*. Cambridge: Cambridge University Press.

Gal, Susan. 1984. "Phonological style in bilingualism: the interaction of structure and use," in Schiffrin (1984), 290–302.

Givón, Talmy. 1979. *On understanding grammar*. New York: Academic Press.

Jacobsen, Teresa. 1986. "¿Aspecto antes que tiempo? Una mirada a la adquisición temprana del español," in Meisel (ed.), 97–114.

Kellerman, Eric. 1979. "Transfer and non-transfer: where are we now?," *Studies in second language acquisition*. 2: 37–58.

Klein, Wolfgang. 1985. *Second language acquisition*, Cambridge: Cambridge University Press.

Klein, Wolfgang and C. von Stutterheim. (n.d.). "Text structure and referential movement," MS, Nijmegen: Max-Planck-Institüt für Psycholinguistik.

Klein-Andreu, Flora. 1986. "La cuestión del anglicismo: apriorismos y métodos," *Thesaurus*, Boletin del Instituto Caro y Cuervo, Tomo XL, 1–16.

Labov, William. 1972. *Sociolinguistic patterns*, Philadelphia: University of Pennsylvania Press.

Levelt, Willem. 1979. "Linearization in discourse," MS, Nijmegen: Max-Planck-Institüt für Psycholinguistik.

Macnamara, J. (ed.). 1977. *Language learning and thought*, New York: Academic Press.

Meisel, Jürgen M. (ed.). 1977. *Langues en contact: pidgins, creoles. Languages in contact*. Tübingen: TBL Verlag Narr.

1983. "Transfer as second-language strategy," *Language & communication* 3: 11–46.

1985. "Les phases intiales du développement de notions temporelles, aspectuelles et de modes d'action," *Lingua* 66: 321–374.

(ed.). 1986. *Adquisición de lenguaje. Adquisição da linguagem*, Frankfurt: Vervuert.

Mougeon, Raymond, E. Beniak, and D. Valois. 1985. "A sociolinguistic study of language contact, shift, and change." *Linguistics* 23: 455–487.

Mühlhäusler, P. 1981. *Pidginization and simplification of language, Pacific Linguistics*, Series B, No. 26.

Muysken, Pieter. 1981. "Creole tense/mood/aspect systems: the unmarked case?," in Muysken (ed.), 181–199.

(ed.). 1981. *Generative studies on creole languages*, Dordrecht: Foris.

Muysken, Pieter and N. Smith (eds.). 1986. *Substrata versus universals in creole genesis*. Amsterdam: Benjamins.

Schiffrin D. (ed.). 1984. *Meaning, form and use in context*. Washington, D.C.: Georgetown University Press.

Seuren, Pieter and Herman Wekker. 1986. "Semantic transparency as a factor in creole genesis," in Muysken and Smith (eds.), 57–70.

Silva-Corvalán, Carmen. 1983. "Tense and aspect in oral Spanish narrative: Context and meaning," *Language* 59: 60–80.

1985. "Modality and semantic change," in Fisiak (ed.), 547–572.

1986. "Bilingualism and language change: the extension of *estar* in Los Angeles Spanish," *Language* 62: 587–608.

1987. "Tense–mood–aspect across the Spanish–English bilingual continuum," in Keith Denning *et al.* (eds.), *Variation in language: NWAV-XV at Stanford*. Stanford: Department of Linguistics, 394–410.

1988. "Oral narrative along the Spanish–English bilingual continuum," in John Staczek (ed.), *On Spanish, Portuguese, and Catalan Linguistics*. Washington, D.C.: Georgetown University Press.

Slobin, D. 1977. "Language change in childhood and in history," in Macnamara (ed.), 185–214.

Traugott, Elizabeth C. 1976. "Natural semantax: its role in the study of second language acquisition," in Corder and Roulet (eds.).

Trudgill, Peter. 1983. *On dialect*. Oxford: Blackwell.

Weinreich, U. 1974. *Languages in contact* (eighth printing). The Hague: Mouton.

Part III
Case studies

12 Morphological disintegration and reconstruction in first language attrition

DORIT KAUFMAN AND MARK ARONOFF

1 Introduction

The need for long term longitudinal studies of attrition within individuals has long been recognized in attrition (Obler 1982; Weltens 1987). Such longitudinal studies allow insight into the cumulative effects of attrition on the linguistic features of the language involved. This chapter is devoted to one such study. The developmental attrition of L1 (Hebrew) in a young child placed in an L2 (English) dominant environment has been monitored longitudinally through naturalistic observations and systematic probes to study the effect of attrition on the lexicon, syntax, morphology, and phonology of L1. The present contribution highlights one aspect of this study – the disintegration and reconstruction of the L1 verbal system. The study is based on daily notes and bi-weekly recordings of primarily naturalistic observations as well as on occasional elicitation activities and probes designed to ascertain the child's competence in L1. The data were collected primarily in the home environment where the use of L1 dominated.

The study focuses on instances of **code mixing**, where linguistic units (words, phrases, clauses) of one language are juxtaposed with units of another language within a single sentence (Sridhar & Sridhar 1980), and **code blending**, where morphemes from one language are combined with morphemes of another language within a single word while the phonological features of the respective source languages are retained (Kaufman & Sridhar 1986). Given that code blended words are necessarily of the child's own creation, it follows that code blending provides a window into the child's morphological competence (Aronoff 1983, 1976). In particular , code blending allows us to gain some insight, through the productive morphology, into the simultaneous process of L1 loss and L2 acquisition in the young child.

Our subject, Michal, a native speaker of Hebrew, entered the United States in July 1985. At 2;6 she was a fluent speaker of Hebrew, whose fluency paralleled that of her Hebrew speaking peers. Her initial exposure to English, which was occasional and not intensive, was increased when at 2;7 she attended nursery school for three hours a day three times a week. At 2;8 the exposure was further increased when she attended a different school for seven hours a day five days a week. At home Hebrew was the exclusive language used by both parents and sisters (seven and eleven years old) for within-family discourse.

The study highlights four stages in the child's linguistic journey from fluency to non-production. First, the onset of attrition (2;9–3;1), three months after initial contact with English. This stage is characterized by L2 nominal and, later, verbal insertions in an L1 morphosyntactic context. (Our focus in this chapter will be on the verbal insertions.) Second, the bilingual stage, which overlaps the first and third periods (3;1–3;2), exhibits native-like fluency in both languages, appropriate for this age level. Developmental errors in L1, at this stage, attest to productivity in the language. The third stage (3;2–3;5) marks the disintegration of the L1 verbal system, accelerated by the child's increasing unwillingness to speak Hebrew. The fourth stage (3;5–4;6) involves the reconstruction process and the development of an idiosyncratic L1 template. This template is based in part on the morphology and syntax of L2 and is incorporated in L2 discourse. These stages are summarized in Table 12.1.

2   The outset

At the outset of the study, prior to the onset of attrition, the child's language at 2;6 exhibits good command of morphology and syntax in keeping with the language of her native speaker peers.[1] The following is a representative sample, selected to illustrate the child's versatile verbal system at 2;6–2;8.[2]

Table 12.1 *Stages in the attrition of the L1 verbal system*

Stage	Age	Months in US
Onset of attrition	2;9–3;1	4–7
Bilingual period	3;1–3;2	7–8
Disintegration of L1	3;2–3;5	8–11
Idiosyncratic template	3;5–4;6	12–24

(1)   *Hi lo yexol-a   li-tfos   et   ha-kadur   šel-a.*
        she no can.PRES-fs to-catch   OM   the-ball   of-her
        "She cannot catch her ball."

(2)   *Ani   roc-a   še-te-lx-i   it-i   li-šon.*
        I   want-fs   that-2.FUT-go-fs   with-me   to-sleep
        "I want you to go to sleep with me."

(3)   *...aval ani roc-a   axšav mašu   la-sot, t-avi-i*
        ... but I   want-fs now something to-do, 2.FUT-brings-fs
            li   et   ze
            to-me OM this
        "... but I want to do something now, bring it to me"

(4)   *Ma   sam-nu   al   ha-madreg-ot?*
        what   put-1pl.PAST   on   the-stairs-fpl?
        "What did we put on the stairs?"

(5)   *Lo, kodem   ne-saxek   axar-kax na-šir,   tov?*
        no, first   1pl.FUT-play then   1pl.FUT-sing   good?
        "No, first let's play and then let's sing, OK?"

(6)   *At te-sapr-i   ...axšav ta-dlik-i.*
        you 2.FUT-tell story-fs ... now 2.FUT-switch on-fs
        "You tell the story ... now switch on."

The child's language at this stage exhibits mastery of the linguistic features typically acquired by monolingual Hebrew speaking children in their third year as discussed in Berman (1985). Note that the child's speech manifests diverse use of verbs and mastery of appropriate inflectional markings to express tense, number, person and gender.

Linguistic features that are characteristic of children her age include pervasive use of infinitives (1,2,3,); ability to construct present, past and future verb forms (1,2,3,4,5,6); assignment of the case marker *et* before definite noun phrase direct objects (1,3); use of bound prefixal preposition *le* "to" used to express dative relation *li* "to me" (3); the use of the definite marker *ha* to mark definiteness in nouns (1,4); genitive or possessive marker *šel* (1) and the subordinator *še* (2). The infinitival prefix *le*, which may also take the form of *la* or *li* according to the phonological properties of the verb it precedes, is appropriately used (*li-tfos, li-šon, la-sot* in 1,2,3).

Other features of her early speech include the use of the negative marker *lo*, which precedes the predicate (1); the third feminine singular suffix *-a*, which is used with both the predicate and the genitive particle *šel* to agree with the subject pronoun *hi* "she"; the preposition *im* "with" when used with the first singular pronoun becomes *it-i* (2). This usually appears in children's language at a later age (Berman 1985), and a common developmental error in younger children is the use of *im ani* (*ani* being the subject form of the pronoun). The discourse conjunction *aval* (3) "but," is appropriately used to contrast this utterance with the previous one. The use of *axšav* (3,6) is common in children's language to mark immediate future, consequently the future tense immediately follows.

3   Onset of attrition

The attrition process initially affected the lexicon. At this stage (2;9–3;1), which started three months after initial contact with L2, L2 nominals were inserted at an increasing rate into an L1 syntactic environment. All the features of L1 morphology and syntax acquired by the child and discussed at greater length in the previous section are still present. Typical utterances of this stage that include nominal insertions are illustrated below (7,8). For an analysis of the implications of the nominal insertions for the attrition of the nominal system see Kaufman & Aronoff (1989).

(7)   2;9 *Ima*   *t-oxl-i*   *et*   *ha*-apple   *šel-i.*
            mommy   2.FUT-eat-2fs   OM   the-apple   of-me
            "Mommy, eat my apple."

(8)   3;0 *Šama-t*   *et*   *ha*-noise   *ha-ze?*
            hear.PAST-2fs   OM   the-noise   the-this?
            "Did you hear this noise?"

3.1.   *L2 verbal insertions*

Semitic morphology, especially verb morphology, is characterized by the combination of consonantal verb roots with a small number of fixed derivational templates in which vowels and syllable structure are specified. There are seven such templates in Modern Hebrew, of which five are most common in children's language (Berman 1978, 1985). For example, the root *k-t-v* may occur in the following forms: *katav*, "wrote," *nixtav*, "was written," *(h)ixtiv*, "dictated," *(h)itkatev*, "corresponded." The semantics of the individual templates is a complex matter, which we will not address here. In addition to the templates, there are also affixes, both derivational and inflectional. Verbs in Hebrew are marked for tense – present, past or future – and agree with the subject noun in person, number and gender. Children initially produce the imperative form followed by the infinitive, which requires no person, gender or number marking and is preceded by the infinitival prefix *le, li,* or *la* "to," depending on morphophonological considerations. For example: *le-kapel* "to fold," *li-vdok*, "to check," *la-zuz* "to move." The infinitive is widely used in children's early language possibly because it is uninflected and is salient in the input (Berman 1985).

Code blended insertions of L2 verbs into L1 began just prior to and continued through the bilingual period:

(9)   3;0 *Im   ze   it-laxlex   ani   a-kliyn   ot-am.*
               if   this 3s.FUT-get.dirty   I   1s.FUT-clean OM-they
               "If this gets dirty. I'll clean them."

(10)   3;0 *Ani bala-ti   et   ze   xazak.*
               I   blow.PAST-1s   OM this hard
               (English verb *blow* inflected as a Hebrew verb)
               "I blew this [candle] out hard."

(11)   3;0 *Lo   la*-flaš.
               no   to-flush
               "Don't flush."

(12)   3;1 ... *az   lo   yexol-im le*-step   *al   ha-šeleg*
               ... then no can-mpl to-step on   the-snow
               "... then people can't step on the snow"

The examples above show three different types of L2 verbal insertions. First, (9), an uninflected form of the verb "clean" is blended with the L1 bound morpheme of the first person singular future prefix *a*. Second, (10), the English verb "blow" is treated as a two consonantal Hebrew verb CVCV (like the verbs *kara*, "read," *bala*, "swallow") and is inflected accordingly. These examples suggest that, at this stage, the child still has control of L1 verbal inflection and verb formation rules. The third, and most pervasive type of L2 verbal insertions involves the code blending of the L1 infinitival bound prefix *le*, *li*, or *la* with the stem form of the L2 verb (11, 12). It is unclear how the decision to use one form or another of the infinitival prefix is made by children (to the best of our knowledge, no research has been published on children's acquisition and use of the various forms of the infinitival prefix). In this case of *la*-flaš and *le*-step (11, 12) standard Hebrew phonological rules are violated as the use of *li*- would be required in both cases (cf. *li-floš* "invade," *li-stor* "contradict, slap"). This may suggest that children's use of the infinitival prefix is not motivated by phonological rules but is probably acquired with the verb as one unit. The code blending of the bound infinitival prefix with the English verb, however, suggests that the analysis of the verbal unit as prefix + verb has been made.

Table 12.2 *L2 verbal insertions*

L2 verb	Child's form	Child's L2 verb root
clean	*a*-kliyn	*k-l-n*
blow	bala-*ti*	*b-l-*
flush	*la*-flaš	*f-l-š*
step	*le*-step	*s-t-p*

Table 12.2 illustrates the child's incorporation of L2 verbs into L1 morphosyntactic contexts. The L2 verbs are possibly treated as derivations CVCVC or CVCV and are inflected accordingly.

4   The bilingual period

By the age of 3;1, seven months after initial exposure to L2, the child was what could be termed a balanced bilingual – at ease with the use of both L1 and L2. The period of balanced bilingualism was extremely short and occurred between 3;1 and 3;2. This period was characterized by fluency in both languages. Instances of code switching – intersentential switching from one language to another – were frequent and were made irrespective of the input, which was exclusively Hebrew (in the home environment). Code mixing – intrasentential switching – consisted almost exclusively of L2 words inserted in an L1 environment. This is consistent with the process that had begun during the first stage of attrition. The following is a sample of typical utterances of this period. These are generally longer and reflect the code switching, which is characteristic of this stage in our sample.

(13)   3;1 First I want to bring the paper and then I bring two papers. Where my other papers?[3] *ulay ani e-ese al ze. ani rak e-mca iparon ve-*crayon *ani rak roc-a li-rot efo. ani crix-a iparon, ulay* crayons maybe I 1s. FUT-do on this. I just 1sFUT-find pencil and-crayon, I just want-fs to-see where. I need-fs pencil, perhaps crayons

"Maybe I will do it on this. I'll just find a pencil and a crayon, I just want to see where. I need a pencil, perhaps crayons"

(14)   3;1 I can do myself, and you know what? I can open that.
... *ve-ani   yexol-a   li-sgor   et   ze   gam*
... and-I   can.PRES-fs   to-close   OM   this   also
"... and I can also close this"

(15)   3;1 *At*   *yexol-a*   *la-kaxat* some papers off?
                you   can.PRES-fs to-take   some papers off?
                "Can you take some papers off?"

L1 syntax is still intact. Features that are still present in the child's speech include: the infinitival prefix, correctly realized as *li* (13, 14) and *la* (15) according to the verb stem; the preposition *al* "on" (13); the object marker *et* (14) and appropriate verbal inflections (13, 14, 15).

L1 developmental errors due to overgeneralization, and paradigmatic factors typical in children of up to the age of 4;0 are now featured in the child's speech, attesting to productivity in L1 morphology:

(16)   3;1 *Ani *šata-ti*   *et*   *ze* all up. (correct form: *šati-ti*)
                I   drink.3msPAST-1s OM this all up
                "I drank it all up."
(17)   3;2 *Ze*   *ma*   *še-*raca-ti.*   (correct form: *raci-ti*)
                this   what   that-want.3msPAST-1s
                "This is what I wanted."
(18)   3;2 *Hu*   **irbac*   *li.*   (correct form: *irbic*)
                he   hit.*ms   me
                "He hit me."

In examples (16 and (17), the CC-verb roots *š-t-* "drink" and *r-c-* "want," which should be inflected as *šatiti* and *raciti*, are modeled on the morphologically unmarked third person masculine singular PAST form *šata*, *raca*, and on regular tri-consonantal roots, rendering *šatati* and *racati* (see Table 12.3).

In (18), the correct form *irbic* is unique for the third masculine singular PAST form; all other forms of the past tense for this verb are *irbac* + suffix, hence the paradigmatic error. For a comprehensive and detailed analysis of children's developmental errors see Bar-Adon (1959).

Table 12.3 *Child's 2-C defective verbs modeled on the canonical 3-C pattern*

	Normative form		Child's form
	Canonical 3-C verb	2-C verb	2-C verb
3ms.PAST	CaCaC	CaCa	CaCa
	katav	*šata*	*šata*
1s.PAST	CaCaC-ti	CaCi-ti	CaCa-ti
	katav-ti	*šati-ti*	*šata-ti*

5   The disintegration of L1

The stage which follows the brief period of balanced bilingualism shows the initial signs of the disintegration of L1 morphology and syntax. This is coupled with the child's evident diminishing interest in speaking Hebrew, an unwillingness that was often explicitly expressed during this period in utterances such as *"I don't like to speak Hebrew," "I don't like to speak Hebrew"* (3;4). Linguistically, the child's utterances are becoming increasingly L2 dominant, even though her parents and siblings continue to use L1 exclusively.

5.1   L1 verbal insertions

Verbal insertions at this stage consist of L1 verbs inserted in L2 morphosyntactic contexts, and the disintegration of the L1 system accelerates. The prolific number of L1 verbal insertions made at this stage dramatically demonstrates this disintegration. The verbal insertions consist of deviant but recognizable forms of L1 verbs, devoid of appropriate morphological inflections. These verbs reveal traces of the L1 system:

(19)   3;5 Don't *a-xofef*   *me roš.*
          don't 1s.FUT-wash.ms.PRES   me head
          "Don't wash my head [hair]."

(20)   3;6 I didn't *i-zuz.*
          I didn't *i*-move
          "I didn't move."

(21)   3;6 I *sader-et*   my chair.
          I arrange-fs.PRES (OM) my chair
          "I am arranging my chair."

(22)   3;6 I'm *me-nagev*-ing myself. I want to *i-nagev* myself. Can you *it-labeš* me?
          I'm PRES-dry-ing myself. I want to *i*-dry myself. Can you dress (reflexive) me?
          "I'm drying myself. I want to dry myself. Can you dress me?"

Because of the code mixing in these utterances, we cannot be certain what Hebrew forms should have occurred here. The important point is that the actual forms that the child used would occur in neither normative, nor colloquial Hebrew, and are different from developmental forms used by younger children in the process of acquisition. In order to illustrate the extent to which these verbal forms deviate from normative use; Table 12.4

Table 12.4 *Child's L1 deviant forms*

Child's form	Normative form (predicted from context)
a-xofef	*ta-xfef-i* 2.FUT-wash-2fs
i-zuz	*zaz-ti* move.PAST-1s
sader-et	*me-sader-et* PRES-arrange-fs.PRES
me-nagev-ing	*me-nagev-et* PRES-wipe-fs.PRES
i-nagev	*le-nagev* to-wipe
it-labeš (reflexive)	*le-(h)albiš* to-dress (causative)

presents possible normative forms the child could have used in these contexts, as compared with the forms that were actually used.

The child's L1 inflectional and derivational morphology is disintegrating. Traces of the system are occasionally attested to in prefixes (19, 22) and suffixes (21) that mark tense, person and gender, although it is unclear whether the affixes play a functional role in the utterances. The use of *me-* in the code blended *me-nagev*-ing (22), for example, is redundant when the L2 suffix "-ing" marks the present progressive. It is, however, possible that, as Hebrew has no present progressive, the L2 suffix is juxtaposed to mark the progressive nature of the action, and the L1 *me-* is still functional in marking the present, as is the *-et* (21) in marking person and gender. Her misuse of the derivational templates (22) attests to loss of their morphosemantic distinctions. (For further discussion of children's knowledge of the morphology and semantics of the Hebrew verb system see Berman (1980 and 1982).) It is important to note, however, that her knowledge of the Semitic verb root has not been affected. Although the templates and the inflections are inappropriately used, the verb root is present and is recognizable. This knowledge is retained even in later stages of attrition, as will be illustrated in the next sections.

In sum, the transition period between the use of correctly inflected L1 verbs and the emergence of the idiosyncratic template (see Section 6) is characterized by the use of a multitude of verbal forms which contain traces of L1 verbal morphology that have remained in the system.

6   Reconstruction of L1: the idiosyncratic template

The variety of verbal forms used soon gives way to a single idio-syncratic verbal template, similar to an actual L1 form, adopted by the child and overgeneralized to all L1 verbs. This template is iCaCe(C); for example, *inagev* "wipe." The last consonant may be eliminated if the root is bi-consonantal; for example, *inake* "clean." This idiosyncratic stem has the same form as the colloquial third person masculine singular Future form of the verb template which is called Piel in traditional Hebrew grammar. Since Piel is one of the most productive templates in children's speech and in the colloquial language, the choice of this particular stem form is reasonable. It may also be important to note that in colloquial informal speech, of the kind the child is mostly exposed to as spoken by her sisters, and to a lesser extent by her parents, the prefix *i-* is quite pervasive. The standard Hebrew prefixes *hi-, yi-* and *ye-* appear as *i-* in colloquial speech (see Table 12.5). In addition, in the colloquial speech of preschoolers and school age children, the first person singular Future form of five of the seven templates are also pronounced with an initial *i-* rather than standard *e-* or *a-* (a form which probably originated because of phonetic assimilation with the immediately preceding *i-* of *ani* "I" (Bar-Adon 1959). It is quite possible, then, that the child has selected the one form she found most dominant in the speech of those around her and has overgeneralized it across different verb patterns.

Table 12.5 shows the correspondences between the colloquial prefix *i-* and various standard prefixes. We have omitted obscure forms that are not common in Modern Hebrew, although they may be found in grammars. It is interesting to note that there is no prefix of the form *i-* in the standard language.

Table 12.5 *Saliency of the prefix* i *in colloquial Hebrew*

Prefix	Occurrence	Normative form	Colloquial form
hi	PAST Hif'il	*hixtiv*	*ixtiv*
yi	3m.FUT Kal,	*yixtov*	*ixtov*
	Nifal	*yikatev*	*ikatev*
ye	3m.FUT Piel,	*yesader*	*isader*
	Pual	*yesudar*	*isudar*
e	1s.FUT Kal,	*extov*	*ixtov**
	Nifal	*ešatef*	*išatef**
a	1s.FUT Piel	*asader*	*isader**

* The asterisked forms are common only in the language of pre-schoolers and school children.

The child has, thus, lit on one particular form of the verb which she uses to the exclusion of others, regardless of the context, and regardless of the verbal forms she is exposed to through the input. This form is treated as an L2 stem and conforms to the morphosyntactic L2 environment, while retaining L1 phonetic form. This template becomes very productive in the child's reconstruction of L1. Evidence for this productivity lies in the fact that the template is used even with roots that are uncommonly used in this form in L1 (for example, at 3;9, *išatef*) and, moreover, with roots that never occur in this form in the Hebrew language (for example, at 3;11, *idapes*). Table 12.6 shows the first occurrence of each verb used in the iCaCe(C) form. These forms are shown here without the L2 bound morphemes pervasively used as suffixes to mark person and tense on the idiosyncratic L1 predicate. The most prolific use of these forms occurred between 3;5 and 3;11.

Table 12.6 *The first occurrence of each verb used in the iCaCe(C) form (shown here without L2 suffixation)*

3;1	*ikapel*	fold	3;9	*ikašet*	decorate
3;5	*isaref*	burn		*inake*	clean
	ikarer	cool		*ixabes*	wash
	isader	arrange		*icalcel*	ring
	inagev	dry, wipe		*išatef*	rinse
3;6	*igared*	itch		*ixaded*	sharpen
	isarek	comb		*igalgel*	roll
	inagen	play (instrument)	3;11	*itate*	sweep
3;7	*ikalef*	peel		*isaxek*	play
	ixabet	turn off		*itafer*	sew
	isaben	soap		*idapes*	type
	išaber	break	4;1	*ikalkel*	spoil
	igamer	end		*ivarex*	bless
	ixamem	warm	4;5	*icalem*	take photos
3;8	*ixaten*	marry	4;6	*ibalbel*	be confused
	ixatex	cut			
	ixasot	cover			

In order to get an insight into the emergence of this form, one verb has been selected. The verb root *k-p-l*, "fold" (transitive) and its occurrence in the data are illustrated and discussed here.

(23)   3;1 Hey can you *i-kapel et   ze?   at   ye-xol-a   le-kapel et   ze?*
            Hey can you fold   OM   this? you PRES-can-fs to-fold OM this?
(24)   3;4 Can you *kapel* this?

(25)   3;6 Can you *ikapel* this?
(26)   3;6 I don't want you to *ikapelet*.
(27)   3;8 Look I *ikapel*-ed it nice, right?
(28)   3;8 Can you *ikapel* the blintz for me?
(29)   3;8 No, first i*kapel* it for me.
(30)   3;8 Look at how I *ikapel* it.
(31)   3;9 I want to *ikapel* one.
(32)   3;9 I'm *ikapel*-ing yours and mine, right?
(33)   3;9 I was just *ikapel*-ing them.
(34)   3;11 Look I can *ikapel* this.
(35)   4;4 I'm *ikapel*-ing my shirt. That's how I *ikapel* my shirt.

The first occurrence of this form took place during the bilingual period. The request (23) was initiated in L2 but a switch to L1 occurred at the verb. L2 syntactic rules concerning modals exclude the use of "to" or *le* before the verb. Hence, it is unclear whether the *i* preceding the verb is a compromise between L1 and L2 syntactic rules or whether the third person masculine singular colloquial Piel form was selected here as a stem. The sentence was then repeated in correct L1 form. More productive and frequent use of this form occurred as of 3;4. In (24) the *i* was eliminated. Based on other examples in the data, one explanation that seems plausible is that the *i* was perceived as an infinitive form equivalent to "to" + verb stem, and according to L2 rules its use was inappropriate, as in (24), where the *i* was dropped. Other such examples were the bound stems *sarek* "comb," *xasot* "cover," *sader* "arrange," mostly in use up to age 3;6. As of 3;7 however, the iCaCe(C) form was used almost exclusively.

In the form *ikapelet* (26) it is unclear whether *ikapel-et* represents "verb-fs.PRES," (as in *me-kapel-et* "PRES-fold-fs.") or an unanalyzed verb + object marker with a missing object (as in *kapel et ha-mapit* "fold OM the-napkin"). In either case, traces of the L1 morphosyntactic system are attested. From the age of 3;8 *ikapel* is treated as a realization of the idiosyncratic verb template and is used with appropriate L2 suffixes to convey past tense (27), present tense (30,35) present progressive (32,35), past progressive (33), imperative (29), and infinitive (31).

The following is a sample of typical utterances of this period. The single template of the L1 predicate is now used as an L2 verb and is juxtaposed with L2 suffixes to mark person, number and tense.

(36)   3;7 Look my legs are dry without *inagev*-ing.
                                    dry-ing
(37)   3;7 My room is *isader*-ed.
                        arrange-ed

(38)   3;8 When the light *ixabe-z* I'm going to fall asleep.
                  turn.off-s

(39)   3;9 Lytal finished *inagen*-ing and you didn't *inagen* yet.
                  play-ing (an instrument)   play

(40)   3;9 I *ikalef*-ed them Ornat.
                  peel-ed

(41)   4;0 Daddy, *ixamem* this for me.
                  warm

(42)   4;1 Why does it *igared*? It *igared*-z me.
                  itch   itch-es

(43)   4;4 When it *icalcel*-z I will turn it off.
                  ring-s

The rich L1 derivational and inflectional system has been reduced to a single form. This form, however, is very productive and is pervasively used in the child's system. The form attests to the child's knowledge of the Semitic verb system at this stage of attrition.

7   Conclusion

The longitudinal study of attrition in the fertile mind of a young child has revealed a remarkable ability to accommodate. In the early L1 dominant period, L2 verbs are quite effortlessly adapted to the L1 template system. In the later L2 dominant period, this template system is modified idiosyncratically and without benefit of a direct model, so that L1 verbs may be accommodated in turn to the L2 system. The resulting system, which, while perfectly intelligible to all those in the child's family environment, is entirely her own, is a powerful reminder of the fact that languages are individual creations constrained only by the social need to communicate. Attrition in this circumstance is the incorporation of L1 into L2.

Notes

We would like to thank Ellen Broselow, Robert Hoberman, Elite Olshtain, S.N. Sridhar, and especially Ruth Berman for comments on an earlier version of this paper.
1   The examples selected for this chapter all illustrate utterances that were not elicited directly.
2   We use the following abbreviations PRES – present; FUT – future; OM – object marker; fs – feminine singular; ms – masculine singular; 1s – first person singular; 2fs – second person feminine singular; 3s – third per-

son singular; 3ms – third person masculine singular; fpl – feminine plural; mpl – masculine plural; 1pl – first person plural.
3   We cannot tell whether the absence of the copula here is due to Hebrew interference, English phonology or universal factors (Ferguson 1971; Berman & Grosu 1976).

References

Aronoff, M. 1976. *Word formation in generative grammar*. Linguistic Inquiry monograph No 1. Cambridge, MA: MIT Press.
Aronoff, M. 1983. "A decade of morphology and word formation." *Annual Review of Anthropology* 12: 355–75.
Bar-Adon, A. 1959. "Children's Hebrew in Israel (leshonam hameduberet shel hayladim beisrael)," doctoral dissertation, Hebrew University, Jerusalem, Israel.
Berman, R. A. 1978. *Modern Hebrew Structure*. Tel Aviv, Israel: University Publishing Projects.
     1980. "Child language as evidence for grammatical description: preschoolers' construal of transitivity in the verb system of Hebrew." *Linguistics* 18: 677–701.
     1982. "Verb-pattern alternation: the interface of morpholgy, syntax, and semantics in Hebrew child language," *Journal of Child Language* 9,1:169–191.
     1985. "The acquisition of Hebrew." in D.I. Slobin (ed.), *The crosslinguistic study of language acquisition*. Hillsdale, NJ: Lawrence Erlbaum Associates, 255–371.
Berman, R. A., and A. Grosu. 1976. "Aspects of the copula in Modern Hebrew," in P. Cole. (ed.), *Studies in Modern Hebrew syntax and semantics*. Amsterdam: North Holland, 261–285.
Ferguson, C. 1971. "Absence of copula and the notion of simplicity: a study of normal speech, baby talk and pidgins," in Dell Hymes, (ed.), *Pidginization and creolization of languages*. London: Cambridge University Press.
Kaufman, D., and M. Aronoff, 1989. "Morphological interaction between L1 and L2 in language attrition," in S. Gass and C. Madden, (eds.), *Variations in second language acquisition: Psycholinguistic issues*. Avon, England: Multilingual Matters Limited, 202–215.
Kaufman, D., and S. N. Sridhar. 1986. "The process of becoming a bilingual: simultaneous language loss and language acquisition." Paper presented at LSA/AAAL Annual Conference, New York, NY.
Obler, L. K. 1982. "Neurological aspects of language loss as they pertain to second language attrition," in R.D. Lambert and B.F. Freed, (eds.), *The loss of language skills*. Rowley, MA: Newbury House Publishers, 60–79.
Sridhar, S. N., and K. K. Sridhar. 1980 "The syntax and psycholinguistics of bilingual code mixing," *Canadian Journal of Psycholinguistics* 34, 4: 407–416.
Weltens, B. 1987. "The attrition of foreign language sklls: A literature review," *Applied Linguistics* 8, 1: 22–36.

13 Assessing first language vulnerability to attrition

EVELYN P. ALTENBERG

1 Introduction

This chapter addresses the issue of which aspects of first language grammar are most vulnerable to attrition. Three untimed tasks are used to examine the first language knowledge of two proficient German–English bilinguals for the purpose of outlining methodological approaches to the investigation of this issue. The first experiment is an untimed sentence judgement task which investigates the vulnerability of first language (German) surface word order under the influence of second language (English) word order. The second task, also an untimed sentence judgement task, examines the vulnerability of first language selectional restrictions under the influence of second language idiomatic verb usage. The third task is an untimed fill-in task which assesses the vulnerability of first language gender and pluralization information and the relationship of this information to the factors of frequency and predictability. The experimental data will be useful in drawing preliminary conclusions regarding first language vulnerability to attrition as well as highlighting potentially fruitful areas for future research. Some of the issues for which these types of tasks and their findings have relevance will first be briefly outlined.

The competence/performance issue, of central importance in all psycholinguistic research, is of special significance in research on proficient bilingualism. This is because, on the one hand, the proficient bilingual must have a knowledge of two distinct sets of grammatical rules and forms, one for each of his/her languages, since no two languages are so similar that they can be described by the same descriptively adequate grammar. On the other hand, while the proficient bilingual can certainly function exclusively in one of his/her languages at will, a number of studies have shown that it is difficult, if not impossible, for one language to be completely deactivated while the other is being used. (See, for example, Blair & Harris 1981; Sridhar & Sridhar 1980; and Altenberg & Cairns 1983 for evidence of language interaction in the areas of the bilingual's lexicon, syntax, and phonology, respectively.) Consequently, any bilingual data must be assessed to determine if they result primarily from the bilingual's knowledge of one language, or from the interaction of two systems during on-line language processing.

While processing effects can never be ruled out entirely, some tasks are less prone to show interaction effects than others. Thus, Altenberg & Cairns (1983) found no evidence of language interaction in an untimed, metalinguistic judgement task, but did find evidence of interaction in lexical decision reaction times. They propose that, while the bilingual automatically activates two linguistic systems during processing, a "language check mechanism" is used to ensure that only the output of the contextually appropriate processing system plays a role in the final conceptual representation of input. (See Sridhar & Sridhar 1980 for further support for such a mechanism, as well as research on transfer in second language acquisition, where similar comparison mechanisms have been proposed, e.g. Sharwood Smith 1983.) In the untimed judgement task, subjects presumably had time to interrogate the output of the language check mechanism; in the lexical decision task, they did not. Thus, an untimed judgement task is particularly suited to an investigation of first language rules and forms, as it appears to minimize the effects of language interaction during processing. Further, untimed tasks are likely to minimize performance slips of the tongue (or pen) and, unlike production tasks, judgement tasks have the advantage of telling the researcher not only which structures are possible, but also which are not (Gundel & Tarone 1983). They also allow one to establish degrees of grammaticality. Such a task, with highly proficient bilingual subjects who are given time to think about the well-formedness of stimuli and need not produce sentences but merely evaluate them, decreases the likelihood of finding L1–L2 interaction effects, or, indeed, of finding any incorrect L1 responses at all. Any inappropriate L1 responses that do appear, then, are of particular interest.

Since the two judgement tasks described below were designed to investigate transfer from L2 to L1, two questions dealing with transfer need to be considered: (1) How does the process of transfer operate? and (2) Which aspects of a language are most likely to be transferable?

Both Schachter (1983) and Andersen (1983),rt dealing with second language acquisition, view L1 information as imposing on the learner's L2 acquisition process. That is, they incorporate transfer into a model of learning. As such, their notions of transfer do not extend readily to the area of L1 loss. Corder (1983), on the other hand, suggests that inadequacies in the second language lead to learners borrowing from their first language when necessary, and successful, probably frequent, borrowings ultimately affect the learner's L2 grammar. While Schachter, Andersen, and Corder all limit their claims to second language acquisition, Corder's model can be extended most readily to the domain of first language loss. That is, if one assumes that there is no hypothesis testing in first language attrition because no active learning is taking place, then evidence of the existence of transfer in first language loss provides support for Corder's view of transfer as successful borrowing.

In recent years, researchers have begun exploring the issue of what determines transferability from one language to another, and a number of relevant factors have been proposed. For example, Kellerman (1983) suggests that transfer is more likely to occur if L1 and L2 are perceived as being close (say, Italian and Spanish) than if they are perceived as being distant (for example, English and Chinese). Similarity between specific L1 and L2 structures is apparently a necessary condition for transfer, as shown by a variety of studies (e.g. Cowan 1986; Gass 1983; Weinreich 1953; Wode 1978; and Zobl 1980a). It is important to note that any requirement of similarity between L1 and L2 structures implies that there is a stage during which a comparison of aspects of L1 and L2 is made (Sharwood Smith 1983).

Eckman (1977) discusses the factor of linguistic markedness, while Jordens & Kellerman (1978) and Kellerman (1983) propose that psycholinguistic markedness plays a role in determining transferability. Along these lines, Zobl (1980b) and Sharwood Smith (1983) suggest that those structures which lead to overall processing simplicity will be transferred most readily. Unfortunately, as Sharwood Smith points out, "Without good theories of markedness, we have to resort to ad hoc definitions to suit our current empirical findings" (229). Andersen (1982) further suggests that frequency is a factor which plays a role in transfer. While these constraints on transfer have been proposed primarily to account for the influence of the first language on the second language, they are likely to be equally significant in an investigation of the influence of the second language on the first language. The experiments described below investigate the roles of predictability, frequency, and transfer from L2 in first language attrition.

2 Syntactic judgement task

The purpose of the untimed syntactic judgement task is to determine if the fluent bilingual's knowledge of first language syntactic rules can be altered under the influence of a second language. While Haugen

(1953) suggests that syntax is least likely to be borrowed, Sharwood Smith (1983) reports that the Utrecht Project found syntactic loss in the area of adverbial placement among English speaking children residing in Holland. Similarly, Costello (1978) reports on the partial assimilation to English of three syntactic rules in Southeastern Pennsylvania German. His subjects were adults who acquired English as a second language in school when they were between the ages of approximately five and ten. In the present study, the question is whether any first language syntactic loss can be demonstrated among adults who learned the second language after the critical period and who have maintained high levels of first language proficiency, and, if loss is found, to determine which structures prove to be most vulnerable to transfer from the second language. Note that Gass (1983), Kellerman (1983), and Sharwood Smith (1983) all observe that surface features are involved in syntactic transfer.

2.1   Subjects

Two subjects who were expected to show mild attrition were selected, so that those aspects of grammar which they have lost are likely to be those that are most vulnerable. The subjects are a married couple, both native speakers of German, born in Germany, who have been living in the United States for over forty years. Though they continue to use German with one another on a daily basis, and in informal situations with family and friends, they have not been part of a German-dominant language community for more than forty years. Therefore, their German may be expected to have suffered some attrition. Both subjects demonstrate fluent though non-native use of English, which is used daily in both formal and informal situations, and they are literate in both German and English. Subject A learned English upon her arrival in the United States at age twenty-five. Subject B studied English in school in Germany between the ages of fifteen and sixteen; his English improved upon his arrival in the US at age twenty-nine. Both subjects participated in all three of the tasks described in the paper.

2.2   Materials and procedure

For the syntax task, subjects were asked to evaluate four types of German sentences and four types of English sentences: sentences whose surface word order is the same in English and German (EG) (e.g. *Das ist leicht zu machen, That is easy to do*); sentences whose word order is grammatical in English but ungrammatical in German (E*G) (e.g. **Barbara kann* *lesen hindi, Barbara can read Hindi*); sentences whose word order is grammatical in German but ungrammatical in English (*EG) (e.g. *Barbara kann hindi lesen, *Barbara can Hindi read*); and sentences whose word order is ungrammatical in both English and German (*E*G) (e.g. *Sie wohnt in einem Haus blauen, *She lives in a house blue*). The last group was constructed using Spanish word order so that the sentences, while ungrammatical, would still be linguistically plausible structures. An English version of the syntactic judgement task was included in order to be certain that the relevant English structures are in fact perceived by subjects to be grammatical in English.

An example of each type of structure used in the task is presented overleaf in Table 13.1. There were three tokens for each structure type listed. English sentences were changed slightly (e.g. by using a different noun) so as not to be exact translations of the German sentences. Filler sentences were included to ensure equal numbers of grammatical and ungrammatical sentences in each task. German and English sentences were presented to subjects in a random order, in written form, with at least thirty sentences separating grammatical and ungrammatical versions of the same sentence. Subjects were instructed to indicate each sentence's acceptability on a scale ranging from one (**vollkommen annehmbar, completely acceptable**) to five (**vollkommen unannehmbar, completely unacceptable**). The German sentences were judged first and the English sentences were judged a few days later. In order to establish English norms, two monolingual English subjects were also given the English judgement task. German norms for all tasks were established by reference to literature on German syntax (e.g. Hawkins 1985; Kufner 1962; Lederer 1969) and to German speakers and linguists. Two E*G structures (#4 and #21) are moderately acceptable in German.

2.3   Results and discussion

The overall results for each subject are indicated in Table 13.2 on p. 195. The overall scores reveal that subjects have a firm grasp of syntax in both languages. That is, in each language, grammatical sentences were judged, on the whole, as better than ungrammatical sentences. This finding is not surprising, as one expects syntax to remain largely intact when a language is used on a daily basis.

Scores for the E*G and *EG groups on the German task are of particular interest, as these are the structures with the potential to show English influence. It is clear, by comparing EG and *EG scores, that the ungrammaticality of a structure in English did not affect its status as grammatical

Table 13.1 *Examples of each structure used in the syntactic judgement task*

EG	E*G	*EG
1.	Barbara kann lesen hindi. Mary can read Spanish.	Barbara kann hindi lesen. Mary can Spanish read.
2.	Ich bleibe zu Hause weil es ist kalt. She is staying home because it is hot.	Ich bleibe zu Hause weil es kalt ist. She is staying home because it hot is.
3.	Does he go to the theater?	Geht sie ins Kino? Goes he to the theater?
4.	Die Rolle wurde gesungen von einem Tenor. The role was sung by a baritone.	Die Rolle wurde von einem Tenor gesungen. The role was by a baritone sung.
5.	Der Mann, dessen Gepäck steht da, kommt gleich zurück The woman whose suitcase is standing there, will come right back.	Der Mann, dessen Gepäck da steht, kommt gleich zurück The woman whose suitcase there standing is, will come right back.
6.	Es ist zu spät, zu gehen ins Kino. It is too early to go to the theater.	Es ist zu spät, ins Kino zu gehen. It is too early to the theater to go.
7. Das ist leicht zu machen. This is easy to do.		Das ist in jedem Laden zu finden. This is to find in every supermarket.
8. Die Leute sind nicht da. The boy is not here.	Er nicht arbeitet zu Hause. She does not work at home.	Er arbeitet nicht zu Hause. She works not at home.
9. Komm mit! Come along!		Komm du doch mit! Come you along!
10.	Dieser Anzug trägt gut. This dress wears well.	Dieser Anzug trägt sich gut. This dress wears itself well.
11. Ich lese nicht gerne solchelangen Bücher. He doesn't like to read such long articles.		Solche langen Bücher lese ich night gerne. Such long articles he doesn't like to read.
12. Ich gab der Frau das Buch. He gave the man the letter.	Ich gab das Buch zu der Frau. He gave the letter to the man.	
13. Der Film, den wir gestern Abend gesehen haben, war grossartig. The show that we saw last week was great.	Der Film wir gestern Abend gesehen haben, war grossartig. The show we saw last week was great.	
14. Ich weiss nicht, was ich sagen soll. He does not know what he should say.	Ich weiss nicht, was zu sagen. He does not know what to say.	
15. Er weckt die Kinder auf. She wakes the children up.	Er weckt auf die Kinder. She wakes up the children.	
16.	Wen glaubst du, dass ich gesehen habe? Whom do you think that we have seen?	Was glaubst du, wen ich gesehen habe? What do you think whom we have seen?
17. Auf was wartest du? For what are we waiting?	Was wartest du auf? What are we waiting for?	
18.	Das Mädchen wurde ein Buch gegeben. The boy was given a book.	Dem Mädchen wurde ein Buch gegeben
19. Was für Bücher lesen Sie? What novels do you read?	Was für Bücher sind Sie lesend? What novels are you reading?	
20. Es ist leicht, den Jungen zu sehen. It is easy to see the girl.	Der Junge ist leicht zu sehen. The girl is easy to see.	
21. Wilhelm sah den König und dankte dem König. William saw the king and thanked the king.	Wilhelm sah und dankte dem König. William saw and thanked the king.	

Table continued opposite.

Table 13.1 (*continued*)

E*G*

22. Das Spanisch ist leicht.
    The French is easy.

23. Sie fahren durch das
    Japan.
    They're traveling in the
    France.

24. Sie nicht arbeiten schwer.
    She not works hard.

25. Sie wohnt in einem Haus
    blauen.
    She lives in a house pink.

26. Studieren viel.
    Studies a lot.

27. Sie mich kennen.
    He me knows.

28. Paul mir gab das Geld.
    Paul me gave the book.

29. Den Dienstag gehe ich ins
    Kino.
    The Wednesday I am
    going to the store.

30. Ich kenne nicht zu jemand.
    I don't know to anyone.

31. Die Studenten sind in der
    Klasse von Geschichte.
    The students are in the
    class of mathematics.

32. Ich brauche sechzig und
    sieben Pfennig.
    I need eighty and seven
    cents.

Table 13.2 *Average responses of each subject in the syntactic judgement task*

	EG	E*G	*EG	*E*G
Bilingual subjects				
German				
Subject A	1.06	2.57	1.10	2.88
Subject B	1.00	3.24	1.10	4.12
English				
Subject A	1.26	1.11	2.37	3.06
Subject B	1.06	1.26	3.42	4.51
Monolingual subjects				
English				
Subject C	1.40	1.53	4.67	4.91
Subject D	1.34	1.49	4.67	4.30

in German. Subjects' knowledge of what is grammatical in L1 is firm. However, subjects' knowledge of what is ungrammatical in L1 is somewhat less secure: both subjects rated E*G sentences as slightly better than *E*G sentences, suggesting the influence of English. Their judgements on the English task similarly suggest the influence of German, with English *EG structures rated as more acceptable than *E*G structures. Further, a comparison of bilingual and monolingual English judgements reveals a greater difference between monolingual and bilingual scores for *EG structures than for *E*G structures. These findings all suggest the influence of English and German on one another. (Note that children acquiring a first language also reveal correct knowledge of grammatical sentences but uncertainty regarding ungrammatical sentences (Hakes 1980).) More specifically, a few E*G structures were judged by subjects to be fairly acceptable in German. Acceptability was determined here both by the structure's average rating and by the difference in score between the ungrammatical E*G structure and its EG or *EG grammatical counterpart. Other E*G structures are of special interest because they were judged as strongly unacceptable in German. These two groups of structures, at the extreme ends of the acceptability continuum, are worth noting here, as they provide data on which aspects of syntax are most and least vulnerable to attrition.

Both subjects judged E*G structure #16, which involves the grammaticality of wh-questions with embedding, as fairly acceptable in German. Subject A also judged structure #5, which involves verb position in a relative clause, and #18, which deals with case in a passive sentence, as acceptable. Subject B judged structure #4, involving verb position in a passive sentence, as acceptable. (Structure #4 is acceptable in colloquial German.) Similarly, #21, which involves the grammaticality of conjoined sentences with deletion of identical noun phrases, was judged as acceptable by both subjects, and is considered to be moderately acceptable in German in short sentences. In all these cases, subjects' ratings of the English sentences indicate that they know the E*G structures are grammatical in English. Further, in interviews conducted a few weeks after testing, both subjects stated that all of these E*G structures except #16 were fairly unacceptable in German and expressed surprise at their own responses on the judgement task regarding these structures.

Both subjects rated the following E*G sentences as highly unacceptable in German: #8, involving negative placement; #13, involving sentences where the German relative pronoun is deleted; #17, involving preposition stranding; and #19, which involves the progressive tense. Subject B also judged #12, sentences with to-datives, as highly unacceptable.

In the ungrammatical version of #18, the object in a passive sentence is put in the nominative case; that is, it is treated as a surface subject, as it would be in English, whereas in German the object retains its accusative case in passive structures. The fact that one of the subjects found the E*G sentences of #18 to be fairly acceptable suggests either that case information in general is vulnerable to attrition (which possibility is supported by the acceptability of #21, where case information is lost in conjoined sentences), or that surface grammatical relations are vulnerable to attrition. The acceptability of structures #4 and #21 may be due to the fact that they are somewhat acceptable in German. Their acceptability also suggests that a marginally acceptable L1 structure may become more acceptable if it coincides with an L2 structure. It is important to note here that the constraints on transfer described earlier are not very specific. While one might argue that German structures #4, 5, 16, and 18 are more marked, linguistically and/or psycholinguistically, than their English counterparts, and that the English and German structures are similar to one another in those cases where rule changes occurred, this is nonetheless an ad hoc, after-the-fact description, not an explanation. It leaves unexplained, for example, the fact that Subject A found a change in verb position in relative clauses (#5) acceptable, but not a change in verb position in infinitive clauses (#6).

The data also reveal a great deal of variability from subject to subject. For example, Subject A found *to*-datives (#12) fairly acceptable, while Subject B found them completely unacceptable; Subject B found a change in verb position in passives (#4) more acceptable than did subject A. However, one subject did not show more overall attrition than the other subject. Rather, judgements varied depending upon which structure was being rated. This variability is found here even with subjects whose communication in L1 is predominantly with one another.

It is important to consider two further questions. First, is it the case that the relevant German rule, such as that of verb position in a relative clause, is particularly vulnerable to attrition, or is it the case that the English verb position rule is particularly intrusive? Researchers have taken different stands on this issue: Kellerman (1983), discussing second language acquisition, makes the strong claim that only the guest language (L1), not the host language (L2), plays a role in determining transferability, while Zobl (1980a) suggests that formal features of L2 (the host language) control the activation of transfer from a first language. The second question is: do the relevant E*G structures show the effects of transfer from English, or are the structures showing the effects of universal changes, say of simplification? Future research can address both of these questions, using the sentence judgement task, by including appropriate control groups. In this case, German L1, English L2 speakers could be compared with German L1 speakers with different L2s.

The findings suggest that future research focusing on structures #4, #5, #16, and #18 is likely to be most fruitful. Another possible direction for future research to take is to examine the vulnerability of marginally acceptable L1 structures, perhaps by comparing judgements of marginally acceptable L1 structures that have L2 counterparts with judgements of marginal L1 structures that do not have L2 counterparts.

The experiment described next uses the sentence judgement task to examine the effects of L2 on L1 verb usage.

3   Verb usage task

3.1   *Materials and procedure*

Jordens & Kellerman (1978) investigate the transfer of idiomatic verb uses from the first language to the second language. Ostyn (1972) similarly finds changes in selectional restrictions in American Flemish. In the present experiment, the uses of two verbs were investigated using a variation of a Jordens & Kellerman task. The verbs *nehmen* "take" and *brechen* "break" were selected as these verbs were used by Jordens & Kellerman. Eighteen sentences using *brechen* were constructed, half with the verb used in ways that are acceptable in German (e.g. *Sie brechen ihr Versprechen jedesmal* "They are always breaking promises"), and half with the verb used in ways that are likely to be unacceptable in German (e.g. **Wann wird das Wetter brechen?* "When will the weather break?"). Sixteen sentences with *nehmen* were also constructed, half of them with acceptable uses of the verb (e.g. *Der Schneider nahm sein Maß* "The tailor took his measurements") and half with uses likely to be unacceptable in German (e.g. **Nimm Herz!* "Take heart!"). Subjects were asked to rate the acceptability of each German sentence on the same acceptability scale used in the syntax task, with instructions to pay particular attention to the question of whether the verb can be used this way in German. Sentences with *brechen* and *nehmen* were rated separately. Subjects were also asked to indicate, on a three point scale, how certain they were that they understood the English translation of each sentence, and post-test interviews were used to determine whether or not subjects knew the meaning of each English translation. In addition, subjects indicated whether or not English and German translations of the same sentence have the same meaning. The sentences and results are listed in Table 13.3 opposite.

Table 13.3 *Stimuli, verb usage task*

Sentences with *brechen*
Unacceptable German sentences
 1. *Sein Fall wurde von einem Baum gebrochen.* "His fall was broken by a tree." (A)
 2. *Sie brachen ihm die Neuigkeit.* "They broke the news to him." (A, B)
 3. *Er hat seine Verlobung gebrochen.* "He broke off the engagement." (A, B)
 4. *Er ist der Mann, der in Monte Carlo die Bank gebrochen hat.* "He is the man who broke the bank at Monte Carlo." (A, B)
 5. *Der Elektriker hat den Stromkreis gebrochen.* "The electrician broke the electrical circuit." (A, B)
 6. *Wann wird das Wetter brechen?* "When will the weather break?" (A, B)
 7. *Sie brachen ihr Fasten.* "They broke their fast."
 8. *Endlich wurde die feindliche Geheimschrift gebrochen.* "At last they broke the enemy code." (A, B)
 9. *Die Concorde hat die Schallmauer gebrochen.* "The Concorde broke the sound barrier." (B)

Acceptable German sentences
10. *Er brach sich das Bein.* "He broke his leg."
11. *Sie brechen ihr Versprechen jedesmal.* "They are always breaking promises."
12. *Einiges Alkohol war nötig, um das Eis zu brechen.* "A few drinks were needed to break the ice."
13. *Er brach das Schweigen, als er zu sprechen begann.* "He broke the silence when he began speaking."
14. *Ellen brach sein Herz.* "Ellen broke his heart."
15. *Sie brachen das Gesetz.* "They broke the law."
16. *Der Tag brach an.* "Dawn broke."
17. *Bei den Olympischen Spielen brachen die Ostdeutschen einen Rekord.* "At the Olympics, the East Germans broke a record."
18. *Der Sturm brach los.* "The storm broke."

Sentences with *nehmen*
Unacceptable German sentences
 1. *Die Idee hat ihn mit Überraschung genommen.* "The idea took him by surprise." (A)
 2. *Dieser Roman nimmt in Washington platz.* "This novel takes place in Washington."
 3. *Die Kinder nahmen Wechseln.* "The children took turns."
 4. *Er nahm einen Eid vor Gericht.* "He took an oath in court." (A)
 5. *Nimm Herz!* "Take heart!"
 6. *Kannst du einen Wink nehmen?* "Can you take a hint?"
 7. *Nimm Mut!* "Take courage!"
 8. *Es wird mir zu lange nehmen, das zu tun.* "It will take me too long to do that." (B)

Acceptable German sentences
 9. *Er nahm sich die Mühe, ihnen zu helfen.* "He took the trouble to help them."
10. *Er nahm sich ein Zimmer für die Nacht.* "He took a room for the night."
11. *Er nahm ein Bad.* "He took a bath."
12. *Bitte nehmen Sie Platz.* "Please take a seat."
13. *Er nahm das Geld.* "He took the money."
14. *Er nahm sich Zeit, die Arbeit fachgerecht zu machen.* "He took the time to do the job right."
15. *Er nahm einen tiefen Atemzug.* "He took a deep breath."
16. *Der Schneider nahm sein Maß.* "The tailor took his measurements."

Note: Parentheses following translations of unacceptable German sentences indicate which subject, if any, judged that sentence as acceptable in German.

3.2   *Results and discussion*

The results indicate that some unacceptable German verb uses have come to be accepted by the subjects. A verb usage was considered accepted by a subject if it met all three of the following criteria: (1) the sentence was rated as completely acceptable in German; (2) the German and English sentences were judged as meaning the same thing; and (3) subjects indicated, on the questionnaire and in follow-up oral interviews, that they understood the idiomatic meaning of the English sentences. Under these conditions, both subjects judged seven out of the nine ungrammatical German sentences with *brechen* as acceptable in German (though not the same seven sentences). With *nehmen*, however, Subject A judged only two of the eight unacceptable sentences as acceptable in German while Subject B accepted only one.

Thus, there are two findings of interest here. First, the results indicate that verb usage is vulnerable to attrition. Here, uses of verbs which violate German selectional restrictions were considered to be acceptable in German. One direction for future research to take, then, is to examine the vulnerability of selectional restrictions in greater detail. One can speculate that certain restrictions, say abstractness, might be more or less vulnerable than other restrictions, such as animacy. Sentence judgement tasks lend themselves readily to the testing of such hypotheses.

The second finding of interest is that *brechen* was far more vulnerable to attrition than *nehmen*. A possible explanation for this is the greater phonetic similarity between *break* and *brechen* than between *take* and *nehmen*. Haugen (1953) states that "if a native word is similar in sound to a desired foreign word, it is often given meanings of the foreign word" (380). Zobl too (1980a) indicates the importance of morphological similarity in transfer. This explanation assumes that transfer from L2 to L1 is taking place, and, coupled with the findings of the syntax task, supports Corder's view of transfer as simply borrowing.

The third task was used to investigate subjects' knowledge of aspects of first language morphology, with particular attention to the roles of frequency and predictability in attrition.

4   Gender and plural tasks

Word frequency is a well known variable affecting lexical processing. Both Forster's (1976) search model of lexical retrieval and Morton's (1970) logogen model incorporate elements designed to account for the effects of frequency on lexical retrieval. Further, Andersen (1982) suggests that low frequency items will be lost in language before high frequency items. It is reasonable, then, to hypothesize that word frequency plays a role in the retention of information about a word's gender and plural form. (Note, though, that Brown (1973) found that the frequency of morphemes in speech had no effect on the order in which morphemes were acquired by the child during the process of first language acquisition.)

Predictability of form is another factor which may be of relevance to attrition. German has a variety of ways to pluralize nouns. For example, the *-(e)n* suffix is used to form the plural for all nouns ending with the suffix *-keit* (e.g. *Kleinigkeit, Kleinigkeiten*), while most one syllable masculine nouns have *-e* plurals (e.g. *Hund, Hunde*). While some nouns follow rule governed patterns of this type, others do not. Since overgeneraliz-ation of regular rules to irregular forms is well documented for both first and second language acquisition (e.g.Dale 1976; Richards 1974), it seems reasonable to predict that irregular plural forms are more likely to be forgotten than regular, predictable plural forms. Thus, the expectation here is that idiosyncratic information regarding pluralization, which in-formation must be part of an individual noun's lexical representation, will be lost earlier than pluralization information involving morphological rules.

4.1   Materials and procedure

A list of high frequency words and a list of low frequency words were constructed. Each list was further subdivided into nouns with pre-dictable plural forms and nouns with unpredictable plural forms. Word frequency was established using Meier's (1964) word frequency count for German. Meier lists, in order of frequency, the eight thousand most frequent words in the corpus of over ten million words. Both the high and low frequency words used in this task were selected from this list in order to ensure that even the low frequency test items were likely to be known to the subjects. There were 56 high frequency words, ranging in fre-quency from 14,529 to 700 occurrences in the corpus, and 56 low fre-quency words, ranging in frequency from 162 to 101 occurrences. There were 20 feminine, 16 masculine, and 20 neuter high frequency words, and 19 feminine, 16 masculine, and 21 neuter low frequency words. Words whose gender is predictable (e.g. by meaning or by suffix) were not used. As far as possible, equal numbers of concrete and abstract words were included in each category.

The nouns fall into two groups with regard to the formation of the plural: 34 high frequency words (e.g. *Tag* "day") and 22 low frequency words (e.g. *Pfeil* "arrow") have predictable plural forms, and 22 high frequency words (e.g. *Gesicht* "face") and 34 low frequency words (e.g. *Beitrag* "contribution") have unpredictable plural forms. Predictability was based on Lederer (1969) and Bauer & Bauer (1967). Subjects were presented, in a random order, with the singular form of each noun, and asked to fill in, in the spaces provided, each noun's gender (*der*, *die*, or *das*) and its plural form. Post-test interviews with subjects indicated that they knew the meanings of all but one of the nouns on which they made errors; this noun was eliminated from the analysis and the scores adjusted accordingly.

4.2   Results

The results are indicated on Table 13.4. What is immediately striking is that far fewer errors were made regarding gender than plural information, even though gender was unpredictable in all cases. While the small number of overall gender errors makes it difficult to draw further conclusions regarding frequency, the number of gender errors for

Table 13.4 *Percentage of inccorect responses, gender and plural task*

| | Gender (all forms were unpredictable) | |
	High frequency words	Low frequency words
Subject A	2	9
Subject B	2	0

| | Plural | | | |
| | High frequency words | | Low frequency words | |
	Predictable	Unpredictable	Predictable	Unpredictable
Subject A	3	14	14	21
Subject B	3	5	5	9

| | Mean Plural Scores, Subjects A and B | |
	High frequency words	Low frequency words
Predictable	3	9.5
Unpredictable	9.5	15

Subject A is greater for low than for high frequency words. (Subject B had only one error on gender.)

Turning now to the plural forms, one finds more errors among low frequency than among high frequency words. Further, there are more errors for unpredictable nouns than for nouns whose forms are rule governed. The most errors were found among low frequency, unpredictable plural forms.

The findings lead to a number of tentative conclusions. First, frequency appears to be a factor in the vulnerability of lexical information to attrition. Second, unpredictability appears to be an additional factor leading to loss. In this case, an unpredictable plural form is presumed to be part of the lexical representation of an individual word, while a predictable plural form follows from the application of morphological rules. Thus, idiosyncratic lexical information may be more prone to attrition than morphological rules. What is surprising is that even predictable forms were subject to error. The further investigation of frequency and predictability as factors in language loss appears to be a fruitful direction for future research to take.

The findings also indicate that the attrition process is selective. Not all lexical information is equally susceptible to loss, as evidenced by the greater number of plural over gender errors. Since, as discussed above, researchers have suggested that L1 and L2 similarity is a necessary condition for transfer, one can speculate that German gender may be less vulnerable to attrition under the influence of English because English nouns have no gender (H. S. Cairns, personal communication). Selectivity is further apparent with individual words as well as overall: some words showed loss only of gender information (e.g. *Prozent* ''percent'', Subject A); many showed loss only of plural information (e.g. *Paradies* ''paradise'', Subject B).

5   Discussion and conclusion

Since these three tasks were preliminary studies, their findings must be interpreted cautiously and their limitations are obvious: future research of this type will require more subjects, more tokens, and possibly a monolingual German control group (although, in this case, one could not be certain that the judgements of monolingual German speakers today would parallel those that would have been made by these subjects forty years ago). Nonetheless, some tentative conclusions are possible.

It is clear that judgement tasks are useful in discovering areas of first language loss. For these subjects, while the tasks revealed that most L1 knowledge remained intact, there were changes in some syntactic rules which may be due to transfer from the second language. However, no proposed constraints on transfer are specific enough to account for these changes. The tasks also revealed changes in L1 verb usage under the influence of L2, and support the notion that such changes are more likely to occur in cases where L1 and L2 verbs are phonetically similar. The occurrence of such transfer in L1 loss lends support to Corder's view of transfer as borrowing, and does not support any model in which transfer is incorporated solely into the language learning process. The fill-in task reveals the loss of plural information and the possible loss of gender information. The suggestion that L1 and L2 similarity is a necessary condition for transfer is supported by the greater vulnerability of plural over gender information to attrition. Frequency and unpredictability of forms appear to play an important role in the loss of such information. Finally, all three tasks reveal variability of loss among subjects, tasks, forms, and structures.

Note

My thanks to Edward G. Fichtner, Harry Lederer, and Dana McDaniel for essential information regarding the facts of German, as well as for many helpful comments. Thanks also to Helen Smith Cairns and Carolyn Sobel for many helpful comments and suggestions. Special thanks to my subjects for their participation in this study.

References

Altenberg, E. P., and H. S. Cairns. 1983. "The effects of phonotactic constraints on lexical processing in bilingual and monolingual subjects," *Journal of Verbal Learning and Verbal Behavior* 22: 174–188.

Andersen, R. W. 1982. "Determining the linguistic attributes of language attrition," in R. D. Lambert and B. F. Freed (eds.), *The loss of language skills*. Rowley, MA: Newbury House Publishers.

Andersen, R. W. 1983. "Transfer to somewhere," in Gass and Selinker (eds.), 177–204.

Bauer, E. W., and B. Bauer. 1967. *Lebendiges Deutsch*. New York: Holt, Rinehart and Winston.

Blair, D., and R. J. Harris. 1981. "A test of interlingual interaction in comprehension by bilinguals," *Journal of Psycholinguistic Research* 10: 457–467.

Brown, R. 1973. *A first language: the early stages.* Cambridge, MA: Harvard University Press.

Corder, S. P. 1983. "A role for the mother tongue," in Gass and Selinker (eds.), 85–97.

Costello, J. 1978. "Syntactic change and second language acquisition: the case for Pennsylvania German," *Linguistics* 213: 29–50.

Cowan, J. R. 1986. "Toward a psychological theory of interference in second language learning," in B. W. Robinett and J. Schachter (eds.), *Second language learning.* Ann Arbor: The University of Michigan Press.

Dale, P. S. 1976. *Language development.* New York: Holt, Rinehart and Winston.

Eckman, F. R. 1977. "Markedness and the contrastive analysis hypothesis," *Language Learning* 27(2): 315–330.

Forster, K. I. 1976. "Accessing the mental lexicon," in R. J. Wales and E. C. T. Walker (eds.), *New approaches to language mechanisms.* Amsterdam: North-Holland.

Gass, S. 1983. "Language transfer and universal grammatical relations," in Gass and Selinker (eds.), 69–84.

Gass, S., and L. Selinker (eds.). 1983. *Language transfer in language learning.* Rowley, MA: Newbury House Publishers.

Gundel, J. K., and E. E. Tarone. 1983. "'Language transfer' and the acquisition of pronominal anaphora," in Gass and Selinker (eds.), 281–296.

Hakes, D. 1980. *The development of metalinguistic abilities in children.* New York: Springer Verlag.

Haugen, E. 1953. *The Norwegian language in America.* Philadelphia, PA: University of Pennsylvania Press.

Hawkins, J. A. 1985. *A comparative typology of English and German.* Austin: University of Texas Press.

Jordens, P., and E. Kellerman. 1978. "Investigations into the strategy of transfer in second language learning," *AILA Congress,* August 1978.

Kellerman, E. 1983. "Now you see it, now you don't," in Gass and Selinker (eds.), 112–134.

Kufner, H. L. 1962. *The grammatical structures of English and German.* Chicago: The University of Chicago Press.

Lederer, H. 1969. *Reference grammar of the German language.* New York: Charles Scribner's Sons.

Meier, H. 1964. *Deutsche Sprachstatistik.* Hildesheim: Georg Olms Verlagsbuchhandlung.

Morton, J. 1970. "A functional model for memory," in D. A. Norman (ed.), *Models of human memory.* New York: Academic Press.

Ostyn, P. 1972. "American Flemish: a study in language loss and linguistic interference," doctoral dissertation, University of Rochester, *Dissertation Abstracts International* 33/05: 2356-A.

Richards, J. C. 1974. "A non-contrastive approach to error analysis," in J. C. Richards (ed.), *Error analysis.* London: Longman.

Schachter, J. 1983. "A new account of language transfer," in Gass and Selinker (eds.), 98–111.

Sharwood Smith, M. 1983. "On first language loss in the second language acquirer: problems of transfer," in Gass and Selinker (eds.), 222–231.

Sridhar, S. H., and K. K. Sridhar. 1980. "The syntax and psycholinguistics of bilingual code mixing," *Canadian Journal of Psychology* 34: 407–416.

Weinreich, U. 1953. *Languages in contact*. The Hague: Mouton.

Wode, H. 1978. "Developmental sequences in naturalistic L2 acquisition," in E. Hatch (ed.), *Second language acquisition*. Rowley, MA: Newbury House.

Zobl, H. 1980a. "The formal and developmental selectivity of L1 influence on L2 acquisition," *Language Learning* 30(1): 43–57.

Zobl, H. 1980b. "Developmental and transfer errors: their common bases and (possibly) differential effects on subsequent learning," *TESOL Quarterly* 14(4): 469–479.

14 Compensatory strategies of child first language attrition

DONNA TURIAN AND EVELYN P. ALTENBERG

1 Introduction

A growing interest in the area of language loss or attrition has been seen in recent years (e.g. Lambert & Freed 1982; Seliger 1984). However, relatively little research has been devoted to the phenomenon of first language loss in young children. In this chapter, we describe the attrition of a young child's first language, focusing in particular on the question: How does the child first language attriter compensate for native language deficiencies? Our data will also be used to address a number of pertinent ancillary questions: (1) Does the use of certain compensatory strategies indicate that the child has a conscious awareness of language loss? (2) Are the compensatory strategies used by first and second language attriters culture and language bound?, and, especially, (3) Are the compensatory strategies used by the child first language attriter the same as those used by child and adult second language learners? If children are found to use the same compensatory strategies as adults, then this fact would suggest that the use of these strategies is not dependent upon advanced cognitive development. Further, if the same compensatory strategies are used in coping with language loss as with language acquisition, the implication is that the cause of incomplete linguistic knowledge (here, the process of acquisition versus attrition) is not a factor in selecting the strategies that are used to cope with it.

Compensatory strategies are described by Tarone (1981) as those strategies used by the second language speaker when he/she desires to communicate a particular meaning to a listener but believes there is a lack in his/her second language linguistic system. We expand this definition to include a lack in the speaker's first language linguistic system.

A number of typologies of the compensatory strategies used by child and adult second language acquirers have been devised (e.g. Tarone 1981; Bialystok 1983; Faerch & Kasper 1980). We will briefly describe here a few relevant studies and some of the pertinent compensatory strategies which these studies observed. (The interested reader is referred to

Poulisse, Bongaerts & Kellerman 1984 for a comprehensive review of typologies of compensatory strategies.)

Bialystok (1983) distinguishes between L1 and L2 based strategies. Her high school and adult subjects, speaking in L2, resorted to the L1 based strategies of language switching, foreignizing (applying L2 morphology and/or phonology to L1 lexical items), and transliteration (''the use of L2 lexicon and structure to create a usually non-existent literal translation of an L1 item or phrase''; Bialystok 1983; 106). They resorted to the L2 based strategies of word coinage, description (i.e. circumlocution), and semantic contiguity (use of a similar but inexact L2 lexical item when the correct item is not known to the speaker).

Haastrup and Phillipson (1983) investigated the compensatory strategies used by Danish high school students who were studying English. They found the L1 based strategies of borrowing, anglicizing, and literal translation, and the L2 based strategies of generalization, paraphrase, and word coinage. The cooperative strategy of appealing for assistance was used to different degrees by learners.

Galvan and Campbell (1979) studied two children in the Culver City immersion program. They found that a non-native Spanish speaking child, who was acting as an interpreter for a monolingual English speaking adult, heavily used circumlocution and paraphrasing (L2 based strategies). They also found syntactic constructions in L2 based on the stronger language: *Ahora mi mama traeme a la escuela* ''Now my mom brings me to school.'' Here the Spanish pre-verbal placement of the pronoun, *me trae*, is replaced by the English word order, ''brings me.''

Schachter (1974), in her study of English relative clause usage in adult ESL students, found that avoidance was used to deal with a difficult L2 structure. And Grosjean (1982) concludes that the avoidance of difficult words and constructions in the weaker language is found repeatedly in bilingual children. Strictly speaking, as Poulisse *et al.* point out, avoidance is not a compensatory strategy since it does not, in fact, compensate for a linguistic deficiency. We would also not wish to include it under the umbrella term ''communication strategy,'' as has been proposed by Poulisse *et al.*, since it is not a strategy used to enhance communication, although their use of the term ''message adjustment strategy'' seems reasonable. Nonetheless, avoidance is not unlike the strategies outlined above in that it is used by individuals to cope with incomplete linguistic knowledge. For this reason and for the sake of simplicity, we will continue to refer to all of our subject's strategies, including avoidance, as compensatory strategies.

2   Subject

The subject is the first author's son Joseph. Joseph simultaneously acquired Russian and English from birth, the parents using Ronjat's (1913) "une personne, une langue" strategy. The father spoke exclusively Russian inside and outside the home to Joseph and the monolingual mother spoke English. When Joseph was six months old, the mother returned to work full time, and a monolingual Russian babysitter cared for him. By the age of three and one half, Joseph had acquired Russian as his preferred and dominant language. During his solitary play, he would speak aloud to himself in Russian. When he was overheard talking in his sleep, it was in Russian. Russian speaking peers were chosen to interact with him, and the language used was Russian. Thus, by age three, Joseph was a non-balanced bilingual: his English was halting; his Russian was proficient.

The mother went on sabbatical from her work when Joseph was 3:6, and consequently the Russian speaking primary caretaker was replaced by Joseph's English-speaking mother. There were additional abrupt changes in Joseph's life causing restriction in the use of L1: a family move to a more monolingual English suburban area; half-day attendance five days a week by Joseph at a nursery school in which L2 (English) was used; activities such as weekly gymnastics classes, puppet shows, plays, interacting with new friends, and seeing videotapes daily in which L2 was exclusively used. Factors remaining the same were that the father continued to speak only Russian to Joseph within and outside the home, and also read nightly from Russian books to Joseph. Thus, L1 input and exposure decreased from eight hours a day to one hour, when the father returned home from work. On weekends, the input and exposure to Russian remained the same. The child's attitude towards Russian continued to be positive. He expressed the following remarks to a new acquaintance: "My father's name is Gresha." "My father was born in Russia." "My father speaks Russian." "I speak Russian and English." Joseph also commented, "Mommy, I wish you spoke Russian. Then you could teach other people how to speak Russian" (age 3:9).

3   Methods

The underlying assumption upon which this study is based is that restriction in language input and use "leads to reduction in linguistic form and the creation of gaps in the individual's linguistic repertoire" (Andersen 1982: 87). Clark (1982) appropriately suggests that, for the purpose of studying language change, at least two measurement occasions are needed to establish the nature, direction, and extent of any change in performance. Gardner (1982) further emphasizes the need for multiple measures of language competence. He refers to achievement assessment of two different times, with an incubation period between them; the incubation period is that time during which previously acquired language is either strengthened or reduced.

Time 1 in this longitudinal study involved a period during which Joseph's linguistic proficiency in Russian prior to attrition could be assessed. It is important to note that such an assessment of language abilities is more essential for the child L1 attriter than for the adult L1 attriter, since for the typical adult a certain level of first language proficiency can be assumed. The Time 1 data were obtained by videotaping Joseph in a variety of natural situations, when he was 3:0 to 3:7 years of age. The videotaping took place in both his and his grandparents' home, with family members and friends present and participating. Time 2 data were obtained when Joseph was 4.3 and 4.4 years of age. The data serve a dual purpose: to document his attrition in Russian, and to reveal the compensatory strategies that he used to overcome L1 deficits. Time 2 data were obtained in a number of ways. First, the interaction between Joseph and a sixty-year-old native Russian monolingual speaker was tape recorded. Joseph was brought to the speaker's home and was told that she would watch him for a short time. The mother then left for one half hour and during that time, Joseph, if he wanted to communicate, had to use Russian. Additional Time 2 data were obtained by observations of Joseph communicating with his father. Unexpected data were elicited when Joseph spontaneously created a game in which the mother was to ask him in English how to say something in Russian.

Researchers have used a variety of procedures to identify the use of a compensatory strategy. For example, Ervin (1979) compares a learner's attempts to convey the same meaning in both L1 and L2. Others, for example Tarone (1977) and Poulisse *et al.* (1984), use introspective techniques such as asking the learner where he/she experienced a problem. These two techniques are not possible here due to the subject's young age and to the natural approach used to collect the data. Consequently, we rely primarily on two methods in identifying compensatory strategies: (1) a comparison of Time 1 and Time 2 data, and (2) an analysis of the Time 2 data themselves, as the data are characterized by cues such as false starts, hesitations, and overt comments. Furthermore, given the limited nature of our data, we are assuming for both Time 1 and Time 2 data that Joseph's correct use of an item or structure signifies his acquisition of that item. That is, we are assuming that there are no covert errors (Corder 1971).

4   Results

4.1   Russian language abilities prior to attrition

The Time 1 data appear in the Appendix at the end of this chapter. Briefly, the data at Time 1 are characterized by correct use of infinitives and correct use of present tense forms. Negatives are used correctly. Nouns are appropriately declined in the nominative, genitive, accusative, and dative cases, and adjectives are appropriately declined in the masculine nominative case. (Only these cases are used by Joseph in the Time 1 data.) The few occurrences of conjunctions, prepositions, and adverbs are all used correctly. One sentence (Time 1 #37), while technically grammatical, is nonetheless almost unintelligible, probably because of the difficult concept which Joseph wanted to express. (He wanted to say, "Can you make me look into the camera and see myself?," thinking that he could simultaneously be behind the camera and in front of it while having his picture taken.) Thus, Time 1 data reveal fluent, fluid, and grammatical use of Russian.

4.2   Russian language abilities after attrition

The Time 2 data also appear in the Appendix. Before dealing with the central issue of compensatory strategies, it is necessary to establish that by Time 2, language loss had indeed occurred. Attrition is seen, for example, in the loss of nominative–accusative control. Compare Time 1 #21 and #63, where the accusative suffix correctly appears in Joseph's speech, with Time 2 #12, #18, #34, and #55, where the accusative suffix is incorrectly replaced by the nominative singular form. Attrition can also be seen in a comparison of verb forms at Time 1 and Time 2. At Time 1, the present tense form is correctly supplied in #5, #21, #25, #31, and #37, while an incorrect form is used for the present tense at Time 2 #28 and #55 (although a correct present tense suffix is seen at Time 2 #32).

Further evidence of attrition is seen in Time 2 #14, #16, #18, and #102. Here Joseph responds "I forgot" when asked to say particular items in Russian. This indicates that Joseph believes he previously knew these Russian items.

Finally, what is most salient in even a brief comparison of Joseph's Time 1 and Time 2 data is that the Time 2 data are characterized by a reduced ability to be quick and easy and expressive. There are "more frequent hesitations, pauses, repairs, false starts, etc. than an LC [language competent] of the same language" would have (Andersen 1982: 112).

See, for example, the use of fillers in Time 2 #65 and #71, and a false start in Time 2 #110.

We turn now to an examination of those strategies which Joseph used to compensate for his language loss.

4.3   Compensatory strategies

We found compensatory strategies of three general types: interlingual strategies, intralingual strategies, and discourse strategies. While Bialystok (1983), as indicated above, distinguishes between L1 and L2 based strategies, we prefer the terms interlingual and intralingual strategy, as used by Poulisse *et al.* (1984), because in the acquisition literature, L1 is the stronger and L2 the weaker language, whereas in this study of first language attrition, L1 is the weaker and L2 the stronger language. On the other hand, the terms inter- and intralingual strategy, as defined below, are more general, and hence more useful in allowing us to compare attrition strategies to acquisition strategies.

In the discussion which follows, each type of strategy will be defined. Unfortunately, as Poulisse *et al.* (1984) point out, a plethora of clear and unclear definitions, synonyms, and near synonyms exists in the literature dealing with compensatory strategies. Consequently, wherever relevant and appropriate, we shall use those terms and definitions already proposed in the literature.

4.3.1   Interlingual strategy

"A strategy which results in the interpolation of another language, either the learner's native language or another foreign language" (Poulisse *et al.* 1984). We would omit the word "foreign" from the definition above, to allow for the inclusion of other second or native languages.

(a) **Code switching**: The alternation of two languages (Fallis 1976).

Joseph code switches in both the Time 1 and Time 2 data. There are, however, important differences between the switches before and the switches after attrition. At Time 1, #7, #14, #51, and #63, Joseph appropriately code switches in order to address the listener in his/her native language. He occasionally, though rarely, switches to English when speaking with his bilingual father (Time 1 #1, #31, and #63). In these cases, code switching is apparently used for emphasis, a rhetorical device for which code switching is commonly used by proficient bilingual speakers. (See, for example, Fallis 1976.) Note that out of Joseph's twenty-six Time 1 utterances, there are only seven instances of code switching, all of them appropriate.

A different picture emerges with code switching at Time 2. What is most striking is that Joseph continuously switches into English when addressing a monolingual Russian speaker. In fact, out of Joseph's thirty-two utterances in this particular conversation, there are nineteen utterances which contain at least one switch from Russian to English, and many of these contain numerous switches. The switches described here are unrelated to topic, interlocutor, or environment, and appear to be manifestations of language loss. Seliger (1984) suggests that language attrited speakers code switch even in the presence of a monolingual speaker who is unable to understand the switched elements. The switches in additional Time 2 data further indicate that they are qualitatively different from the Time 1 switches. There are two switches which occur when Joseph is speaking to his father. The first, Time 2 #3, appears to be motivated solely by linguistic need. The second, Time 2 #8, is used to request assistance in saying *baked apple* in Russian.

Thus, code switching at Time 1 is used by Joseph in order to address an individual in his/her L1, or for emphasis. Further, it is rarely used. At Time 2, code switching is basically used as a strategy for coping with an inability to say something in Russian. As such, it is used frequently and relied upon heavily.

(b) **Lexical borrowing**: Borrowing "lexical items from another language, usually adapting the lexical item to the phonological, lexical, semantic, and morphosyntactic structure of the borrowing language" (Andersen 1982).

It is important to note that not all the lexical items to be discussed here and below appear both in Joseph's Time 1 and Time 2 data. Consequently, we cannot be certain whether the lexical strategies noted are triggered by Time 2 attrition or lack of acquisition at Time 1.

Joseph used *basement* and *name* as Russian words, adapting their pronunciation as follows: /bésmInter/ (Time 2 #9) and /námʌ/ (Time 2 #24).

(c) **Syntactic transfer**: Syntactic constructions based on the syntax of another language.

Prescriptively, in English, *That is I* is correct and not *That is me*. However, Joseph, as many other English speakers do, says *That is me*. In Russian, this option is not available and only "That is I," the nominative, is used. Joseph, nonetheless, said in Russian "That is me" (Time 2 #67). This error clearly suggests transfer from English. His incorrect use of the accusative in place of the nominative is particularly striking here, since the Time 2 data, as noted above, are characterized elsewhere by incorrect use of the nominative case rather than the accusative.

Transfer from English is also seen in Time 2 #24, where Joseph, instead of using the Russian idiom "How are you called?," uses English syntax and says in Russian "What is your name?"

4.3.2 Intralingual strategies

"A strategy occurring in L1 and L2 speech, the use of which is not bound to the particular linguistic form of a given language, but reflects general approaches to solving linguistic problems" (Poulisse *et al.* 1984).

(a) **Analogical leveling**: "A highly regular form or construction will be chosen to replace an irregular form or construction" (Andersen 1982: 103).

Analogical leveling is seen in Joseph's incorrect usage of the infinitive form with the verbs "to shave" (Time 2 #3) and "to sleep" (Time 2 #28). Both of these are irregular verbs which should have been in their present tense forms.

(b) **Lexical innovation**: The creation of new lexical items (Andersen 1982).

Lexical innovation occurred when Joseph combined *medvedi* "bears" and *deti* "children" to create *medvedeti* "bear children," meaning "baby bears" (Time 2 #78).

(c) **Approximation**: "The use of a single target language vocabulary item or structure, which the learner knows is not correct, but which shares enough semantic features in common with the desired item to satisfy the learner" (Poulisse *et al.* 1984).

In Time 2 #71, Joseph used a related but incorrect word, *smotrish* "to look" instead of *vidish* "to see." Joseph also replaced *babushka* /bábʌ ška/ "old woman" with *babochka* /bábə tška/ "butterfly" (Time 2 #90). This, however, is probably not a lexical error so much as it is a pronunciation error, since incorrectly inserting the /t/ in "old woman" will change the word to sound like "butterfly."

4.3.3 Discourse strategies

We suggest the following definition: language based strategies which are not intralingual or interlingual. The speaker steps away from a manipulation of linguistic structure and towards a strategy that is focused on the speaker/listener interaction.

(a) **Overt comments**: A comment made by the speaker regarding a linguistic deficiency.

Joseph often overtly commented on his linguistic inadequacies at Time 2: *I forgot what you call him* (Time 2 #102); *I forgot* (Time 2 #14, #16, and #18); *Only* morkovka *I can say* (Time 2 #34).

(b) **Appeal for assistance**: "The learner asks for the correct term" (Poulisse *et al.* 1984).

There were several occasions on which Joseph appealed for assistance: *Papa, how do you say baked apple in Russian?* (Time 2 #8); *How do you say tape in Russian?* (Time 2 #88); and *Papa, how do you say toothbrush in Russian?* (Time 2 #56).

(c) **Deliberate wrong answer**: Interestingly, there were three occasions when Joseph clearly did not know a particular word in Russian but deliberately gave a wrong answer by using English (Time 2 #30, #44, and #52). Donna: *How do you say how in Russian?* Joseph: *How, the same way you say it in English.* D: *Tooth.* J: *Tooth, the same way you say it in English.* D: *Foot.* J: *Foot, the same way you say it in English.* It is important to note that Joseph was not treating these words as lexical borrowings, because the phonology used here was English, not Russian.

(d) **Avoidance**: "A strategy of getting around target language rules or forms which are not yet an established part of the learner's competence" (Poulisse *et al.* 1984). (We would delete the word *yet* here, in order to make the definition applicable to language attrition.)

Joseph used a variety of avoidance techniques, ranging from changing the topic to no verbal response at all. For example, Joseph changed the topic in Time 2 #118, when he asked, "Where is my mother?" This question did not naturally follow from the preceding utterance, in which he had commented that he had the same clock at home. Joseph appears to be entirely abandoning any attempts to produce Russian utterances in Time 2 #118, when he asks, "Will you read to me?" and then begins singing. Here, Joseph expects the answer to be affirmative, and indicates not only by his question but also by his singing a desire to distance himself from any further prospective conversation. He wants the woman to read to him, and he wants to listen. Similarly, Joseph indicates, in Time 2 #106, that he is tired of playing the Russian question and answer game by saying, in English, *I think I'm tired of doing this.* Finally, Joseph uses an extreme avoidance strategy in Time 2 #75, where he does not respond at all to questions addressed to him in Russian.

5   Conclusion

We began this paper by raising the question: How does the child first language attriter compensate for native language deficiencies? We found compensatory strategies of three types: interlingual strategies, intralingual strategies, and discourse strategies. The interlingual strategies are code switching, lexical borrowing, and syntactic transfer. The intralingual strategies are analogical leveling, lexical innovation, and approximation. Finally, the discourse strategies are overt comment, appeal for assistance, deliberate wrong answer, and avoidance.

The ancillary questions raised at the beginning of this paper can also now be addressed. First, the data indicate that the three-year-old child can have a conscious awareness of language loss. Joseph's desire to avoid continued conversation in Russian indicates his awareness of discomfort with the situation (though this does not necessarily imply that he was conscious of what was causing his discomfort). However, Joseph does respond *I forgot* when asked to say particular items in Russian. It is clear here that Joseph believes that loss has occurred.

Second, the compensatory strategies observed in this and other studies do not appear to be language bound and may not be culturally bound, since they have been observed with speakers of a variety of first languages, e.g. Danish (Faerch & Kasper 1980), Russian (Joseph), Hungarian (Varadi 1973, as cited in Poulisse *et al.* 1984), English (Bialystok & Frohlich 1980).

Third, we were particularly interested in observing whether the same strategies are used in child first language loss as in child and adult second language acquisition. Table 14.1 (opposite) lists all the strategies used by Joseph and cites child and adult L2 acquisition studies which have observed the same strategies. It is clear from Table 14.1 that L2 acquirers use the same intralingual and interlingual strategies as does Joseph. (Note that the strategies used by Joseph are a subset of the strategies which have been reported in the L2 literature.) With respect to the discourse strategies, we find appeals for assistance and avoidance used in second language acquisition. However, it should be noted that in the Schachter study, subjects were avoiding a specific syntactic construction in the weaker language, while Joseph was avoiding the use of the weaker language altogether. We have informally noted numerous occasions in which adult second language acquirers have made overt comments regarding their L2 linguistic deficiencies, and speculate that occasionally, though rarely, deliberate wrong answers may be given by adult learners to compensate for a lack of L2 knowledge.

Thus, on the whole, the data support the conclusion that the same compensatory strategies are used in first language attrition as in second language acquisition, and that children use basically the same compensatory strategies as do adults. Therefore, these findings suggest that the cause of incomplete linguistic knowledge (process of acquisition versus attrition) is not a factor in selecting the strategies that are used to cope with the deficiency. The findings also imply that the cognitive immaturity

Table 14.1 *Compensatory strategies used by Joseph*

I INTRALINGUAL STRATEGIES

1 **Code switching**
Bialystok 1983 – adults
Faerch & Kasper 1980 – ages 12 to adult
2 **Borrowing**
Bialystok 1983 – adults
Faerch and Kasper 1980 – ages 12 to adult
Haastrup & Phillipson 1983 – adults
3 **Syntactic transfer**
Bialystok 1983 – adults
Haastrup & Phillipson 1983 – adults
Galvan & Campbell 1979 – ages 11 and 12

II INTERLINGUAL STRATEGIES

1 **Analogical leveling**
Anderson 1982 – adults
2 **Lexical innovation**
Bialystok 1983 – adults
Tarone 1981 – adults
Faerch & Kasper 1980 – ages 12 to adult
3 **Approximation**
Tarone 1981 – adults
Bialystok 1983 – adults

III DISCOURSE STRATEGIES

1 **Overt comment**
2 **Appeal for assistance**
Haastrup & Phillipson 1983 – adults
Tarone 1981 – adults
Galvan & Campbell 1979 – ages 11 and 12
3 **Deliberate wrong answer**
4 **Avoidance**
Tarone 1981 – adults
Schachter 1974 – adults
Grosjean 1982 – children
Faerch & Kasper 1980 – ages 12 to adult

Note: Each strategy is followed by references, where available, to child and/or adult L2 acquisition studies which have observed the same strategy.

of children does not result in their using qualitatively different strategies from adults; that is, the cognitive development of a three-year-old child is sufficient for use of the same compensatory strategies as are used by the adult. Thus, this finding, coupled with the suggestion that strategies are not language bound, suggests that all individuals may rely on a universal set of coping strategies.

Finally, it is important to note that none of the already existing typologies of compensatory strategies is completely adequate in describing Joseph's strategies. For example, while we found the Poulisse *et al.* distinction between intralingual and interlingual strategies to be more general and useful than the Bialystok L1 based and L2 based distinction, we found Andersen's definition of borrowing to be more helpful than Poulisse *et al.*'s. We conclude that a single typology, useful in describing the strategies that speakers use in compensating for linguistic deficits of all types, does not yet exist, and we suggest that the strategies used by first language attriters provide a fruitful arena in which to test the universality of typologies as they continue to be developed.

Appendix

Appendix transcription key

J	Joseph (bilingual, Russian and English)
G	Gresha, subject's father (bilingual, Russian and English)
D	Donna, subject's mother (monolingual, English)
GP	Grandpa, subject's maternal grandfather (monolingual, English)
GM	Grandma, subject's maternal grandmother (monolingual, English)
A	Alla (monolingual, Russian)
Jaime	Jaime (monolingual, English)

Note 1: Each Time 1 and Time 2 Russian utterance is followed, in parentheses, by its English translation.
Note 2: Russian transliterations are based on the *United States government printing office style manual* 1984.

Time 1 data, age 3

January 1984

1. J: No you. *Ty prinesi.* (You bring it.)
2. G: *Ty khochesh' chtob ya prines?* (Do you want me to bring it?)
3. J: *Da.* (Yes.)
4. G: *Okey. Ya prinesu.* (Okay, I will bring it in.)
5. J: *Chto ty skazal tak? Ya delayu domik. . .i nuzhno. . .*(What did you say? I am making a house. . .and I need. . .)
6. D: Beautiful, Joseph.
7. J: Look at the picture. It has to be only one. It has to be.
8. D: Only one roof. That's right. Only one. You should put your little television there so you can see what you're checking, or you can tell by looking, I guess. OK.
9. G: Come on Joseph.
10. D: OK Joseph. Mommy's going to bring you money. Here.
11. J: That's gonna be for you mommy.
12. D: OK. Take a penny. Find a penny. That's not a penny. The pennies are copper. This is a penny.
13. J: That's my. . .mama two pennies. This one's for daddy.
14. J: *Odin goluboy . . .Ya skushal belyy. . .Ty budesh' skushat'? Ty skushay etot.* (One is blue. I ate the white one. Will you eat it? You eat this one.)
15. G: *Mozhet my ikh nazad polozhim. Ty brosish' monetku. U tebya yest monetka yeshche?* (Maybe we'll put them back. You put money in. Do you have any money left?)

16. G: *Net my tak ne mozhem polozhit'. Nado zdes otkryt'. Smotri. Vot zdes' otkryt'.* (No we can not do it like this. It has to be open. Look. It opens here.)

17. J: *Ya – Ya – Ya!!!* I – I – I!)

18. G: *Ty otkroesh'?* (You will open?)

19. J: *Podymi menya.* (Pick me up.)

20. G: *Ne . . .Otvertku nado prinesti.* (No . . .We have to use a screwdriver.)

21. J: *Ya khochu otvertku.* (I want a screwdriver.)

22. G: *Otvertku khochesh'a?* (Do you want a screwdriver?)

23. J: *Tvoy.* (Yours.)

24. G: *Moyu? Okey.* (Mine? Okay.)

25. J: *Papa, ya khochu smotret' v kameru.* (Daddy, I want to look in the camera.)

26. D: Hurry up Joseph so we have a nice picture tonight. Come on. I want a nice picture.

27. J: *Ya khochu posmotret'. . .* (I want to see. . .)

28. G: *Tam nichego net.* (There's nothing there.)

29. J: *Pochemu?* (Why?)

30. G: *Ya ne znau pochemu.* (I don't know why.)

31. J: *Tam yest chto-to. Ty posmotrel i tam yest chto-to . . .Stop! Seychas' ty vidish' chto-to?* (There is something. You looked there and there is something. . .Stop! Now do you see something?)

32. G: *Seychas' ya vizhu Iosika.* (Now I see Joseph.)

33. J: *Ya khochu posmotret' sam!. . .Ya khochu posmotret' sam.* (I want to see it myself. . . I want to see it myself.)

34. G: *Kak zhe ty uvidish' Iosika, kogda ya delayu tvoyu fotografiyu.* (How can you see Joseph when I take your picture?)

35. J: *Ya ne khochu chtoby ty delal.* (I don't want you to take it.)

36. G: *Pochemu?* (Why?)

37. J: *Ya khochu sdelat' sam. Ty mozhesh' menya sdelat' sam?* (I want to do it myself. Can you make me there make myself?)

38. G: *Da.* (Yes.)

39. J: *Pozhaluysta, sdelay.* (Please make it.)

40. G: *Obozhdi minutku.* (Wait a moment.)

41. D: We're going to take pictures now.

42. GP: Want to remove all of this?

43. GM: All right. Give me that thing back honey.

44. J: *Ya khochu posmotret'.* (I want to see.)

45. G: *Tishe. Poydi syad' k dedushke na koleni. Potom tebya po televizoru.* (Quiet. Go to grandpa and sit on his lap. Then I'll show you yourself on TV)

46. J: *Papa, yesli ya syadu na mamu, budet eto?* (Daddy, if I sit on mommy will it be on that?)

47. G: He wants to look in camera.

48.	GM:	Oh.
49.	GP:	I've got some little beach chairs.
50.	GM:	No you don't. The sand chairs she doesn't want. She doesn't go to the beach.
51.	J:	Mommy.
52.	D:	What is it darling?
53.	J:	I want to look in the camera.
54. IO	D:	Daddy will let you look in the television like you did last night and saw all the pictures. Remember?
55.	G:	OK.
56.	D:	So if you sit with grandpa, you'll see Joseph and grandpa together, OK?
57.	J:	No. I want to be by myself.
58.	GP:	What is the name of the dust remover?
59.	D:	Endust.
60.	G:	*Posmotrish', kogda budesh' smotret' sebya na videolente.* (You'll see it when we are going to watch ourselves on the videotape.)
61.	J:	*Net! Seychas' khochu posmotret'!* (No! Now I want to see it!)
62.	G:	*Yeshche raz nazhmi.* (Push one more time.)
63.	J:	*Ya ne khochu muzyku. Mne ne nuzhno . . .* [To Jaime] Turn it off. *Ya vyklyuchil eto, ya vyklyuchil . . .Big volk ne kushay menya. Velosiped ne kushay menya! Ne kushay menya! A-a-a! Krichi na pomoshch'! Papa krichi na pomoshch'!* (I don't want music. I don't need it . . . I turn it off. I turn it off . . .wolf . . .don't eat me. Bicycle don't eat me! Don't eat me! Ah. Ah. Ah. Call for help! Daddy, call for help!)

Time 2 data, age 4.2

March 20, 1985

1.	*Ya khochu sobachku, papa.* (I want a doggie, daddy.)
2.	*Ya ne znayu.* (I don't know.)
3.	See how you *britsya.* (. . .shave.)
4.	Mommy, wait. I'm going to see daddy *britsya.* (. . .shave.)
5.	*Ty znaesh'* how many babies I'm going to have? *Raz, dva, tri, chetyre, pyat', shest', sem', vosem'. Net ne vse mal' chiki. Chetyre mal' chika i chetyre devochki.* (Do you know . . .? One, two, three, four, five, six, seven, eight. No, not all boys. Four boys and four girls.)

March 21, 1985

6.	*Ya spryatal tvoi botinki.* (I hid your shoes.)

March 22, 1985

7.   *Papa, ya khochu molochko.* (Papa, I want milk.)
8.   Papa, how do you say baked apple in Russian?

March 23, 1985

9.   *A ty na beysmente?* (Are you in the basement?)

March 25, 1985

10.   D: How do you say I like apples in Russian?
11.   J: *Ya lyublyu yablochki.* (I like apples.)
12.   J: *On lubit knizhka. Ona lubit knizhka.* (He likes books. She likes books.)
13.   D: How do you say we love books?
14.   J: I forgot.
15.   D: How do you say they love books?
16.   J: I forgot.
17.   D: How do you say I love the blue book in Russian?
18.   J: I forgot. [He thinks] *Ya lyublyu goluboy knizhka. Ya lyublyu goluboy domik. Ya lyublyu goluboy mama.* (I love the blue book. I love the blue house. I love the blue mama.)
19.   D: How do you say I will go to school tomorrow?
20.   J: *Ya poydu v school tomorrow.* (I will go to...)
21.   D: Where is daddy?
22.   J: *Gde papa?* (Where is daddy?)
23.   D: What is your name?
24.   J: *Chto tvoy nama?* (What is your name?)
25.   D: When will daddy come home?
26.   J: *Kogda papa pridet doma?* (When will daddy come home?)
27.   D: Why are you sleeping?
28.   J: *Pochemu ty spat'?* (Why are you sleeping?)
29.   D: How do you say how in Russian?
30.   J: How, the same way you say it in English.
31.   D: Give me a lot.
32.   J: *Ya khochu mnogo.* (I want a lot.)
33.   D: Give me a carrot.
34.   J: *Morkovka.* Only *morkovka* I can say. (Carrot... carrot...)
35.   D: Mouth.
36.   J: *Rotik.* (Mouth.)
37.   D: Ears.
38.   J: *Ushki.* (Ears.)
39.   D: Hand.
40.   J: Um. *Ruchki.* (Hand.)
41.   D: Teeth.

42.   J: *Zubki.* (Teeth.)
43.   D: Tooth.
44.   J: Tooth, the same way you say it in English.
45.   D: Eyes.
46.   J: *Glazki.* (Eyes.)
47.   D: Hair.
48.   J: *Volosiki.* (Hair.)
49.   D: Leg.
50.   J: *Nozhka.* (Leg.)
51.   D: Foot.
52.   J: Foot, the same way you say it in English.
53.   D: I want a toothbrush.
54.   J: *Ya khochu.* I don't know how to say toothbrush in Russian. (I want . . .)
55.   J: *Ya khochu moy knizhka. Ya khochu tvoy knizhka. Ya khochu on knizhka. Ya khochu ona knizhka. Ya poydu v biblioteku. Ty poydet v biblioteku. On poydet v biblioteku. Ona poydet v biblioteku.* (I want my book. I want your book. I want his book. I want her book. I am going to the library. You are going to the library. He is going to the library. She is going to the library.)

March 26, 1985

56.   J: Papa, how do you say toothbrush in Russian?

Time 2 data, age 4.3

April 5, 1985

57.   J: *Moy* name is *Iosik. Posmotri.* (My. . . Joseph. Look.)
58.   A: *Pokazhi mne. Chto eto takoye u tebya? Chto eto? Foto? A kto zhe zdes'? Eto chto takoye? Eto imeniny?* (Show it to me. What is it you have? What is it? A picture? And who is it? What is it? Is it a birthday party?)
59.   J: *Eto* was *kogda moy* birthday. (It. . . when my. . .)
60.   A: *Den' rozhdeniya.* (Birthday.)
61.   J: And look at this.
62.   A: *Posmotri. Skazhi mne a chto eto takoye? Chto zdes'?* (Look. Tell me what it is? What's here?)
63.   J: It's same as this.
64.   A: *Net podozhdi. Ty mne po-russki skazhi. Kto eto?* (No wait. You tell me in Russian. Who is it?)
65.   J: *Moy ah ah* grandmother. *Kogda ya byl vo Floride ah ah kogda ya byl teplenko.* (My. . . When I was in Florida. . . when I was warmish.)
66.   A: *A eto kto?* (Who is this?)
67.   J: Grandpa. *Eto menya.* Hey look, *posmotri.* This is alligators. (. . . That's me. . . .look . . .)

68. A: *A eto chto?* (And what is this?)
69. J: *Eto* bird. I like that bird. *Ya lyublyu.* (This is a. . .I love.)
70. A: *A eto gde?* (And where is it?)
71. J: Wherever you see a shirt on. *Kogda ty smotrish. Ah ni kurtochka. Tam ya* in Florida. *Posmotri. Eto moy mama.* And look at this. *Ty skazala mne chto budet mne podarok.* (. . .When you look . . .no jacket. There I . . .Look. It is my mother . . .You told me that there will be a gift for me.)
72. A: *Konechno. Ya prigotovila tebe podarok. Ty popey kompot. Ya sama sdelala.* (Of course. I prepared you a gift. You drink compote. I made it myself.)
73. J: *Eto* too much. (This is. . .)
74. A: *Vot tebe malen' kaya chashechka. Skazhi eto mnogo?* (Here is a smaller cup for you. Say, it is too much?)
75. J: *Eto mnogo.* (It is too much.)
     [Alla asks a few questions. No answers are given.]
76. J: *Oranzhevaya.* (Orange.)
77. A: *Chto zdes' narisovano?* (What is drawn here?)
78. J: *Tri medvedeti.* (Three bear children.)
79. A: *A eto?* (And what's that?)
80. J: *Eto* look like a *volk.* (It. . .wolf.)
81. A: *A mozhet eto mama medved?* (And maybe it's a mama bear.)
82. J: Or papa *eto.* (. . .father.)
83. A: *Chto ty delayesh?* (What are you doing?)
84. J: I go to dot. Oy. I made an accident. By accident from *trinadtsat'* to *pyatnadtsat'.* (. . .thirteen. . .fifteen.)
85. A: *A kuda tebe nado?* (And where were you supposed to go?)
86. J: From *trinadtsat'* to *chetyrnadtsat'.* Do you know I have a tape? (. . .thirteen. . .fourteen. . .)
87. A: *Ya ne ponimayu.* (I don't understand.)
88. J: How do you say tape in Russian?
89. A: *Ya ne ponimayu tebya. Davay posmotrim knizhku. Znaesh' chto eto?* (I don't understand you. Let's look at the book. Do you know what it is?)
90. J: *Eto babochka.* (This is an old woman.)
91. A: *Chto ona delayet?* (What is she doing?)
92. J: *Brosit.* (She will throw.)
93. A: *Da, ona brosila tarelki. A eto chto?* (Yes, she threw plates. And what is this?)
94. J: Teacup.
95. A: *Eto chaynik.* (This is a teapot.)
96. J: *Chaynik.* (Teapot.)
97. A: *A eto chto?* (And what is this?)
98. J: *Tarelki.* (Plates.)
99. A: *A eto?* (And that?)

100. J: *Kotiki.* (Kittens.)
101. A: *A eto?* (And that?)
102. J: I forgot what you call him.
103. A: *Krokodil.* (Crocodile.)
104. J: *Da, krokodil.* (Yes, crocodile.)
105. A: *A eto chto?* (And what's that?)
106. J: I think I'm tired of doing this.
107. A: *Mozhet poprobuyesh eto?* (Maybe you'll taste it.)
108. J: *Eto* have *sakhar?* (Does it...sugar?)
109. A: *Da, eto konfety.* (Yes, it's candy.)
110. J: *Da,* but they have shu. *sakhar.* I don't want they. *Ya ne khochu eto. Ya* don't like the one that has *sakhar. Ya ne lyublyu to. Ya. Ya ne khochu* my teeth to rotten. (Yes...sugar...I don't want it. I...sugar. I don't like it. I. I don't want ...)
111. A: *Skazhi eto po-russki.* (Say it in Russian.)
112. J: *Zubki.* I don't want. They make my teeth fall out. *Ya ne lyublyu kogda moy zubki vypadayut.* Can I see all the candies do you have? *Ya khochu posmotret'* all the *konfety.* (Teeth...I don't like when my teeth fall out...I want to see...candies.)
113. A: *U menya bolshe netu.* (This is all.)
114. J: *Tol'ko* these? *Tol 'ko eti.* Is this the *podarok?* (Only...? Only these? ...gift?)
115. A: *Net. Vot tebe podarok.* [Presents the gift, a shirt.] *Tebe nravitsya? Poydem v druguyu komnatu.* (No. Here is your gift. Do you like .it? Let's go to the other room.)
116. J: Oh. I have that clock at home.
117. A: *Chto?* (What?)
118. J: *Eti chasy doma. Kogda moy mama. Gde moy mama?. Ty pochitaesh' mne?* [Joseph begins to sing.] (This clock at home. When my mother. Where is my mother? Will you read to me?)

Note

The authors wish to thank Gregory Turian for help in translating, transliterating, and analyzing the Russian data; Barry Rubin for his assistance in analyzing the Russian data; Walter Petrovitz for his assistance in transliterating the data; and Carolyn Sobel for helpful comments and suggestions.

References

Andersen, Roger W. 1982. "Determining the linguistic attributes of language attrition," in Lambert and Freed (eds.), 83–118.

Bialystok, Ellen. 1983. "Some factors in the selection and implementation of communication strategies," in Faerch and Kasper (eds.), 100–118.

Bialystok, Ellen, and M. Frohlich. 1980. "Oral communication strategies for lexical difficulties," *Interlanguage Studies Bulletin* 5: 3–30.

Clark, John L. D. 1982. "Measurement considerations in language attrition research," in Lambert and Freed (eds.), 138–152.

Corder, Pit. 1971. "Idiosyncratic dialects and error analysis," in Jack C. Richards (ed.), *Error analysis*. London: Longman, 158–171.

Ervin, S. 1979. "Communiciation strategies employed by American students of Russian," *Modern Language Journal* 63: 329–334.

Faerch, Claus and Gabriele Kasper. 1980. "Processes and strategies in foreign language learning and communication," *Interlanguage Studies Bulletin* 5: 47–118.

Faerch, Claus, and Gabriele Kasper (eds.). 1983. *Strategies in interlanguage communication*. London and New York: Longman.

Fallis, Guadalupe Valdes. 1976. "Social interaction and code-switching patterns: a case study of Spanish/English alternation," in Gary D. Keller, Richard V. Teschner, and Silvia Viera (eds.), *Bilingualism in the bicentennial and beyond*. New York: Bilingual Press, 53–83.

Galvan, J., and R. N. Campbell. 1979. "An examination of the communication strategies of two children in the Culver City Spanish immersion program," in Roger Andersen (ed.), *The acquisition and use of Spanish and English as first and second languages*. Washington, DC: Tesol, 133–150.

Gardner, Robert. 1982. "Social factors in language retention," in Lambert and Freed (eds.), 24–39.

Grosjean, François. 1982. *Life with two languages*. Cambridge, MA: Harvard University Press.

Haastrup, Kirsten, and Robert Phillipson. 1983. "Achievement strategies in learner–native speaker interaction," in Faerch and Kasper (eds.), 140–150.

Lambert, Richard D., and Barbara F. Freed (eds.). 1982. *The loss of language skills*. Rowley, MA: Newbury House Publishers.

Poulisse, Nanda, Theo Bongaerts, and Eric Kellerman. 1984. "On the use of compensatory strategies in second language performance," *Interlanguage Studies Bulletin* 8: 70–105.

Ronjat, J. 1913. *Le Developpement du language observé chez un enfant bilingue*. Paris: Champion.

Schachter, Jacquelyn. 1974. "An error in error analysis," *Language Learning* 24 (2): 205–14.

Seliger, Herbert W. 1984. "Primary language attrition in the context of other language loss and mixing." Unpublished paper, Queens College, CUNY.

Tarone, Elaine. 1977. "Conscious communication strategies in interlanguage: a progress report," in H. Brown, C. Yorio, and R. Crymes (eds.), *Teaching and learning English as a second language*. Washington, DC, 194–203.

Tarone, Elaine. 1981. "Some thoughts on the notion of communication strategy," in Faerch and Kasper (eds.), 61–74.

Varadi, Tamas. 1983. "Strategies of target language learner communication: message adjustment," in Faerch and Kasper (eds.), 79–99.

15   Language attrition, reduced redundancy, and creativity

HERBERT W. SELIGER

1   Introduction

First language attrition is a ubiquitous phenomenon found wherever there is bilingualism. The phenomenon raises a number of interesting questions for the linguist and the psycholinguist. For the linguist, language attrition, like second language acquisition, provides interesting evidence about the relationships of grammars in contact, be it phonological (Vago, this volume), morphological (Kaufman & Aronoff, this volume), morphosyntactic (Seliger 1986) or syntactic, as in the study to be discussed in this chapter. The phenomenon of language attrition also allows hypotheses about putative language universals and markedness conditions to be tested across languages (Seliger & Vago, this volume).

For the psycholinguist, language attrition raises questions about the relative permanence of acquisition itself, about the cognitive conditions necessary to maintain language in the context of bilingualism, and about the conditions which lead to the dissolution or attrition of language abilities within normal populations of mature speakers as opposed to polyglot aphasics.

Both language attrition and language acquisition must explain how generalizations and overgeneralizations are learned and then unlearned in the gradual evolution of grammars. In both situations, rule constraints and categorization features may be underextended or overextended until the process of acquisition or loss has reached its maximum level of development. In the one case, L1 acquisition, that evolution is supposed to lead to the final state grammar used by the adult native speaker. In the case of first language attrition in the context of bilingualism, that process of unlearning and evolution can lead to reduction in some areas of the grammar and the creation of new forms in others in the first language while the second language may continue to develop. Eventually, as in the case of language death, most of the first language is replaced or absorbed by the second.

In the case of L1 acquisition, the grammar is often too powerful and produces utterances which are the result of overgeneralizing rules. The puzzle for learnability theory is how the child succeeds in unlearning incorrect hypotheses given the paucity of language data which can be regarded as corrective. Language attrition can be seen as a similar puzzle. What linguistic or psycholinguistic mechanisms can explain the "unlearning" or replacement of previously grammatically acceptable rules with those which are not grammatically acceptable in L1?

2   Sources of knowledge for the creation and dissolution of language grammars

Language attrition is selective, affecting some aspects of the grammar more than others. However, it is not haphazard and may be characterized as the unlearning of an L1 grammar through a rule governed process. It may be assumed that this process is affected by the kinds of data or sources of knowledge which are available to the language user and which may be used as evidence in judging the fitness of hypotheses in his grammar. For example, the data available to the first language acquirer are the utterances of language users around him as well as the acquirer's own utterances. He uses the evidence extracted from these data to judge the fit of his grammar with those grammars to which he is exposed.

In this sense, it may be useful to distinguish between data in the form of actual utterances and language knowledge in the form of abstract rules already existing in the grammar of a speaker. The abstract rules of grammar which have already been acquired may be said to be a source of knowledge while the actual utterances of the speaker and those around him may be said to constitute the raw data. It would be illogical to claim that only externally provided language data or the speaker's own utterances would be the sole sources of evidence when other sources of language knowledge such as an incipient grammar, in the case of first language acquisition, or a fully developed grammar, as in the case of second language acquisition or first language attrition, is also available as an evaluative mechanism for judging data.

In the case of first language acquisition, the use of these sources of evidence is thought to be responsible for the rejection of overgeneralized rules and the gradual acquisition of rule restrictions as well as subcategorical constraints on the kinds of data to which rules apply. In the case of first language attrition, evidence may include not only data from the first language, which is usually limited, but all other types of language knowledge such as that developed for the second language.

While in second language acquisition research, the hypothesis testing model seems to be pre-eminent, hypothesis testing requires as a condition that the hypothesis be tested against negative feedback or what has been termed "negative evidence" (Pinker 1984; Chomsky 1981) or "negative input" (Schachter 1984). What these terms basically mean is that some form of correction or evidence is supposed to be present in the context in which the language is used to cue the child or language learner to the deviancy of his utterance and thus lead to a revision of the hypothesis about the underlying grammar.

But suppose the learner, child or adult, does not produce errors and does not hear incorrect utterances but begins to produce correct forms from the very beginning. This is argued to be the case, for example, for the acquisition of the rule for dative alternation such as in the following sentences:

(1)   I gave the apple to John.
(2)   I gave John the apple.

BUT

(3)   I donated the apple to John.
(4)   *I donated John the apple.

Studies in first language acquisition seem to indicate that very little direct negative evidence or correction is present in the language environment of the child which could function as negative feedback and, even when that is present, children seem to be oblivious to correction (Braine 1971). (There is some disagreement as to whether children produce overgeneralizations themselves; cf. Mazurkewich & White 1984). This has led to proposals that the child may be utilizing indirect negative evidence, which according to Chomsky (1981) would be simply the absence or relatively low frequency of ungrammatical forms. The language acquirer therefore has access primarily to direct positive evidence which would be the preponderance of grammatical forms. For the bilingual, however, the type of evidence available is complicated by the fact that the speaker possesses two grammars. Since the speaker is exposed to the second language grammar and to second language "positive evidence" at a higher frequency than he is to first language data, it is only natural that the second language grammar be regarded as a source of knowledge for evaluating forms in the first language.

Schachter (1984) has proposed a different definition of indirect negative evidence from that suggested by Chomsky. Her proposal derives from the context of second language acquisition and assumes that the underlying mechanisim for language development in this context is hypothesis testing. As presented by Schachter (1984), indirect negative evidence is a form of feedback from which the language learner extracts evidence that something is amiss with his utterance. This would then lead, it is hoped, to a revision of the hypothesis upon which the utterance is based. Indirect negative evidence according to this second definition would be a request for clarification or a confirmation check by the interlocutor indicating to the language acquirer that something is amiss without specifying what is amiss. It would be up to the language learner to infer what is wrong with the utterance and revise it accordingly.

One of the problems with arguing for indirect negative evidence according to Schachter's definition is that the learner must deal with three levels of hypotheses at the same time. While creating utterances based on an initial hypothesis, he must then create a second and third level hypothesis which hypothesizes about whether there is indirect negative feedback and what that negative evidence might be about. It would seem a very complicated and uneconomical model given the speed at which conversations take place, the focus on content and not on form, and the need to hold in short term memory a number of hypotheses about several different levels of language at the same time!

Level 1 hypothesis: I think the grammar of this sentence goes like this . . .
Level 2 hypothesis: Is that negative evidence or is that positive evidence out there?
Level 3 hypothesis: What is the negative evidence referring to – what I said or how I said it (content or form?)

15.1   The problem with indirect negative evidence

As stated above, the definition of indirect negative evidence as proposed by Chomsky is basically the absence of data which would be incorrectly predicted by the developing grammar. What this means is that the learner is exposed primarily to positive instances of a form. In other words, it is the absence of anything that would support an over-generalization of a rule that constitutes for Chomsky (1981) what he calls "a kind of negative evidence." That is, "if certain structures or rules fail to be exemplified in relatively simple expressions where they would be expected to be found, then a (possibly marked) option is selected excluding them from the grammar." Since the emphasis in this kind of evidence is on what **is** rather than on what **is not**, this type of evidence may also be referred to as "positive evidence." It will be argued that positive evidence can be direct or indirect and that a type of positive evidence is responsible for the changes which we term language attrition.

Positive evidence can, in the case of the bilingual, logically come from two sources: one is the same external language data to which the monolingual child is exposed. For example, the child is exposed to adults speaking the grammatical form of the language he will eventually acquire, and the bilingual is exposed to the external data of speakers of the second language.

However, in the case of the bilingual, there is a second source of positive evidence which will be referred to as indirect positive evidence. This is the abstract grammar of the second language which the learner has acquired. In this case, it will be argued that when there is a problem in retrieving or accessing information (structures or rules) stored in the first language grammar, the second language grammar becomes an internal source of indirect positive evidence.[1]

In a sense, what is taking place is that both grammars become a source for generating utterances in the first language. Figure 15.2 summarizes the various types of evidence which have been discussed to explain first and second language acquisition as well as first language attrition.

Direct negative	external	correction
Indirect negative (a)	external	absence of deviant data
Indirect negative (b)	external	clarification/miscommunication
Direct positive	external	grammatical data
Indirect positive	internal	inferences from L2 grammar

(a) Chomsky's (1981) definition
(b) Schachter's (1984) definition

15.2   Possible types of evidence for developing grammars

Based on the data in the current study, it will be argued that the bilingual uses both his grammars as potential sources for evidence about the grammaticality of his utterances, and when faced with the need to make a decision about the grammaticality of an utterance in L1, will, if necessary, resort to rules in L2 as a source of **indirect positive evidence**.

3   The case of word order in dative sentences: English and Hebrew

According to the views expressed previously about language acquisition (Braine 1971; Chomsky 1981; Pinker 1984 and 1987; Fodor 1985; Randall 1987), children get little or no direct negative evidence while developing grammars of their first language. That is, the language learner develops rules based on positive instances and does not hear enough negative or deviant instances or utilize external correction in order for such data to act as a significant source of evidence for grammar development.

An argument to support the positive evidence claim is the fact that children supposedly do not produce dative sentences such as (5) but do produce sentences such as (6).

(5)   *John made Susan the choice. (i.e. John made the choice for Susan.)

(6)   John made Susan the table.

The argument is that adults in the environment of the language acquirer do not produce sentences such as (5) but do produce sentences such as (6). In order to arrive at a rule which will produce (6) but not (5), the learner has to acquire with each verb, the lexical subcategories or "verb arguments" that will allow the double object construction sentence with one meaning of "made" but not with the other. (See Mazurkewich & White 1984; and Randall 1987 for discussions of this issue.)

In the case of language attrition, an additional complicating factor in the evidence question is the fact that the bilingual has access to two language systems interacting within the same mind. In the case before us we are concerned with the language attrition of a bilingual English–Hebrew speaker.

Since the language attrition data we will discuss concerns the dative construction, it is necessary to provide some background discussion of (1) the word order of the constituents of dative sentences, and (2) preposition stranding or binding in English and Hebrew.

In the case of dative sentences, English contains what is referred to as the "alternation rule," which allows for sentences such as (1) and (2) above. English speakers must also acquire knowledge of when the verb will allow this alternation in the NP NP arrangement and when not. It is clear that the rules involved in the dative in English consist of much more than syntactic rearrangement and deletion of the preposition.

Whereas the English rule is lexically governed, the Hebrew dative is syntactic and does not contain the double object alternation as in (2) or (6) above. Hebrew prepositions are bound to their objects and move with them, as we see in sentences (7) through (10):

(7)   *Dan natan sefer le-Sarah.*
       "Dan gave (a) book to Sarah"

(8)   *Dan natan le-Sarah sefer.*
       "Dan gave to-Sarah (a) book"

(9)   *Dan natan la sefer.*
       "Dan gave to-her (a) book"

(10)   *Dan natan sefer la.*
       "Dan gave (a) book to-her"

Note that all of the variants except (10) are acceptable. We may conclude the following about Hebrew datives:

(a) Direct and indirect object constituents may alternate in position after the verb unless the indirect object is pronominalized. In that event, it may not occur as the final constituent.

(b) The preposition, *le/la,* which can mean "to" or "for," is always bound to the head noun of the prepositional phrase (PP).

In summary, English dative and the restrictions on alternations are primarily lexical with syntactic implications from the lexical selectional restrictions, while Hebrew dative is primarily syntactic with morphological restrictions carrying syntactic implications. In Figure 15.3 this is shown as Stage I.

4   Data from the dative performance of O

The data to be reported were collected from a bilingual subject (identified as O), female, who immigrated to Israel at age six. At the time of immigration, according to reports from the child's mother, English was the home language and the language used by the child. However, soon after arriving in Israel, the home language switched to Hebrew in order to facilitate the child's adjustment. One must assume that a stage of code mixing preceded that switch to exclusive use of the second language. According to the mother, the child did not speak Hebrew at the time of arrival in Israel.

The child was studied from the beginning of her ninth year, during which tape recorded samples of her speech and random transcriptions were collected approximately every three to four weeks. At these taped sessions, the child related stories and school experiences. During the second year of the study, the subject was then approximately ten and a half, metalinguistic tests were constructed on the basis of an analysis of the discourse protocols.

The metalinguistic tests were also administered to a group of eight monolingual children living in the United States, ranging in age from six to nine years, in order to establish norms for language performance on the tests since the subject immigrated at age six and the data collection began at age nine.

The tests consisted of six parts, which were administered separately and focused on different aspects of the subject's grammar. This discussion will be limited to the findings on a thirty-two item test of acceptability of dative sentences.

4.1   Free discourse sentences

Sentences (11) through (15) are examples from the free discourse data recorded during the first year of the study. They indicate that the subject was able to produce both forms of the dative sentence.

(11)   I'm gonna tell you a few nother things. (NPpro NP)
(12)   I'm gonna tell you a different thing that everyone likes it. (NPpro NP)
(13)   The school gives the girl that she has the birthday a present. (NP NP)
(14)   So she telled it to another girl. (NPpro PP)
(15)   I told it to the girl thats [*sic*] was sitting next to me. (NPpro PP)

It is clear from these examples that the subject was able to produce dative sentences. The errors that occur in these sentences are not due to not observing restrictions pertaining to datives but rather to other aspects of the grammar such as relative clause formation. (For a discussion of the subject's relative clause grammar see Seliger 1989.) What the limited free discourse data on datives does not show, is whether she was able to control for other restrictions on the datives such as the restriction on the movement of the PP and the lexical restrictions on the double object NP construction.

In the metalinguistic tests not all aspects of datives were investigated. Sentences were constructed in the following two categories:

Twenty-one sentences which tested the placement of the PP before or after the direct object or the use of the correct preposition (Hebrew can use one (*le-*) for both possessor or benefactor). Of these, eleven were ungrammatical and of this set two were ungrammatical because the word order was correct but the wrong preposition was inserted (*to* for *for* or *for* for *to*). Example (16) is a case of correct preposition but incorrect word order, while in (17) the word order is correct but the wrong preposition is used.

(16)   *Dick handed to Sally the book.
(17)   *Eric cooked the soup to Ann.

Eleven sentences (six grammatical, five ungrammatical) with the NP NP construction, as in sentences (18) through (22).

(18)   *David made Susan the choice.
(19)   *Ariella answered the teacher the question.
(20)   *Harry made Tom the decision.
(21)   She read the baby the story.
(22)   Dick handed Sally the book.

Of the total of thirty-two sentences to which the subject and the native speakers responded, there were sixteen grammatical and sixteen ungrammatical sentences.

4.2   Findings

Table 15.1 summarizes the performance of the subject and the eight native speakers on the metalinguistic test of grammaticality judgement. For the native speakers, the average number of errors is reported. The native speaker group has been further subdivided into different age ranges, five to seven and eight to nine, since it is possible that grammaticality judgements might differ across such a wide age range. The performance of the first group of native speakers (ages 5–7) may be thought to represent the performance of the subject before the onset of bilingualism and language attrition.

Table 15.1 *Word order and preposition judgements: responses of subject and native speaker (NS) children*

	False positive (11 ungrammatical)	False negative (10 grammatical)
subject	9 (4)	1 (0)
NS (n = 8)	1.25	0
NS (n = 4) (ages 5–7)	1.75	0
NS (n = 4) (ages 8–9)	.75	.25

Table 15.2 *The double object judgements*

	False positive (5 ungrammatical)	False negative (6 grammatical)
subject	4 (1)	2 (0)
NS (n = 8)	1.0	.5
NS (n = 4) (ages 5–7)	1.5	.75
NS (n = 4) (ages 8–9)	.5	.25

False positive = ungrammatical sentences which were accepted as grammatical.

False negative = grammatical sentences which were rejected as ungrammatical.

5   Discussion

5.1   *Word order judgements*

We can see from the results of the judgement test in Table 15.1 that O accepts ungrammatical sentences such as those exemplified by (16) above more than she rejects them (nine out of eleven possible ungrammatical sentences) as well as accepting grammatical sentences. Her performance is compared with the native speakers, who overwhelmingly rejected ungrammatical sentences because of word order problems. In fact, the difference between the five- to seven-year-olds and eight- to nine-year-olds is not great and it is clear that word order grammaticality ability is present in the younger group.

What is interesting for our purposes is to consider why both word orders are acceptable by the subject. In other words, O's grammar accepts a syntactic arrangement in which the PP is the final constituent as well as an arrangement where the PP is placed immediately after the main verb. The native speakers in both age groups did not generally accept this second arrangement, which is considered ungrammatical in English but grammatical in Hebrew.

It is not unreasonable to postulate on the basis of this evidence and what we know about the subject that she is relying on the Hebrew rule for unrestricted placement of the PP. This can be explained by the fact that the subject had experienced increasing difficulty in accessing evidence from English. Her exposure to English language data either as direct positive evidence, negative evidence or indirect negative evidence is very limited but at this point her own second language grammar (Hebrew) becomes the source of indirect positive evidence for making grammaticality judgements about the first language (English).

The progression of this development is shown opposite in Figure 15.3. In the initial stages of bilingualism, autonomy is maintained between the two languages. Dative alternation in Hebrew remains syntactically based while the alternation in English is lexically determined with syntactic implications.

At the intermediate stage (see Figure 15.3, Stage II), the subject utilizes indirect positive evidence from Hebrew. When the speaker experiences increasing difficulty retrieving English and has increasingly limited access to positive or negative evidence in English, she turns to Hebrew as a source. At this point, an equivalency relationship is established between the rules in the two languages. In a sense, the learner has established a syllogism which states that if A is equal to B and B is equal to C then A must also be equal to C. In this case, if one form of dative alter-

Stage I. Autonomous rules in a coordinate system

HEBREW (syntactic)   ENGLISH (lexical-syntactic)

$[NP\ V\ NP_{DO}\ PP] \longleftrightarrow [NP\ V\ PP\ NP_{DO}]\ [NP\ V\ NP_{DO}\ PP] \longleftrightarrow [NP\ V\ NP_{IO}\ NP_{DO}]$

Stage II. Intermediate stage: Indirect positive evidence from Hebrew

$[NP\ V\ PP\ NP] \longleftrightarrow [NP\ V\ NP\ PP] \Longleftrightarrow [NP\ V\ NP\ PP] \longleftrightarrow [NP\ V\ NP\ NP]$

Stage III. Final stage: Redundancy reduction and attrition

Some rules in H and E are fused.

$[NP\ V\ PP\ NP] \Longleftrightarrow [NP\ V\ NP\ PP] \longleftarrow [NP\ V\ NP\ NP]$

Stage I. Rules retain autonomy in each language. Hebrew rules for dative are syntactic with some morphological constraints. English rules are controlled by lexical subcategorization with syntactic implications.

Stage II. Because of inaccessibility of L1 data, L2 grammar becomes a source of indirect positive evidence affecting grammaticality abilities in L1. (Word order and lexical subcategorization rules affected.)

Stage III. Where near equivalencies are found for L1 and L2 rules, rules are collapsed or fused into one in the direction of less marked in a crosslinguistic sense. Since datives in both languages can be expressed using a PP and since movement of PP with bound preposition is less marked, it is more economical to maintain that version of the rule which requires fewer rule restrictions on movement (i.e. the Hebrew rule).

15.3   Redundancy reduction for the dative in language attrition

nation is equal in the two languages (the final placement of the PP), then the other must be as well, especially since there is no L1 (English) evidence to indicate the contrary. That is, the equivalency relationship between the rules in English and Hebrew is established because of the absence of contradictory positive evidence from English.

This brings us to the final stage in the attrition development (Stage III in Figure 15.2). The Hebrew rule for PP placement includes within it the more restrictive rule for English PP placement. The separate English rule now becomes redundant and the grammar rule for datives with PP is reduced to that rule which covers both cases. This outcome might also be explained on the basis of a variant of the Uniqueness Principle (Chomsky & Lasnik 1977) which states that when two forms have the same meaning, that which is supported by the data is maintained. In the case of first language attrition, most of the supporting data come from the second language. PP movement is accepted into English as part of the dative alternation rule. That is, in the process of reducing the redundancy between the two languages, the speaker has created a new rule which combines elements from both languages.

5.2   *Double object sentences*

What remains to be examined is whether the lexical sub-categorization restrictions on the dative NP NP construction have been affected by language attrition. It is difficult to tell from O's free discourse utterances. Upon close examination of her sentences ((11) through (15)) we see that in none of them was it necessary for her to deal with a problem which causes difficulties in first language acquisition, the combined problem of animacy and word order. For example, we may assume that the child understands that in order for a noun to function as an indirect object it must have the quality of being a possessor or benefactor of the direct object. Roeper *et al.* (1981) found this to be a factor in the comprehension of sentences such as

The cow gave the dog the pig.

In such sentences, children who have not yet acquired the dative alternation rule and have no contrasting cues will use a linear strategy to interpret the first object as the direct object and second as the indirect object instead of the opposite. In this sentence, since both objects are animate and capable of filling the role of "possessor," the child assigns grammatical role according to word order.[2]

An examination of O's responses on the metalinguistic test indicates that she accepted sentences such as (18), (19) and (20). These sentences are ungrammatical for different reasons. In (18) and (20), the use of *made* ignores the restriction that the object must be capable of being possessed by the indirect object. In the case of abstract words such as *choice* and *decision*, that requirement is not observed. It is possible that the subject is interpreting these sentences as predicate objective sentences.

At the same time, the subject rejected grammatical sentences such as (21) and (22) while both the younger and older monolingual children had an average error rate of less than one error for five sentences. We might explain the rejection of sentences (21) and (22) on the basis of the linear strategy described by Roeper *et al*. In the case of sentence (21), it is likely that the subject understands that the verb *read* requires an inanimate object. If the sentence is interpreted in a linear order then this sentence cannot make sense because the role of direct object is assigned to the first noun following the transitive verb. It is possible that sentence (22) seems strange to her as well for the same reason. This interpretation of the data was supported to some degree by one of the monolingual children in the younger group who rejected sentence (21) and laughed saying, "How can you read a baby?"

6   Conclusion

An analysis of a bilingual child's performance in free discourse and on metalinguistic judgement tasks indicates that the processes involved in language attrition are not unlike processes found in first language acquisition, where the learner must adjust rules in order to limit the overgeneralization of learning. That is, in first language acquisition it is necessary for the acquirer to "unlearn" rules which are too inclusive or overgeneralized in order to arrive at the final state grammar. This unlearning process is triggered by the acquirer's contact with positive evidence from L1.

In the case of first language attrition in the context of bilingualism, the unlearning process is initiated by a lack of access to L1 data and the growing dominance of L2. Unlearning here is triggered by indirect positive evidence from L2 projected onto L1. In this particular case, Hebrew word order rules for the placement of the PP are combined with and partially replace the English rules involved in dative alternation through a process which reduces the redundant rule in one of the languages (English).

Notes

1   Indirect positive evidence can become direct positive evidence when the process is externalized and enough speakers of an attrited form of L1 reinforce the new grammar of L1 which results from the attrition process. This we recognize as the beginning of an immigrant dialect of an overseas language, as in the case of Finnish speakers in the US, and eventually as the source of language death.

2   Roeper *et al.* (1981) claim that this construction is learned at a much later stage. However, it would be necessary to consider which aspects of the dative alternation restrictions are acquired and at what ages. It would seem that more concrete sentences such as (2) or (6) would be acquired earlier than the grammatical ability necessary to judge sentences (18) through (22).

References

Braine, M. 1971. "On two types of models of the internalization of grammars," in D. Slobin (ed.), *The ontogenesis of grammar*. New York: Academic Press.

Chomsky, Noam. 1981. *Lectures on government and binding*. Dordrecht: Foris.

Chomsky, N., and H. Lasnik. 1977. "Filters and control," *Linguistic Inquiry* 8: 425–504.

Fodor, J. D. 1985. "Why learn lexical rules?" Paper presented at the 10th Annual Boston University Conference on Language Development, October 25–27.

MacWhinney, Brian. 1987. "Applying the competition model to bilingualism," *Applied Psycholinguistics* 8, 4: 315–328.

Mazurkewich, Irene. 1984. "Dative questions and markedness," in F. Eckman, L. H. Bell, and D. Nelson (eds.), *Universals of second language acquisition*. Rowley, MA: Newbury House Publishers, 119–131.

Mazurkewich, Irene, and Lydia White. 1984. "The acquisition of the dative alternation: unlearning overgeneralizations," *Cognition* 16: 261–283.

Pinker, Steven. 1984. *Language learnability and language development*. Cambridge, MA: Harvard University Press.

1987. "Resolving a learnability paradox in the acquisition of the verb lexicon," Lexicon Project Working Papers 17. Center for Cognitive Science, MIT.

Randall, Janet. 1987. "The catapult hypothesis: grammars as machines for unlearning." Unpublished paper presented at the Max-Planck-Institut für Psycholinguistik, Nimegen: Conference on the Structure of the Simple Clause in Language Acquisition, Parasession on Verb-Argument Structure.

Roeper, Thomas, Steven Lapointe, Janet Bing, and Susan L. Tavakolian. 1981. "A lexical approach to language acquisition," in Susan L. Tavakolian (ed.), *Language acquisition and linguistic theory*. Cambridge, MA: MIT Press, 35–58.

Schachter, Jacquelyn. 1984. "A universal input condition," in William E. Rutherford (ed.), *Language universals and second language acquisition*. Amsterdam: John Benjamins Publishing Co., 167–183.

Seliger, Herbert W. 1986. "Deterioration and creativity in childhood bilingualism". Paper presented at symposium on Bilingualism across the life span. Linguistic Society of America Summer Institute, New York.

1989. "Deterioration and creativity in childhood bilingualism," in L. Obler and K. Hyltenstam (eds.), *Bilingualism across the life span*. Cambridge: Cambridge University Press, 173–184.

16 Paradigmatic regularity in first language attrition

ROBERT M. VAGO

1 Introduction

This chapter is concerned with the role of paradigmatic coherence in the attrition of a first language morphophonemic system in the context of bilingualism. It aims to characterize paradigm-internally induced changes in formal terms, specifically, as instances of rule simplification, rule reordering, rule loss, and lexical restructuring. The primary motivation underlying these structural innovations is claimed to be derived from two basic principles: reducing allomorphic variation and minimizing rule opacity. Both strategies maximize paradigmatic regularity.

The empirical data for this study were obtained from a thirty-six-year-old Hungarian–Hebrew bilingual Israeli woman who was born in Hungary and immigrated with her parents to Israel at age 5;10. The subject's primary language was Hebrew (L2); her usage of Hungarian (L1) was severely limited, confined almost exclusively to conversations (several times a week) with her parents, for whom Hungarian remained the preferred and dominant language of communication.

The Hungarian attrition data were gathered and analyzed in two stages. The methodology employed in the first stage was paradigm elicitation. In tape recorded interviews conducted in Hungarian by the present investigator, the subject was supplied individual nominal and verbal stems and was instructed to provide the various inflections that constitute paradigmatic sets in Hungarian. The information thus obtained was then analyzed and compared with the respective facts in the standard dialect of Hungarian. Independent investigation confirmed that there were no significant differences between the Hungarian spoken by the subject's parents and the standard dialect of Hungarian as concerns the inflectional phonology and morphology. On the assumption that the subject's first language dialect agreed in essential detail with her parents' dialect from the period of initial acquisition in Hungary through the onset of attrition in Israel, the standard dialect of Hungarian may reasonably be identified as the base-line grammar with which the subject's grammar may be compared. On this basis, any structural deviation from the standard may be identified as an attrition phenomenon.[1]

There are both advantages and disadvantages to collecting data by means of paradigm elicitation. On the positive side is the systematic nature of the methodology: homing in on the paradigmatically related forms carves out a more complete testing ground and paints a more accurate picture of morphophonemic disintegration. As a result, potential problem areas may be brought to the fore that otherwise might escape the attention of the investigator. On the negative side is a serious limitation: paradigm elicitation leaves unresolved the crucial question of whether the prompted deviations, if found, constitute only performance problems relating to retrieval, production, and exclusively intraparadigm influences, or whether they are characteristic of the deeper system of competence as well.

In recognition of the possibility that the attrition data obtained by means of paradigm elicitation might be indicative of problems at the level of performance but not of competence, a second stage of data collection and analysis was devised. In subsequent interviews the subject was asked for grammaticality judgements on individual word tokens – not in the context of paradigms – that she had previously produced in response to paradigm elicitation. The subject's own data that were presented to her at this phase consisted of a target group, i.e. those forms that had previously been identified as deviations from standard Hungarian, as well as a control group, i.e. those forms that had been judged as "correct" in relation to standard Hungarian.

The results of the second phase were in line with expectations: some of the target forms were judged to be grammatical, others ungrammatical. The subject's attrition data reported here are exclusively those that were judged by the subject to be grammatical. We may therefore be reasonably assured that the subject's imputed grammar has undergone attrition at the level of competence. The ensuing sections lay out the formal details of attrition in this individual morphophonemic system.[2]

2   Rule simplification

Consider the singular possessive paradigms of standard Hungarian given in (1), where the first noun represents consonant final stems, the second vowel final stems:

(1)			/bot/ "stick"	/haza/ "home"
1sg	/m/	bot-o-m	hazá-m
2sg	/d/	bot-o-d	hazá-d

3sg	/a/	bot-j-a	hazá-j-a
1pl	/unk/	bot-unk	hazá-nk
2pl	/átok/	bot-otok	hazá-tok
3pl	/u+k/	bot-j-u-k	hazá-j-u-k

Throughout this work, Hungarian examples are cited orthographically; vowel length, in particular, is indicated with diacritic marks. The morphophonemic analyses are expressed in terms of the generative phonology theoretical framework and are based on Vago (1980).[3]

The surface representations in (1) evidence a number of morphophonemic changes, of which the following is of interest here: in the third person singular and plural forms an epenthetic glide shows up between the stem and the vowel initial suffix. It will be noted that only in these two contexts does the initial suffix vowel constitute a separate morpheme. On this basis, it is possible to predict the appearance of the glide /j/ by the following rule:

(2) $\emptyset$/→ j / [STEM] + _____ V +

The subject's version of the singular possessive paradigms of the two representative stems is presented in (3):

(3)

	1sg	bot-o-m	hazá-m
	2sg	bot-o-d	hazá-d
	3sg	bot-j-a	hazá-j-a
	1pl	bot-j-unk	hazá-j-unk
	2pl	bot-j-otok	hazá-j-átok
	3pl	bot-j-u-k	hazá-j-u-k

It is readily observed that a glide is inserted before **any** vowel initial suffix. In particular, epenthesis obtains even before the first person plural and second person plural suffixes. The obvious explanation is that the subject applied a more general version of rule (2), that given in (4):

(4) $\emptyset$/→ j / [STEM] + _____ V

Rule (4) is applied before another rule which inserts /o/ in the first and second person singular forms following consonant final stems. This sequencing explains the fact that /j/ does not appear in 1sg *bot-o-m* and 2sg *bot-o-d*.

In sum, the rule of /j/ epenthesis is represented in the subject's grammar of attrited Hungarian in a simplified form, leading to overapplication. The principal motivation appears to be paradigmatic uniformity/ regularity: in singular possessive forms, /j/ precedes all vowel initial morphemes following a nominal stem.

3   Rule reordering

Standard Hungarian contains the following two rules:

(5)   [V, +low] → [+long] / _____ + [+segment]
(6)   h → ∅// _____ { #, C}

Rule (5) states essentially that low vowels become long at the end of a morpheme, except word finally; thus, /a/ is lengthened to /á/ and /e/ (phonologically [+low]) is lengthened to /é/. For example, the underlying final /a/ of the stem for "home" (cf. nominative *haza*) appears as /á/ in the inflected forms given previously in (1); for the lengthening of /e/, cf. nominative *kefe* "brush," singular possessives *kefé-m, kefé-d, kefé-j-e, kefénk, kefé-tek, kefé-j-ük*.[4]

Rule (6) accounts for the fact that, with some exceptions, nouns ending in /h/ at the underlying level lose their /h/ in word final position and before a consonant initial suffix, that is syllable finally. Thus, for example, the final /h/ of the stem for "bee" does not show up in the nominative and dative cases, but is retained before a vowel initial suffix:

(7)   Nominative: *méh* [meː] "bee"
        Dative: *méh-nek* [meːnɛk]
        3sg poss.:   *méh-e* [meːɦɛ]

As seen, /h/ is indicated in the spelling, whether or not it is pronounced. It should also be noted that it is not possible to insert /h/ prevocalically by general rule; cf. Vago (1980).

In standard Hungarian, rule (5) precedes rule (6). Thus, in the derivation given in (8), the vowel lengthening rule (5) cannot apply to the underlying representation, since the low vowel is not in morpheme final position. Rather, /h/ is deleted by rule (6), yielding a morpheme final short low vowel:

(8)   Underlying   /cseh + nek/ "Czech, dative"
        Rule (5)   ---   (non-applicable)
        Rule (6)   cse + nek
        Surface   [čɛnɛk]

The relevant alternations of the above stem are as follows:

(9)   Nominative: *cseh* [čɛ] "Czech"
        Dative: *cse-nek* [čɛnɛk]
        3sg poss.:   *cseh-e* [čɛɦɛ]

Data elicited from the subject reveal that the subject's grammar contains both rules (5) and (6): she produced alternations like *haza* "home, nominative,'' *hazá-m* ''home, 1sg poss.,'' etc. – cf. (1) above – as well as the alternations given in (7). But significantly, she had deviant forms in those cases where the two rules potentially interact:

(10)   Nominative: /cseh/ → [čɛ]
      Dative: /cseh + nek/ → [čeːnɛk]
      3sg poss.: /cseh + e/ → [čɛfiɛ]

The above attrition facts follow on the view that the ordering of the two rules (5) and (6) is reversed from the sequencing that obtains in the standard dialect. First, rule (6) deletes syllable final /h/; note that setting up final /h/ is justified by the fact that /h/ alternates with /0/ in (10). As a consequence, a context is created in which the low vowel lengthening rule (5) is applicable. For example:

(11)   Underlying /cseh + nek/
      Rule (6) *cse + nek*
      Rule (5) *csé + nek*
      Surface [čeːnɛk]

In sum, rule reordering is another formal attribute of attriting first language grammars, for which the reduction of opacity/maximization of transparency appears to be the primary motivating force. Thus, with respect to the case above, in the standard language the rules apply in counter-feeding order, the result of which is that the low vowel lengthening rule is opaque, since a short low vowel appears in positions where it should have been lengthened. In contrast, in the attrited system the rules apply in feeding order, bringing about a transparent low vowel lengthening rule.[5] Note that this is accomplished at the expense of introducing morphophonemic variation into paradigms, i.e. the length alternation of low vowels. In other words, at least for the case under discussion, the minimization of opacity/maximization of transparency principle supersedes the paradigmatic uniformity principle.

4 Rule loss

Another type of attrition phenomenon that affected the morphophonemic rule system of the subject's grammar may be characterized as rule loss. Three relevant examples follow.

Consider first the alternation between the relative sequencing of the consonants /r/ and /h/ in the following standard forms:

(12)   a. /tehr/ ''load''
      b. Nominative: *teher*

c. Dative: *teher-nek*
d. 3sg poss.:   *terh-e*

(12a) gives the underlying representation of a stem that represents the class ending in /h/ plus a liquid consonant. In the nominative case (12b), a general rule (cf. below) inserts a vowel to break up the otherwise impossible syllable coda cluster /hr/; this rule also applies before a consonant initial suffix, as in the dative inflection (12c). However, in prevocalic position, as in example (12d), where epenthesis is not motivated since the stem final consonant can be gathered into the onset position of the following syllable, a metathesis process applies that switches the /h/ and the liquid:

(13)   h L → L h / _____ + V   (L = liquid)

The above rule saves syllable final /h/ from undergoing deletion; cf. rule (6) above.

The subject's data evidenced no trace of the metathesis process:

(14)   a. /teher/
        b. Nominative: *teher*
        c. Dative: *teher-nek*
        d. 3sg poss.:   *teher-e*

It will further be noted that the epenthetic (second) vowel appears in all contexts, in particular before vowel initial suffixes as well. It seems reasonable to assume that the attrited grammar lost metathesis rule (13) and restructured the underlying form of the stem for "load," as indicated in (14a).[6] As a consequence, the stem acquired a uniform paradigmatic shape.

Rule loss need not necessarily lead to the restructuring of underlying representations. As a case in point, consider the palatalization of verb stem final /t/ before the imperative/subjunctive morpheme /j/ in the standard dialect of Hungarian:

(15)   t → č / _____ + j (in verb stems)

Cf. for example /fűt+j+m/ → *fűtsem* [füːččɛm] "I should heat it" and /szépít+j+m/ → *szépítsem* [seːpiːččɛm] "I should beautify it." Independent evidence establishes that the stems in these forms are *fűt* and *szépít* (derived from the adjectival root *szép* "beautiful") and that the imperative/subjunctive morpheme is /j/ (e.g. *véd* "protect," *védjem* "I should protect it").

The palatalization process is followed by an independently motivated rule which assimilates /j/ to a preceding strident consonant (e.g. *néz* "see," *nézzem* "I should see it"). The joint application of /t/-palatalization and /j/-assimilation derives the geminate strident consonants in the phonetic interpretation of the orthographic examples *fűtsem* and *szépítsem* cited above.

Paradigms elicited from the subject reveal no traces of the palatalization rule formalized in (15). The definite subjunctive paradigms of the verbal stems *fűt* and *szépít* are reproduced in (16).

(16) *fűtjem*   *szépítjem*
      fűtjed   *szépítjed*
      fűtje   *szépítje*
      fűtjük   *szépítjük*
      fűtjétek   *szépítjétek*
      fűtjék   *szépítjék*

In contrast, the /tj/ cluster is pronounced as [čč] in standard Hungarian by virtue of /t/-palatalization and /j/-assimilation.

The attrition data contain no evidence whatsoever for the palatalization of /t/ in verb stem final position. The unambiguous conclusion is that the /t/-palatalization rule has been eliminated from the subject's attrited grammar.

A third instantiation of rule loss comes from the behavior of the instrumental suffix. In the standard dialect of Hungarian the initial consonant of the instrumental suffix fully assimilates to a preceding consonant; in postvocalic position it shows up as /v/. For example:

(17)   Instrumental
      fal "wall"   *fal-lal*
      ház "house"   *ház-zal*
      haza "home"   *hazá-val*

On the assumption that the underlying representation of the instrumental suffix begins with /v/, the postconsonantal assimilations are produced by a rule something like the following:

(18)   C + v
       1 2 3 → 1 2 1

The above rule is missing in the subject's grammar, as suggested by the fact that the initial consonant of the instrumental suffix stays /v/ even after consonant final stems: cf. for example *ház-val, fal-val* in place of the standard forms in (17). In this case, as in the previous one, rule loss is not accompanied by lexical restructuring.

In sum, a number of morphophonemic innovations in the attrition data are due to rule loss. In a subset of the cases reanalysis at the lexical level results as well. In each of the samples considered here, rule loss has reduced or eliminated allomorphic variation.

5   Lexical restructuring

Lexical restructuring, that is modifying the underlying representations of individual morphemes, is perhaps the most common attribute of the attrition of morphophonemic systems. Alternations that are unproductive, lexically conditioned, or otherwise marked are particularly prone to reanalysis, whose overall effect is a more regular alternation pattern. Several cases of these types are examined below.

In standard Hungarian, nominal stems participate in a number of morphophonemic alternation patterns, based in part on whether the following suffix, if any, begins with a consonant or vowel. Three such patterns are exemplified in (19).

(19)		"horse"	"sky"	"ox"
a.	Nominative	ló	ég	ökör
	Dative	ló-nak	ég-nek	ökör-nek
	Inessive	ló-ban	ég-ben	ökör-ben
b.	Plural	lov-ak	eg-ek	ökr-ök
	Accusative	lov-at	eg-et	ökr-öt
	3sg poss.	lov-a	eg-e	ökr-e

The stem shapes in (19b) obtain before vowel initial suffixes, i.e. in case the stem final consonant can be gathered into the onset of a following syllable. The stem shapes in (19a), on the other hand, obtain word finally and before consonant initial suffixes, i.e. in contexts where the stem final consonant cannot be syllabified into onset position. With respect to the paradigmatic shapes of the three representative stems, we may note that in the first case /ló/ alternates with /lov-/, in the second /ég/ alternates with /eg-/, and in the third /ökör/ alternates with /ökr-/. Independent evidence leads to the conclusion that the first and second alternation types are to be described in terms of lengthening, the third one in terms of epenthesis; cf. Vago (1980) for details.

The alternations found in (19) are leveled out in the attrition data obtained from the subject. The equivalent forms are presented in (20).

(20)		"horse"	"sky"	"ox"
a.	Nominative	ló	ég	ökör
	Dative	ló-nak	ég-nek	ökör-nek
	Inessive	ló-ban	ég-ben	ökör-ben

	b. Plural	lóv-ak	ég-ek	ökör-ök
	Accusative	lóv-at	ég-et	ökör-öt
	3sg poss.	lóv-a	ég-e	ökör-e

On the view that in the standard dialect the alternation of the representative stems for "horse" and "sky" are derived by lengthening and that of the stem for "ox" by epenthesis, the attrition data in (20) involve the following adjustments in the underlying representations of the pertinent stems:[7]

(21)   a. /lov/ → /lóv/
         b. /eg/ → /ég/
         c. /ökr/ → /ökör/

Although the attrition corpus elicited from the subject contains other stems that pattern on a par with those in (20) – over a dozen examples for each of the three classes – it also contains several stems for which the alternations evident in the standard dialect are retained. This fact strongly suggests that the sporadic allomorphy reduction in the attrited grammar is due to restructuring on a case by case basis rather than to the outright loss of morphophonemic rules.

6   Conclusion

Rule simplification, rule reordering, rule loss, and lexical restructuring have been claimed to characterize attrition in a first language morphophonemic system. These formal mechanisms are well-known to be operative in the course of normal linguistic change (cf. for example Kiparsky 1968; King 1969) and may best be seen as desired strategies to increase paradigmatic uniformity and rule transparency, both contributory agents of paradigm regularity.

As a final and particularly poignant piece of evidence for the reality of paradigms as coherent linguistic units which may define the domain of attrition processes, consider the fact that the subject of the present study was repeatedly unable to produce the third person singular forms of Hungarian plural possessive paradigms, e.g. the form *botjai* in the representative paradigm adduced in (22); she had no trouble with the other inflections.

(22)   Stem + Pl + Poss.

bot	– jai	– m	"my sticks"
bot	– jai	– d	"your (sg) sticks"
bot	– jai		"his/her/its sticks"

bot	– jai	– nk	"our sticks"
bot	– jai	– tok	"your (pl) sticks"
bot	– jai	– k	"their sticks"

The subject's stumbling is explained as an attempt to generalize from the paradigmatically related forms: she was groping for an overt possessive marker where in point of fact there was none.

Notes

This work is a substantial revision of a preliminary draft which appeared as Vago (1986) and was read at the 1987 Annual Meeting of the Linguistic Society of America in New York. Many thanks to Miklós Kontra for comments.

1   It should be pointed out that none of the deviant forms which are claimed here to be due to attrition can be attributed to transfer from the L2 system. Furthermore, the fact that these forms did not occur in the dialect spoken by the subject's parents effectively argues against grammatical change through imitation. Imperfect acquisition may rather safely be ruled out as well: the morphophonemic alternations discussed in the present study are in general under control by monolingual Hungarian children by the time they reach first grade, the approximate age of the subject when she emigrated from Hungary. See for instance the studies of MacWhinney (1978) and Gósy (1984) and their references.

2   Previous investigations of attrition involving Hungarian as the first language in a bilingual setting are concerned with structural changes (as well as sociopsychological factors) at the societal level. See in particular Gal's (1979) detailed study of a Hungarian–German bilingual community and Kontra's (1985) excellent review of the extensive literature dealing with Hungarian–American English bilingualism.

3   The analytical points are cast within the assumptions of linear generative phonology solely because of the general familiarity of this theoretical model. Clearly, the conclusions concerning the attrition of the formal aspects of Hungarian morphophonemics must be reinterpreted if nonlinear phonological theory is used as the basis of description. Also, some of the descriptive statements about the standard dialect of Hungarian given here are oversimplified; the reader is referred to Vago (1980) and references cited there for a more thorough discussion.

4   For arguments against analyzing the /a/ ~ /á/ and /e/ ~ /é/ alternations in terms of shortening, cf. Vago (1978).

5   For a discussion of feeding and bleeding rule interactions cf. Kiparsky (1968), of opacity and transparency Kiparsky (1971).

6   Hungarian has only two other stems that are subject to metathesis: /pehly/ *pehely* "fluff" and /kehly/ *kehely* "chalice." In the subject's grammar the behavior of these stems paralleled that of the stem for "load" as indicated above in (14).

7 The underlying representation of the consonant /v/ that appears in the instrumental suffix discussed in the preceding section and in the stem class exemplified in (21a) is controversial, but not at issue here. It is claimed to be abstract /w/ in the linear analysis of Vago (1980, 1982), as an empty C timing unit in the non-linear analysis of Vago (to appear).

References

Gal, Susan. 1979. *Language shift: social determinants of linguistic change in bilingual Austria*. New York: Academic Press.

Gósy, Mária. 1984. *Hangtani és szótani vizsgálatok hároméves gyermekek nyelvében*. Budapest: Akadémiai Kiadó.

King, Robert D. 1969. *Historical linguistics and generative grammar*. Englewood Cliffs: Prentice-Hall.

Kiparsky, Paul. 1968. "Linguistic universals and linguistic change," in Emmon Bach and Robert Harms (eds.), *Universals in linguistic theory*. New York: Holt, 171–202.

1971. "Historical linguistics," in William Dingwall (ed.), *A survey of linguistic science*. College Park: Linguistics Program, University of Maryland, 577–642.

Kontra, Miklós. 1985. "Hungarian–American bilingualism: a bibliographic essay," *Hungarian Studies* 1/2: 257–282.

MacWhinney, Brian. 1978. *The acquisition of morphophonology*. Chicago: University of Chicago Press.

Vago, Robert M. 1978. "The lengthening of final low vowels in Hungarian," *Ural-Altaische Jahrbücher* 50: 144–148.

1980. *The sound pattern of Hungarian*. Washington, DC: Georgetown University Press.

1982. "Abstract /w/ in Hungarian," in Ferenc Kiefer (ed.), *Hungarian general linguistics*. Amsterdam: John Benjamins, 589–599.

1986. "Paradigmatic errors in first language attrition," *CUNYForum* 12: 204–214.

(to appear). "Empty consonants in the moraic phonology of Hungarian," *Acta Linguistica Hungarica*, vol. 38.

Index

ability, innate language 37, 38
Aboriginal languages, death of 113
acceptability judgement tests 18, 21, 27
access, loss of fluent 19, 140, 145, 149
accommodation 187
acculturation, degrees of 4, 105–6
acquisition
    compared with attrition 22–4, 164,
        207–8, 217–18
    hypothesis testing in 228–31
    manner of 56, 81
    orders of 46
    relative permanence of 227–40
    research 22–7
    second language: recreation stage 5;
        restructuring stage 5; transfer in
        190–1
    theories of language 12
adult language attrition, lexical retrieval
    difficulties 139–50
adult second language learners,
    compensatory strategies 207–8, 217
Afrikaans 80
agreement rules, breakdown in 8, 79
Albanian, in Greece 68, 101
allomorphic reduction 11, 68, 79–80, 241,
    248, 249
American English
    and Hebrew 26–7, 139–50, 175–88
    and Hungarian 250
    and Spanish 151–71
Amerindian communities 68
Amish 126–36
analogical leveling 10–11, 214
analytic forms, preferred to synthetic 68,
    74
anglicizing 208
aphasia 3, 37, 40
    bilinguals and 53–65
    classification of 57–8
    compared with sociolinguistic language
        decay 109–10
    etiology of 56–7, 61
    language in 37–40
    polyglots and 53–65, 227
    recovery patterns 55, 60–2

and stages in child language
    development 39, 46
approximation 214
Arvanitika 164
aspect 68, 74–5
assimilation, partial 192
assistance, appeals for 208, 215
attitude, change in 103; see also motivation
attrition
    adult language 139–50
    first language, overview 3–15
    onset of 178–80
    see also loss
Australian English, Standard 121
autonomy, degree of 6
avoidance 208, 215

Bhojpuri
    Continental 72
    of Guyana 71
    in Mauritius 71–2, 80
    of Trinidad 71
Bigouden, South, subdialect 99–109
bilingual continuum 151, 161–4
bilingual development, and role of
    Universal Grammar (UG) 4–6
bilingual language history questionnaire 54
bilingual period 180–2
bilingualism 3
    and communicative efficiency thesis 81
    compound and coordinate, and attrition
        5–6, Fig. 1.1
    and performance/competence issue
        17–21, 189–90
biogenetic law (Haeckel) 32, 36
biuniqueness 106
borrowing 80, 102–4, 153, 204
    contact as 67; see also lexical borrowing
Boumaa Fijian 113–24
    dialect leveling in 114–17
Bozal Spanish 80
brain
    damage and language loss 31, 39, 40; see
        also aphasia
    learning and maintenance factors 54

brain (*cont.*)
  organization and loss of L1 in
    aphasia 63
Breton
  aphasia 108–9
  in France 68, 99–112
  literary 99–100
  loss of initial consonant mutations 106–7
  morphology 102–6
  morphophonology 106–8
  phonology 100–2

calquing, *see* loan translation
Cape York Creole 113
category leveling 11
category switch 11
change
  acceleration of 153
  and attrition 115–17, 118–20, 249
  diachronic language 31; and
    acquisition 33
  as discourse strategy 125–37
  externally induced 7–10
  intergenerational language 81
  internally induced 10–11
  permeability to 153–4
  studies of child language 209–10
child
  conscious awareness of language loss,
    and use of compensatory strategies
    207, 217
  developmental errors of 181–2
  first language attrition 175–88;
    compensatory strategies of 207–26
child language 31, 34, 35, 81, 164, 177–8
  compared with aphasics 39, 46
  learning continuum 167
  studies of change 209–10
choice, language 110
Chomskyan linguistic model 12, 17–30
Church, and dialect leveling 115
circumlocution 208
clause subordination, diminished
    frequency 79
code blending 175
code mixing 6, 10, 175, 180
code switching 6, 10, 110, 212–13
cognitive development, and compensatory
    strategies 207, 218
cognitive factors, in change due to contact
    153, 154, 166–7
cognitive load 43
colonialism, linguistic 103
communication extension, and dialect
    leveling 115
communication function 120–1
communication efficiency thesis, in
    bilingualism 81
compensatory strategies 212–15

of child first language attrition 207–26
  and child's conscious awareness of
    language loss 207, 217
  cognitive development and 207, 218
  culture and language relativity 207, 217
  discourse 214–15
  interlingual 212–14
  intralingual 214
  same for L1 attrition and L2 acquisition
    217–18
  typologies 207–8
competence 7
  and bilingualism 189–90
  and control, eliciting 21–2
  criteria 99
  degree of erosion in 7, 139
  grammatical 18
  multiple measures of 210
  and performance attrition 17–21, 189–90
  permanent 19
  pragmatic 18
competences, diverging 24
complexity 33
contact
  additive model of 67
  and attrition 67–84, 151–71
  and change, factors in 153–4
  interference model 67
  with L1 in an L2 environment 87, 94
  resistance-to-mixture model 67
  situations 14, Fig. 1.2
control 18, 21
  alignment of mechanisms 27
  eliciting competence and 21–2
convergence 7, 167
  definition 153
  as discourse strategy 125–37
coordinate constructions, preferred to
    embedded 68, 75
Cornish 107
Cornouaillais dialect 99–109
correspondence theory (Koffka) 36
creativity 187, 227–40
creole languages 113
creolization, and theory of markedness
    164–5, 167
'creoloids' 80
crosslinguistic influence 7, 22, 23–4
  studies 67–84
Culver City immersion program 208

Danish 208, 217
Darwinism 32, 34, 39
dative alternation rule 229, 232
death, language 3, 102, 113, 227
  of Dyirbal 113, 117–20
  factors in 117–20
  and functional diglossia 80

decay
  direction and hierarchy of 105–10
  and giving of proper names in recessive
    language 103–4
  and monostylism 101
decomposition of complex structures 75
deliberate wrong answers 215
dementia 37, 38, 40
  language in compared with child
    language development 40
  and lexical retrieval 140
  senile 3
deprivation, L1 22, 81, 209–18
'desert island' scenario 22–3
diagrammaticity, as a parameter of
    morphological naturalness 106
dialect
  factors in mixing 114–15
  leveling 113, 114–17
  loss 36
diglossia, functional in language death 80
discourse strategies, convergence and
    change as 125–37
disintegration of L1 182–4
dismantling and reordering process 67–82
dissociation of word meaning 40
dissolution 37, 38, 39
distance, principle of 168
domains
  affective 4
  of progress, shift to dominant language
    104
  shift 42
Dutch immigrants
  in Australia 41
  in France 87–98
Dyirbal 79–80, 113, 117–24
  ergative case marking 9, 79–80
  Traditional, attrition stages in 122–3,
    Fig. 8.2
  Traditional and Young 117–20
dysfunction, partial 101, 108, 109
dysphasia 57

economy of distinctions 114, 120–2, 124
editing test 89, 90
education
  and aphasia 58, 61–2
  compulsory and dialect leveling 115
  compulsory English and language death
    118
elderly, language of the, and regression
    40–1
elicitation tests 17, 19, 21–2, 141–3
emigration, time elapsed since 87, 94
English 7–11
  Aboriginal 113
  and French 44–5
  and German 189–206

and Hebrew, word order in dative
    sentences 231–3; *see also* American
    English
  and Japanese 19–20
  and Pennsylvania German 126–36
  and Russian 209–25
  and Spanish 25
  use of relative clause in adult ESL
    students 208
  variety of 113; *see also* American
    English; Australian English; Old
    English
epistemology 36
ergative case markings, allomorphic
    reduction in 79–80
erosion process, at level of competence 7,
    76, 139
evidence
  indirect negative 229–30
  negative 24, 28
  positive 230–1
  problem of input in attrition 22–4
evolution 32
  of grammars 81, 227–40
exposure, inadequate 81, 209–18

factoring process 75
feeding rule 245, 250
Fijian
  Boumaa 114–17
  Standard 114–17
Finnish 36, 80
  in Minnesota 67, 68–71, 239
Flemish, American 198
Foreign Service Interview (FSI) 89, 90–1
foreignizing 208
forms
  contracting/shrinking 152, 161
  expanding 152
  loss of 152, 162–3, 166
fragmentation of ethnic group, and
    language death 118
free discourse sentences 234–5
French 44–5
  and Breton 100, 105
  Canadian 72, 164
  in Louisiana 67, 72–6
  in Missouri 68, 72–6
  in New England 68, 72–6
  Standard 72–6
  in Virgin Islands 68, 72–6
French Creole, in Mauritius 71
frequency
  and transfer 191, 201
  and vulnerability to attrition 203, 204;
    see also word frequency count
function, extension or reduction of 153
functional loss, and structural loss 42

functional shift, and structural decay
    108–10
functions of language 120–2

Gaelic, *see* Scots Gaelic
gender and plural tasks 201–3
generalization 10, 79, 152, 208
generalizations, learning and unlearning
    of, 227–40
geographic factors 109
German 7–11, 44
    in Australia 41
    case marking 43
    and English 189–206
    and Hungarian 250
    in Iowa 68
    Pennsylvania 68, 125–37, 192; the
        auxiliary *du* 131–3; case usage 128–31;
        in Delaware 129; in Ontario 128;
        word order 133–5
    Standard 126
    in Texas 68
Government and Binding Theory
    (Chomsky) 27
grammar
    core and periphery 12–13
    reduced 102
    shift 24; *see also* Transformational
        Grammar; Universal Grammar
grammars
    in contact 227–39
    evolution of 227–40
    'partially replicated' 81
    possible types of evidence for
        developing 231, Fig. 15.2
    sources for creation and dissolution of
        228–3
grammaticality
    degrees of 190, 195–7
    judgement 235–9, 242–9
    judgement test (Koster) 89, 91–3, 96–7
group studies 85–171
Guugu Yimidhirr 113

handedness, in aphasia 57, 60–1, 62, 63
Hebrew
    and American English 26–7, 139–50,
        175–88
    and English, word order in dative
        sentences 231–3
    and Hungarian 241–9
hemiplegia 37
hemispheric damage, in aphasia 57, 60, 63
Hindi
    in Fiji 68
    in Guyana 68, 71
    in Mauritius 68
    in Trinidad 68, 71

Hungarian 7–11, 217, 241–51
    and American English 250
    in Austria 68, 164
    and German 250
    and Hebrew 241–9
Huntington's chorea 37, 39–40
hypothesis testing, in language
    acquisition 228–31
hypothetical texts, 159–60

identity function 120–2
idiosyncratic template 184–7
immigrant communities 3, 4, 42–3, 67–8
    contact and attrition 68–76
immigrant languages 125–37
indigenous communities 3, 68
    contact and attrition 76–80
    minority 42
individuals, attrition within 165, 168,
    175–88
Indo-European languages 34, 79, 80
inflection, reductions in 68, 105–6
innovation
    lexical 214
    phonological 100–1
input
    in attrition 22–4
    'negative' 229–30
    and parameter resetting 25–7
interaction effects 189–90
interference 7, 47, 80, 95, 100
    asymmetry of 102–3
    model of contact 67
interlanguage 5, 19–20, 22, 45
interlinguistic factors
    in change due to contact 153, 154
    in contact 7, 165–6
intermarriage, and dialect leveling 114
interpretation, of attrition data 17–30
intralinguistic factors
    in change due to contact 153, 154
    in contact 10, 166
invariable forms 74

Jambun English 117, 121
Japanese 19–20
jargon aphasia 39

Kannada 77
knowledge 7, 18, 21
Konkani 68
Kriol 113

'language check mechanism' 190
lateral dominance for language 62
Latin 107
learnability, and attrition 17–30, 227–40

learning factors
  imperfect 43
  and language loss 12, 44–5
  'residual' 44
lexical borrowing 10, 102, 213
lexical creativity 104–5, 214
lexical decision reaction times 148, 190
lexical enrichment 102, 104
'lexical fading' 107
lexical hybridization 10
lexical restructuring 248–9
lexical retrieval
  difficulties in adult language attrition
    139–50
  features of the process 145–9
  Inherently Neutral Specificity (INS) 148
  and language attrition 140–1, 178
  logogen model (Morton) 201
  options 145–7, Fig. 10.1
  reduction in accessibility 140, 145, 149
  search model (Forster) 201
lexical similarity, and language loss 44
lexicon, externally induced change 10
linguistic aspects, of first language
    attrition 6–11, 44–5
linguistic environment, impoverished 41
literature, language death and absence of
    L1 88
loan translation 8–9
loss 31–51
  across generations of speakers 42
  in aphasics 53–63
  at the individual level 165, 168
  functional and structural 42
  L1 in an L2 environment 87–98
  regression and language 37–45
  as a result of brain damage 31
  result of: economy of distinctions 120–2
  rule 245–8
  second language/foreign language 43–5,
    46
'lowest common denominator' of
    distinguishing features 123, 124

maintenance, language in bilingual
    context 136, 227–40
Marathi 77
markedness
  and attrition 10, 227
  hierarchy of 165, Table 11.5
  linguistic 191
  psycholinguistic 191
  theory of: and core/periphery
    distinction 12–13; and creolization
    164–5, 167; in UG 12–13, 25–6; *see also*
    analogical leveling
markers, as symbols of the language 114,
    122–3, 124
meaning extension 8

media, and dialect leveling 115; *see also*
    radio; television
memory load, economizing 104
Mendelian genetics 36
Mennonites 127
  Old Order 126–36
'message adjustment strategy' 208
metalinguistic abilities, assessment of 6,
    21, 88, 89, 94, 233–6
metathesis process 246, 250
methodologies 3
monogeny 37
monostylism 101–2
morphemes, frequency and order of
    acquisition 201
morphological complexity 33
morphological disintegration and
    reconstruction 175–88
morphological similarity in transfer 200
morphology
  externally induced change 9
  internally induced change 10–11
morphophonemic system, paradigmatic
    regularity in attrition 241–51
mother tongue shift 42–3
motivation, morphosemantic and
    morphotactic 104, 105
multilingualism 3, 81
Murrinh Patha 113
muscular atrophy 37
mutations, 'default' 107

Nagamese 80
Nahuatl, in Mexico 68
natural languages, fixedness questioned
    23
Natural Morphology 106, 107, 109
Natural Phonology 101, 109
naturalistic observations 175
naturalness parameters 10, 106
neologisms, processing of 104–5
neurolinguistics 26, 53–63
Nijmegen, University of, regression
    studies 43
non-pathological language attrition, types
    87
non-sectarian communities 125–37
null subjects 25

object naming tasks 143, 144–5
Old English 107
ontogeny, and phylogeny of language
    32–7, 38
opacity, reduction of 241–9
overgeneralizations, learning and
    unlearning of 201, 227–40
overlearning 45
overt comments 214

palatalization 246–7
paradigmatic leveling 11; *see also*
    allomorphic reduction
paradigmatic regularity, in first language
    attrition 241–51
paradigms
    elicitation of 241–2
    evidence for reality of 249–50
parameter setting model 12–13, 17–30
    resetting via input 25–7
paraphrase 208
pathology, regression and language 31,
    37–40, 108–9
Pennsylvania German, *see* German,
    Pennsylvania
perception, shift in at level of competence
    19–20, 27
performance
    attrition and competence 7, 17–21,
        189–90
    insecurity 109, 110
periphrastic constructions 68, 74
Pfälzisch 126
phonemes 31
phonetic similarity, and vulnerability to
    attrition 200, 204
phonology
    externally induced change 9
    linear generative assumption 250
phylogeny, and ontogeny of language
    32–7, 38
pidgin languages 164
    and monostylism 102
    restructuring in 81
Piel 184
Pitres, rule of 55
predictability, and vulnerability to
    attrition 191, 201, 203, 204
prepositions, stranding 8, 25, 26–7, 232,
    237
processing theories 20–1, 189–91
production, language 168–9
proper names, giving of in recessive
    language 103–4
psycholinguistics 4–6, 14, 17–30, 227
purism, lack of 103

radio, and language death 117
recall, creativity in 28
recapitulation 31–51
    'attrition variant' 36
    hypothesis 31; problems in 32–7
reconstruction
    of L1 184–7
    morphological disintegration and 175–88
reduction 109
    restriction in language input and use
        and 209–25; *see also* allomorphic
        reduction

redundancy, reduced 227–40
    for dative in attrition 233–6
registers, distinguishing between 45
regression
    hypothesis 31, 46: and aphasia 46
    and language loss 37–45:
        non-pathological 40–5
regularization 10, 79
relative clauses, pronouns in 13
relexification 103
reordering, rule 244–5
restriction in language output and use,
    and reduction 209–25
restructuring
    of grammar 19–20, 68, 80–2
    lexical 248–9
reversion 41
Ribot, rule of 55
rule
    generalization 7–8
    loss 245–8
    reordering 244–5
    simplification 242–3
Russian, and English 209–25

Scots Gaelic, in East Sutherland 68, 76–7,
    164, 169
search model of lexical retrieval (Forster)
    201
second language acquisition, *see*
    acquisition, second language
sectarian communities 125–37
Sele Fara/Zell Pfarre 105
selective blending contact 67
selectivity, in attrition 203, 228–31
semantic contiguity 208
semantic memory search 140–1
semantic transparency 154, 166
semantics, externally induced change 8–9
senile dementia 3
sentences
    double object 238–9
    free discourse 234–5
simplification 33, 79, 151–71
    and attrition 6, 10, 13
    definition 152
    in normal language change 107–8
    rule 242–3
    stages in verb system 162, Fig. 11.3
simplified languages 164
situation (Comrie) 155–9, 168
Slovene Carinthian dialect 103, 105
social factors
    in change due to contact 153–4
    in contact 109–10, 166–7
sociolinguistic aspects, of first language
    attrition 4–6, 17, 99–112
sociolinguistic context, and complexity 35

sociolinguistic language decay, compared
with aphasic disturbances 109–10
sociolinguistic norms 136
South Asian languages 71
Spanish 25, 44, 194, 208
Bozal 80
Hispanoamerican 42, 151–71; verb
system 155–64
speaker perception of language 114, 122–3
speech community
dominant and recessive 103
enclave 67
and morphological complexity 33
speech task, structured spontaneous 21
structural decay, functional shift and 100,
108–10
structural loss, without compensation
107–8
stylistic effects 27, 29, 164
subordinate clause 8, 74–6, 119
Swahili 80
switching, language 135–6, 208
see also code switching
symbols of language, features as 122–3
symmetry, in construction and dissolution
of a language 38
syntactic judgement task 191–8
syntactic loss 192
syntactic transfer 213–14
syntax, externally induced change 7–8
synthetic forms, replaced by analytic 68,
74

tacit knowledge 7, 21
television, and language death 117
tense 152, 165, 168–9
testing techniques 17, 21–2
transfer 5, 7, 166
as borrowing 204
definition 152–3
in second language acquisition 190–1
Transformational Grammar (TG),
hierarchy of sentence structure 38
transliteration 208
transparency
maximization of 241–9
morphosyntactic 81
semantic 14, 154, 166

Trégorrois dialect 99–109

Umlaut 106
uniformity 33, 249, *see also* paradigmatic
regularity
Universal Grammar (UG) 12, 17, 25–7, 82
and cognitive factors 167
constraints on natural grammars 24–7
definition 154–5
innate principles 12
markedness in 25–6
role in bilingual development 4–6
universality, strategy of 154–5
universals in language 31, 36, 37–8, 227
unlearning process 227–40
unmarked forms 10, 12–13, 109
attrition of, *see* markedness
urbanization, and dialect leveling 115
Urdu, in Kupwar 68, 77–9, 80
Utrecht language loss study 21, 192

verb system
distinctive aspectual constructions 68,
74–5
tense–mood–aspect loss 151, 155–60, 165
verb usage task 198–200
verbal insertions
L1 in L2 182–4
L2 178–80
vulnerability to attrition
assessment of first language 189–206
of grammatical structures 90
and level of proficiency 41

Waitabu, Taveuni Island, Fiji 114–17
Wik-Mungkan 113
word
coinage 208
formation rules 102, 104–5
frequency count (Meier) 201
replacement 144
retrieval, *see* lexical retrieval
stress 9, 105–6
word order 8, 68, 79
in dative sentences: English and
Hebrew 231–3
German 189, 192–8
judgements 236–8